MuleSoft Integration for Professionals

Mastering API-Led Connectivity

Radhika Atmakuri
Prasenjit Mondal

ARCCHIE
www.arcchieonline.com

MuleSoft Integration for Professionals

Mastering API-Led Connectivity

Editor: Shambhu
Production Manager: Gaurav Mutreja
Cover design by Freepik and Vecteezy
Formatting & Indexing: Rahul

First Edition: June-2025
Reference: 2307007
Published by Arcchie Publications

ISBN-13 (paperback): 978-81-986981-8-6
ISBN-13 (ebook): 978-81-979768-3-4

Published by ARCCHIE PUBLICATIONS, Greater Noida, U.P. -201 306
and Printed at Repro India Ltd., Mumbai

www.arcchieonline.com

JOIN US ON THE ARCCHIE PUBLICATIONS DISCORD SERVER

Connect with fellow readers, authors, and enthusiasts to discuss all things related to our publications and the exciting world of AI, programming, and learning. Share your insights, ask questions, and engage in vibrant discussions to expand your knowledge and inspire creativity. Take advantage of this opportunity to be part of a dynamic community dedicated to exploring the frontiers of technology and innovation. Join our Discord Server today and be part of the ARCCHIE Publications community!

https://discord.gg/z26SenmpEt

DISCLAIMER

The information contained in this book is for educational and informational purposes only. While the publisher and authors have made every effort to ensure the accuracy and completeness of the information provided, they assume no responsibility for any errors, omissions, or contrary interpretation of the subject matter contained herein. This publication is sold with the understanding that the publisher and authors are not engaged in rendering legal, accounting, or other professional services. If legal or expert assistance is required, the services of a competent professional should be sought. Any trademarks, service marks, product names, or named features are assumed to be the property of their respective owners and are used only for reference. There is no implied endorsement if we use one of these terms. The views and opinions expressed in this book are those of the authors and do not necessarily reflect the official policy or position of any agency, organization, employer, or company. The publisher does not warrant the performance, effectiveness, or applicability of any sites listed or linked to in the book.

DEDICATED TO

To the vibrant MuleSoft community—mentors, colleagues, and pioneers—whose collaborative spirit and shared expertise have made this journey of integration not only possible but profoundly rewarding. For the mentors who guided me, the colleagues who challenged me, and the teams that inspired me every day. This book is a tribute to the spirit of collaboration and innovation that drives our industry forward. For those who dare to envision a seamless digital future, this book is for you. Thank you for your perseverance, creativity, and commitment to building a world where every system speaks a common language.

- *Radhika Atmakuri*

ACKNOWLEDGEMENT

Writing a book is a journey that spans beyond the solitary act of putting words on paper. It's a collaborative effort, a tapestry woven with threads of inspiration, guidance, and unwavering support. As I reflect on the completion of this work, I am deeply humbled and profoundly grateful for the contributions of countless individuals who have illuminated my path. First and foremost, I would like to express my heartfelt gratitude to Gaurav Arora, my colleague, whose unwavering belief in the power of knowledge and innovation has been my guiding star throughout this endeavor. Your boundless encouragement and invaluable insights have been a constant source of inspiration. My gratitude also extends to the team at ARCCHIE for their dedication, enthusiasm, and unwavering commitment to bringing this book to fruition. Your expertise and tireless efforts have transformed my vision into a tangible reality. To my colleagues and peers who offered their insights and feedback, thank you for your thoughtful contributions that enriched the content and depth of this book. Your collective wisdom has left an indelible mark. A special thank you to my family and friends for their enduring patience, understanding, and encouragement during the countless hours spent immersing ourselves in research and writing. Your unwavering support has been the cornerstone of my journey. Finally, I extend my gratitude to the readers, both novice and expert, who will join me on this exploration. It is with the hope that this book sparks your curiosity, broadens your horizons, and inspires you to push the boundaries of knowledge.

-- *Radhika Atmakuri*

ABOUT THE AUTHORS

- **Radhika Atmakuri** is a MuleSoft Architect and Technical Lead with over 19 years of experience in software development and integration. She has worked for companies such as IBM, AST LLC, and Avaya in various roles, including Senior Module Lead, Technical Architect, and Senior Principal Consultant. Radhika is a certified MuleSoft Certified Integration Architect - Level 1, MuleSoft Certified Platform Architect, MuleSoft Certified Developer Integration and API Associate, AWS Cloud Practitioner, and Salesforce AI Associate. She also holds a Master's degree in Computer Science from Osmania University.

- **Prasenjit Mondal** is a MuleSoft Integration Technical Lead with 13 years of experience in Software Development, Integration Solution Design, and Development. He has worked for multiple CMMI Level-5 MNC companies, including IBM, Tata Technologies, and Syntel Ltd., as an Integration Solution Developer, Designer, and Technical Lead, with heterogeneous enterprise application integration scopes that include interactions with SAP ERP, Oracle Database, and Salesforce CRM, among others, using MuleSoft, IBM App Connect, and IBM Integration Bus. Prasenjit is a certified MuleSoft Professional Developer, AWS Cloud Practitioner, Google Cloud Digital Leader, IBM Cloud Technical Advocate v3, and IBM App Connect Professional Developer. He holds a Bachelor of Technology degree in Information Technology from West Bengal University of Technology.

ABOUT THE TECHNICAL REVIEWER

Dr. Gaurav Aroraa is a distinguished Microsoft MVP award recipient and an influential Regional Mentor of Change with AIM NITI Aayog, Government of India. He is a Business Coach and innovation Leader with Business Blaster, Government of NCT Delhi, and he contributes significantly to the startup ecosystem. Dr. Aroraa is a lifetime Computer Society of India (CSI) member. He holds certifications as a Scrum Trainer and Coach, ITIL-F, PRINCE-F, and PRINCE-P, showcasing his expertise in project management and IT service management. Dr. Aroraa is an accomplished open-source developer and an active contributor to the Microsoft TechNet community. With a rich background in technology, he has authored books across diverse fields, addressing both emerging and established technologies. His recent achievements include being recognized as a world record holder for his contributions to books in exceptional and cutting-edge technologies. Dr. Aroraa inspires professionals, educators, and students through knowledge-sharing initiatives and mentorship.

PREFACE

In today's fast-paced digital world, seamless integration of systems has become more than just a technical requirement—it's a strategic necessity. As enterprises grow increasingly reliant on a myriad of applications and platforms, the need to connect disparate systems into a cohesive ecosystem becomes paramount. This book, MuleSoft For Professionals, is born out of a passion for solving these challenges of integration and a desire to empower developers, architects, and IT professionals with practical, hands-on knowledge. Throughout my career, I have witnessed firsthand the transformative power of integration. Whether it was streamlining legacy systems or crafting agile, API-driven architectures, MuleSoft has consistently provided the tools to build robust, scalable solutions. However, mastering such a versatile platform demands more than just familiarity with its components—it requires an understanding of underlying principles, best practices, and real-world application patterns.
This book is designed to be a comprehensive guide that walks you through every facet of MuleSoft. We start with the fundamentals of integration and API design, delving into the nuances of RAML and Mule APIs, and exploring best practices that ensure your solutions are not only functional but also secure and efficient. The journey continues with an in-depth look at DataWeave, split into two parts to cover both fundamental transformations and advanced techniques. Error handling, a critical aspect of building resilient systems, is discussed alongside strategies for meeting non-functional requirements (NFRs) and deploying Mule APIs effectively. I have also dedicated chapters to emerging tools such as Anypoint Code Builder and explored common integration patterns that can be applied to a variety of business challenges. My goal is to provide you with a resource that is both theoretically sound and practically relevant—a guide that you can refer to as you design, develop, and deploy integration solutions in your projects. This book will catalyze your integration journey, inspiring innovative solutions and contributing to your professional growth. Whether you are just starting or looking to deepen your expertise, may the insights and best practices contained within these pages help you achieve excellence in integration with MuleSoft.

Welcome to your journey in mastering integration.

What's Inside This Book

Chapter 1: Introduction to Enterprise Integration – Begin with the fundamentals of integration, understanding why connecting disparate systems is crucial in today's digital era. This chapter lays the groundwork by exploring integration challenges and the strategies needed to overcome them, setting the stage for how MuleSoft transforms integration into a streamlined process.

Chapter 2: Raml – An Inside Story – Dive into the world of RESTful API Modelling Language (RAML). This section details how RAML is used to design, document, and govern APIs. You'll learn about its structure, benefits, and best practices, along with real-world examples that reveal the "inside story" behind effective API design.

Chapter 3: APIs – At a glance – Gain a high-level overview of APIs and their evolution. This chapter explains what APIs are, why they are central to digital transformation, and how they enable communication between systems, with a special focus on their implementation within MuleSoft.

Chapter 4: Mule APIs – Best Practices – Explore the best practices for designing and developing Mule APIs. This chapter provides guidelines on ensuring performance, security, scalability, and maintainability, and shares insights on how to align your API strategy with business needs.

Chapter 5: Secure Properties – Learn how to protect sensitive information in your MuleSoft applications. This section covers techniques for managing secure properties, including encryption strategies and secure configuration management, ensuring your integrations comply with enterprise security standards.

Chapter 6: DataWeave – Part-I – Introduce yourself to DataWeave, MuleSoft's powerful transformation language. This chapter covers the basics, including its syntax, core functions, and everyday use cases for transforming data between various formats, such as JSON, XML, and CSV.

Chapter 7: DataWeave – Part-II – Take your DataWeave skills to the next level with advanced topics. Delve into complex transformations, custom functions, performance optimizations, and real-world scenarios that highlight the versatility and power of DataWeave in solving intricate integration challenges.

Chapter 8: Handling Errors – Understand how to build resilient integrations by effectively managing errors. This chapter outlines various error-handling strategies, including exception propagation, logging, and the use of On Error Scopes, ensuring that your Mule APIs can gracefully recover from failures.

Chapter 9: Non-Functional Requirements – Non-Functional Requirements (NFRs), such as performance, scalability, and security, are critical for enterprise applications. This section offers insights on how to address these requirements within your MuleSoft projects and explains how NFRs influence architecture decisions and overall system design.

Chapter 10: Deploying Mule APIs – Discover the best practices for deploying Mule APIs across different environments. Whether you're targeting on-premises, cloud, or hybrid deployments, this chapter guides you through the deployment process, continuous integration/continuous delivery (CI/CD) practices, and operational considerations.

Chapter 11: Introduction to Anypoint Code Builder – Get acquainted with Anypoint Code Builder, MuleSoft's integrated development environment (IDE) that streamlines API and integration development. Learn how its features boost productivity and enhance collaboration within your development team.

Chapter 12: Integration Patterns – MuleSoft Connectors – Conclude with an exploration of common integration patterns and how they can be applied using MuleSoft. From message routing to data transformation and event-driven architectures, this final chapter provides practical examples and best practices for implementing robust, scalable integration solutions.

For Whom This Book Is Intended

This book is ideal for:

- Novice enthusiasts are seeking to develop REST APIs using MuleSoft.
- Mule developers are expected to build Mule APIs by following best practices.
- The Platform Ops team needs to understand the deployment models available and how they work in the Anypoint Platform.
- Mule Professionals use the MuleSoft out-of-the-box connectors for various integration patterns.
- Mule Professionals implement the Non-Functional requirements for Mule APIs.

Errata

At **ARCCHIE Publications**, we are committed to delivering the highest-quality content in all our publications. We follow best practices to ensure the accuracy of our content to provide our readers with indulgent reading experience. We believe and understand that our readers are our best judges, and we always use their input and feedback from time to time to improve human errors, if any, that may occur during the publishing processes involved. We invite you to participate in our errata submission process to ensure our books remain accurate and up to date. Please help us reach out to readers who might have difficulties due to unforeseen errors. Please write to us at ***errata@arcchieonline.com***.

When submitting errata, please include the following information:
Book Title, Reference#, Author(s), Page Number, Description of the Error, Suggested Correction (if applicable)

The **ARCCHIE Publications** Family highly appreciates your support, suggestions, and feedback.

Sharing Your Perspective and Providing Feedback

Your perspective is invaluable to us, as it helps us enhance our content and gather your feedback. We warmly welcome all forms of feedback. Please feel free to send us an email at **feedback@arcchieonline.com**, mentioning the book title in the subject line of your message.

Book Review Invitation

We kindly invite you to share your thoughts. After you've read and engaged with this book, consider leaving a review on the platform where you acquired it. Your impartial feedback can greatly assist potential readers in making informed decisions. Your reviews provide valuable insights for us at **Arcchie**, helping us better understand your perspectives on our products, and they offer authors the chance to appreciate your feedback on their work.

Piracy

Should you encounter unauthorized reproductions of our publications in any digital format on the internet, we kindly request your assistance in pinpointing their locations or website sources. Please reach out to us at **copyright@arcchieonline.com** and include a link to the infringing material.

If you possess expertise in a particular subject and wish to participate in the creation or contribution to a book, please visit ***authors.arcchieonline.com***. We welcome you and assist you to start your authorship journey with **ARCCHIE PUBLICATIONS**.

TABLE OF CONTENTS

Chapter 1: Introduction to Enterprise Integration 1

Benefits of Enterprise Integration 1

Enterprise Integration Best Practices 6

Conclusion 7

Chapter 2: RAML – An Inside Story 8

RAML Recommendations 8

Conclusion 27

Chapter 3: APIs - At a glance 28

REST APIs 28

Implementing Mule API using RAML 30

Conclusion 48

Chapter 4: Mule APIs – Best Practices 49

Creation of C4E Team 49

C4E Practice Benefits 50

Conclusion 59

Chapter 5: Secure Properties 60

Need of Secured Properties 60

Various ways to Securing Properties in APIs 61

Conclusion 75

Chapter 6: DataWeave Part 1 77

Why DataWeave 77

DataWeave Expressions 79

Conclusion 99

Chapter 7: DataWeave Part 2 100

Data Weave Fundamentals 100

Conclusion 105

Chapter 8: Handling Errors 107

Error Handling in Mule 107

Conclusion 118

Chapter 9: Non-Functional Requirements 119

Applying NFRs using Anypoint Platform 119

Conclusion 132

Chapter 10: Deploying Mule APIs 134

MuleSoftt Deployment Options 134

Conclusion 158

Chapter 11: Anypoint Code Builder 160

Getting Started with Anypoint Code Builder 160

Design an API 162

Conclusion 170

Chapter 12: Integration Patterns – MuleSoft Connectors 171

Integration Patters 171

Best Practices and Anti-Patterns 179

Conclusion 179

Appendix .... i-x

Answers – Test your understandings i

1

Introduction to Enterprise Integration

Enterprise Integration is the process of connecting various business units, systems, and applications within the organization and sometimes outside the organization. Enterprise Integration enables to connect these systems seamlessly to share the data, automate the business process, workflows. Data is the new oil. This notion has been oft repeated. Almost all the enterprises these days hold critical data. The data pertains to their users, critical business functions, transaction data and much more. As different functions of these enterprises get digitized, this data is used in a lot of ways. Enterprises are now increasingly relying on solutions which help improve productivity and efficiency. These solutions require enterprise data. When different enterprises interact with each other or different functions of the same enterprise interact with each other, data is exchanged between them. Using different ways of data exchange between enterprises is referred to enterprise integration.

Benefits of enterprise integration

There are various benefits of using enterprise integration. They are:

1. Start using your data for your benefit - Your data can help you give insights into your business. Make your data available for solutions which can do this. Your organization can become agile, adapting to customer needs faster.
2. Remove dependency on your IT department - Once you create a robust data integration pipeline, consumers of this data can use this data without depending on your IT department.
3. You can also control the access of your information as the data exposure is now controlled.
4. Remove data silos - You might have data related to different departments or functions that when viewed collectively will bring organization wide benefits.
5. Improve productivity and reduce costs - When data is harmonized and made available as a part of the integration pipeline, you will unlock productivity by removing duplication of data.

When we talk about enterprise integration, it is important to note that enterprises factor in a lot of things to finalize the data exchange or integration mechanism:

1) Security - Security is almost always prioritized over other factors as data is extremely critical to enterprises. Data security refers to the safeguards that are built around exchange of data so that it does not fall into wrong hands. It also refers to any legal compliance that must be adhered by the parties involved.

    a) Minimal access rights should be given to users. These rights should be reviewed periodically.
    b) Use secure protocols (SFTP, HTTPS, TLS 1.3 etc)
    c) Your data store should be in a private network.
    d) If you are sharing your data with an external vendor, make sure you do a security audit. You can also check if the vendor is ISO 27001 certified or SOC2 Type 2 assessed.

2) Reusability - Creating reusable assets which can be exposed to the outside world for data integration is an important consideration for most IT teams.

    a) Prefer APIs as integration mechanism. Your APIs should be modular, and you can divide these APIs as System, Process and Experience APIs. When you do this, most of the changes will happen at process (these APIs mimic the business processes) and experience (these APIs will depend on the end user medium, e.g., mobile or web) APIs.
    b) Create user friendly documentation for your integration mechanism.
    c) Have separate sandboxes for UAT and production so that end users can try out the integration.

3) Scalability - The same data set might be used in different apps/solutions. It is important to look at the number of end users that must be supported. These end users might be distributed geographically.

    a) Always load test your solution. Publish the performance metrics for your end users.
    b) The solution should be auto scalable with rules set on CPU and RAM

Let's now look at the different stages of data integration. While enterprises might store data in different data stores and the end users might want to consume this data in different ways, the data integration pipeline would largely have these three different stages:

1) Extract - The data needs to be extracted from the data store. The medium of data extraction would depend on the kind of interface that has been made available to the data consumers. Following interfaces or protocols might be used for extracting data.

    a) APIs – The data might be exposed as REST or SOAP APIs. Exposing the data as API would need a decent tech capability in the IT function of the enterprises. The APIs must be supplemented with user documentation and a sandbox to try out these APIs.

Exposing API is a huge topic and there are various tools that can be used to expose APIs.

b) File based exchanges - The data can be transferred into an SFTP server or any other file-based system like cloud-based filesystems (AWS S3, Azure Blob storage etc.)
c) Access to the data store - Sometimes, the enterprises might give read only access to their data store so that the data can be pulled directly. This is not a something that happens frequently as the data store might be used for various things and pulling data directly might have a performance impact. Sharing the entire data as opposed to the specific data required might not be a good idea as well.
d) Other methods include pushing the data into message queues, auto emailing etc. These are less popular than the other mentioned ways above.

2) Clean the data - Some organizations do this as a part of transformation. You might extract a lot of data from the source data store as a part of the exchange contract (the API exposed might return a lot of unwanted data). Clean the unwanted data before you move to the next stage of the data integration pipeline.

3) Transform - Once the data is extracted, it that must be consumed would most likely be transformed into a format that can be stored at the end user's data store. Transformation is generally a costly operation as it involves changing the format of the data at runtime before storage. A lot of visual tools are available to transform data from one format to another.

   Keep in mind the following factors when you get ready to transform the data:

   a) Make sure that you factor in the performance as transformations can slow down the data pipeline.
   b) No cyclical dependencies - During a data integration pipeline, you might need some data that you will get in the later stages. This can be generally resolved by planning the data integration pipeline stages. You can also keep some static data in a cache or some local store before starting the integration.
   c) Make sure you return proper success or error code so that the pipeline can move forward or abort.

4) Load - The final step of the data integration pipeline is loading the data into the target data store. At this stage, the data is ready to be ingested into the target data store. A few important points to keep in mind at this stage:

   a) Make sure that you stream the data so that your production systems which will ingest this data do not get inundated with huge amounts of data. You can use technologies like Apache Spark, Apache Kafka etc to achieve this.

b) Have a retry mechanism in case you come across infrastructure issues (you database might be busy/unavailable, network issues etc.). This makes the pipeline more reliable and avoids rerunning the entire pipeline again.
c) Record the successful and failed records.

The data pipeline and stages get complicated based on the 'readiness' of the parties involved while moving the data from the source data store to the target data store.

How to integrate data?

Here is a quick checklist that might help you plan the data integration. While the data integration has a lot of complexities and there might be different ways that data integration teams will handle all these scenarios, this checklist will work in most scenarios.

a) Make a list of all the data entities that need to be exchanged. This would depend on the use cases that have to be implemented, so it is a good idea to make a traceability matrix against each use case. This will ensure that no use case is missed during data integration.
b) Break down the entities by listing all the columns/fields within the entity.
c) Finalize the data exchange protocol – API, file-based data exchange, direct data store access or any other protocol depending on the parties involved. Sometimes, multiple protocols might be involved – some entities might have APIs and the others might be shared using file exchange. Document all this meticulously.
d) Frequency of integration – Some entities might require a daily/hourly data exchange while some might require a weekly/monthly exchange. Against each entity, note down the frequency of data exchange.
e) Full synch or delta – A very important aspect is the amount of data exchanged. Let's say you are exchanging the SKU list of a company which includes the pricing information. It might be agreed that the entire SKU list will exchanged every day or to optimize the data exchange, it might be agreed that the entire SKU list will be transferred on the first day followed by a 'delta' exchange every day. Note down the mode of data exchange every entity.
f) Timing – Note down the timing of data exchange for each entity. Factor in the time of integration so that the data is ready by the time it is needed by the solution.
g) Note down any validation that will be done prior to loading the data in the target data source.
h) A lot of times, data might be enriched before loading it to the target data store. For example, the source data store might a field for timestamp of the record, but the target data store might need the 'day in month' field for the record. In this case, the data integration pipeline will have a data enrichment step to compute the 'day in month' field from the timestamp and keep it the ready for the load step.
i) Response codes – this should include the success and error codes so that the parties

involved should know if the integration pipeline was successful. Based on the response code, the data consumer might retry the pipeline after a specific time.

j) Notification mechanism – There should be a reliable notification mechanism that summarizes the integration pipeline every day. This should include the amount of data exchanged, successful ingested records, failed records along with error code. We can build a mechanism of retry the failed records based on the notification mechanism.

k) Cleanup – If the data is kept on a staging server before being ingested into the target data source, it is important to clean it up regularly. Make sure that the cleanup frequency and mechanism is documented properly.

All the parties involved should sign off on this document. Any changes to any of the variables to the data exchange pipeline should be accompanied by a change in this document.

Are there some common data integration patterns?

Yes, enterprise integration has been practiced for some time now and we can learn from the common patterns. In fact, there are five common integration patterns, and you can adapt these patterns based on the business needs.

i) Migration pattern – This pattern is used if you have some data that needs to be permanently transferred to a target data source.

When to use this pattern:

(a) When you are moving to a newer system because of a business process change

(b) Removing the redundant systems and enrolling a vendor for your business process

ii) Broadcast pattern – In the broadcast pattern, data is 'broadcasted' from one system to many systems. The frequency of this data transfer might be real time or near time. In this pattern, the data transfer mechanism is in an ongoing basis.

When to use this pattern:

(a) When the target system must be notified immediately whenever the data changes. For example, an order taking system might need to notify the CRM and internal fulfilment tools as soon as an order is received.

(b) Analytical dashboards which need to be updated real time for important business decisions.

iii) Bi-Directional pattern – In bi-directional pattern, data from two separate systems is harmonized so that they can function as one. This does not mean that these two data systems cease to exist separately, but it only means that they function as a single data set.

When to use this pattern:

(a) When the users across systems must be presented with a uniform view of all the systems
(b) Ensuring consistency among different systems

iv) Correlation pattern - In correlation pattern, we first find the intersection of the datasets in a bi-directional pattern and then synchronize this data. Let's take the example of a large eyeglass store. This store might want to share the data across stores so that a customer can be serviced appropriately across stores. In this case, the data must move across stores in both directions. The store doesn't necessarily have to move the entire data set.

When to use this pattern:

(a) When you have the same 'record' of data across multiple entities/systems.
(b) When you don't want to share the entire data as that might be expensive.

v) Aggregation pattern - In aggregation pattern, data from several systems is aggregated into a single dataset. This resultant data set has all the data that is needed by the consumer of this data. This is a very common pattern that is used by a lot of the reporting frameworks. One important point to note is that this dataset must be updated constantly when the source datasets are updated.

When to use this pattern:

(a) When you must combine data from different sources as reading from these sources separately might be costly
(b) Creating reports or dashboards for an administrator for different data sources

You can choose and adapt these integration patterns based on your requirements. These patterns will help you significantly save the effort and cost for your integration. It will also help you create reusable assets across your IT department.

Enterprise Integration Best Practices

Now that you have a background on enterprise integration, let's talk about some best practices that your organization can adopt:

A. Plan your integration meticulously - Use the checklist given in this book and adapt it for your needs. List all your current applications, entities within the application, fields within the entities and the requirement that the integration must fulfil.
B. Make data available to all - Empower all the functions of your organization by making integration data available to them. This will help them create their own solutions with common underlying data.

C. Use APIs - REST APIs are used extensively across industry. You can use a lot of rapid application development tools to create common, reusable APIs which can then be exposed to developers. This reduces the burden on your IT department.
D. Use Standard connectors - Don't try to build everything from scratch. You can find a lot of connectors - database connectors, REST connectors, cloud connectors - in the open-source community.
E. Ensure data quality - make sure that there is no data loss and have a mechanism to check whether all the data has been ingested successfully. Invest in some tools which can audit the entire system and flag off any errors. Integration testing must be prioritized. Any integration errors are extremely time consuming and difficult to find once the integration phase is over.

Conclusion

Enterprise Integration is a complex topic. We have tried to cover a lot of aspects in this chapter so that you get a good background on the basics of integration. We are now ready to introduce MuleSoft as a powerful framework for integration. As we dive into details on MuleSoft, you will see that this framework makes it a breeze to integrate with disparate systems and create reusable assets for your organization.

In the next chapter, we will learn about Restful API Modeling Language (RAML) and how RAML is important to define an API specification. Also, we learn how RAML can be designed through Anypoint Designer from Anypoint Platform.

Exercise: Test Your Understanding

Answer the following questions and test your understanding of learning from `Chapter 1`:

`Q. 1.` What is enterprise integration?

`Q. 2.` What are the benefits of integration?

`Q. 3.` What is reusability?

`Q. 4.` What is Migration pattern?

`Q. 5.` What are the best practices of Enterprise Integration?

2

RAML - An Inside Story

RAML is a YAML-based language that stands for Restful API Modeling Language. It is used to define the API structure or specification by defining the components of an API, such as resources, methods that will apply to those resources, an example of the API's request and response structure, and other aspects of the API in a human-readable format. RAML is like other API description languages, like Swagger or OAS, Open API. Each language has its syntax and format, and the use of each language depends on one's specific needs and requirements. RAML is commonly used in MuleSoft to define MuleSoft API specifications in the Anypoint Design Center of MuleSoft Anypoint Platform. Anypoint Platform is an API Management platform offered by MuleSoft. RAML serves many services related to MuleSoft API development, such as designing the API specification, mocking the API, testing, and validation, generating the code, versioning, and documenting, which we can discuss in future chapters. RAML is recommended as an API specification-building tool because it offers API specification-driven development. It allows you to follow API design best practices, reuse code, and use design patterns to maintain the API's consistency.

In this chapter, we will learn.

- How to define RAML and its naming conventions
- RAML Fragments and how to define them
- How to use Anypoint Designer from Anypoint Platform to write API specifications using RAML
- Structure of the RAML

RAML Recommendations

Naming Convention
Raml file names recommendation is to use alphanumeric characters using kebab-case, which means using hyphen separated.

Examples:
The RAML file name can be defined by adding the type of API it is, such as experience, process, or system API.

alldrive-mobile-exp-api: This represents an experienced API for mobile applications.

A request-response example can be defined by adding the Example in the rail like below.
get-all-cars-example.json: This is an example of the get method to retrieve all car information.
The data type can be defined based on the entities the application will have, as shown below.

car.raml, order.raml, customer.raml

RAML Fragments
Fragments are reusable components of RAML, making the API's design and build more straightforward and faster. Another important advantage of using fragments is maintaining the consistency of API specification definitions.

Below are some of the fragments we can create at the enterprise level and use them across the APIs:

- Datatypes
- Traits
- Security Scheme
- RAML library
- Resource Type
- Example
- Annotation Type

RAML Fragments can be created by clicking the "**Create"** button from the Anypoint Designer of the Anypoint Platform. We will see how to create and use a RAML library in the API specification.

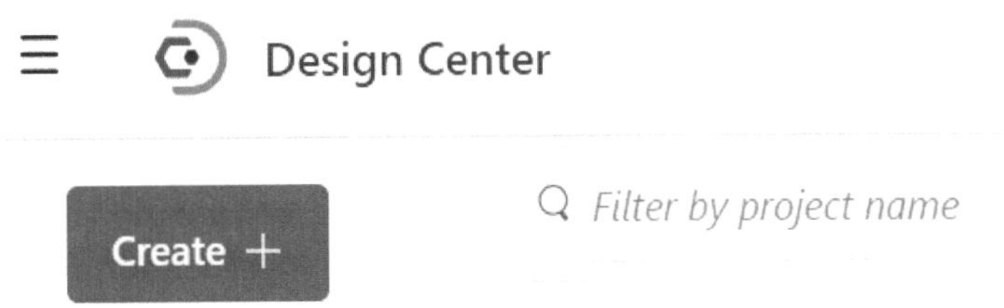

Fig 2.1: Create button in the Design Center

Once you click on the Create button, you will see multiple options from which to select the New Fragment.

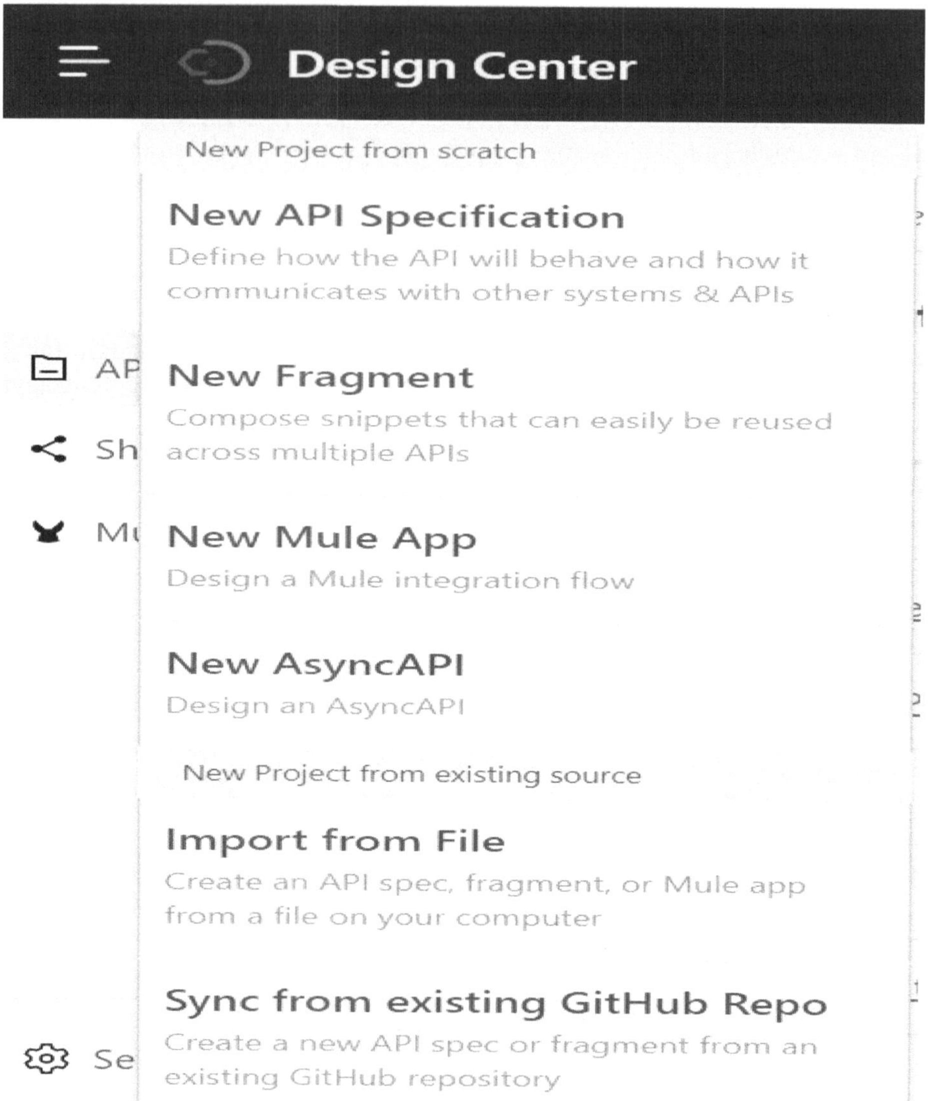

Fig 2.2: Different Options to Create

Once clicked on New Fragment, a popup appears with all the fragment options mentioned above, as shown below.

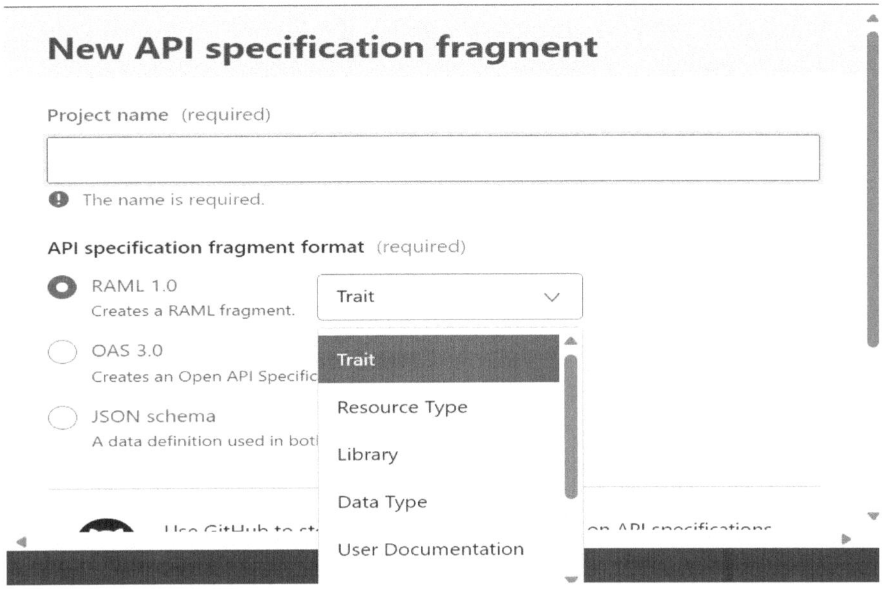

Fig 2.3 Creating Fragment

We can create fragments common for multiple APIs and publish them on exchange.

RAML Library

RAML Library is a collection of reusable components consisting of any number and combination of fragments, such as datatypes, security schemes, traits, and resource types. RAML library is an external file that can be published in exchange and referenced in any other library and API specification.

The Example below creates the RAML library using resource types and Traits fragments.

```
#%RAML 1.0 Library
usage: A collection of common resource types, traits etc.

traits:
  recordNotFoundTrait: !include ../traits/record-not-found.raml

resourceTypes:
  collection: !include ../resourceTypes/collection.raml
  object: !include ../resourceTypes/object.raml


```

Fig 2.4 Library Fragment

Once the library definition is completed, publish the library on exchange using the publish button, as shown below.

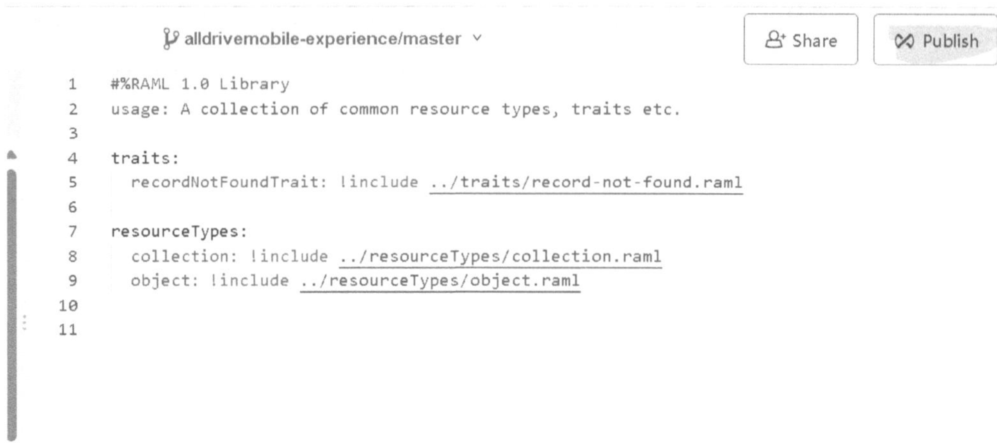

Fig 2.5 Publish Library

The RAML library can be included in the RAML specification as shown in the image Adding API Dependencies below.

As a first step, add the dependencies to the RAML specification by clicking the dependencies button, as shown below.

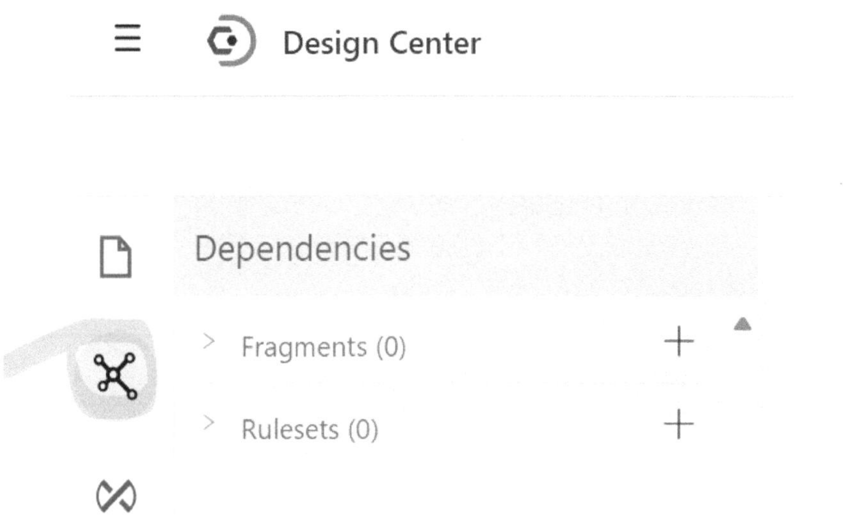

Fig 2.6 Adding API Dependencies

If you click the '+' button next to Fragments, a list of all fragments published in the exchange will be displayed, as shown below.

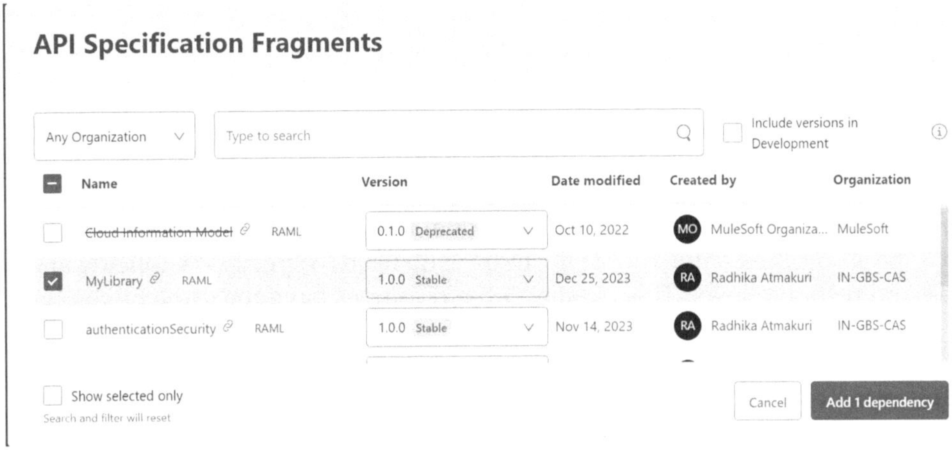

Fig 2.7 Adding Fragment Dependency

Select the fragments from the list required for the API specification and click the Add dependency button. The selected dependencies will be added to the API specification as exchange modules with a folder structure, as shown below. Using the keyword **"uses,"** the dependencies can also be included in the API as a reference.

This is the procedure for adding the fragments as dependencies, which are created and published in the design center as external files.

Fig 2.8 Adding Dependencies to API Specification

Similarly, commonly used traits, security schemes, and basic data types should be referred to and reused through the library fragment.

RAML Media Types

Media Type specifies an API's data format, including how the API accepts the request and produces the response. Although defining the Media Type in the RAML specification is not required, it is best practice to do so. Raml supports various Media Types like application/JSON, application/XML, text/plain, text/HTML, etc.

Below is an example of defining the Media Type

mediaType: application/JSON

It can be defined at the RAML root or individual resource request and response levels. If the media type is specified at the root level, there is no need to specify it explicitly at the resource request and response level. This means all the resources have the same media type, which is defined at the root level.

RAML Concepts

RAML provides a structured way of defining API specifications. Here are the concepts of RAML:

Root: The information we define under root explains the purpose of the API at a high level. Under root element, we define:

Title: The purpose of the API specification
BaseUrl: How the API is going to call
Version: The version of the API specification.

Below is a sample example of a RAML snippet:

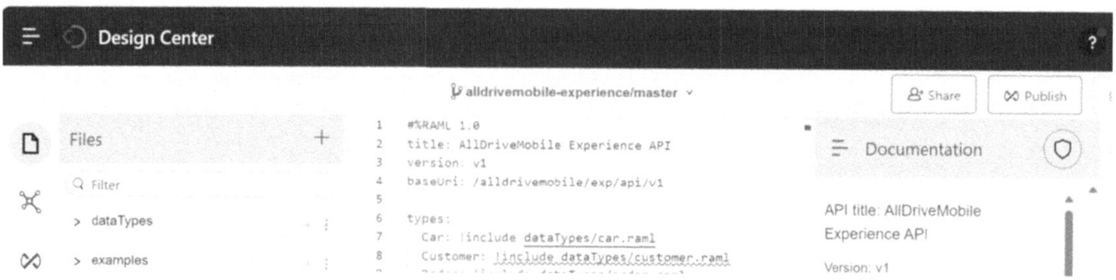

Fig 2.9 Root Element in RAML

Here, the title represents the API specification of an Experience API that is exposed to mobile users. baseUri represents how this API can be accessed, and the version represents the API version.

Resource: A resource in a RAML represents an API endpoint. Resources are always called with a URI. An API can have any number of resources. Resources are defined in lowercase alphabetic. In a resource, we define its purpose, all HTTP methods it supports, and for each method, what kind of request it accepts and what kind of response it provides.

```


/inventories:
  /cars:
    description: |
      Working with cars available in the inventory:
      * Retrieving all cars
      * Retrieving any specific car

    get:
      displayName: Get the list of available cars
      description: |
```

Fig 2.10 Defining Resources in RAML

In the above Example, inventories represent the resource, and cars represent the sub-resource. The description can explain the purpose of the resource, such as that this endpoint provides information about available cars and what operations can be performed.

HTTP Method: HTTP methods, also called verbs, are standard commands clients use to interact with a system. Each method has a specific purpose and acts.

- The most used HTTP methods are GET, POST, DELETE, PUT, and PATCH.
- The GET operation is used to get data from a system, such as a database, ERP, CRM, etc.
- POST operation is used to add the data into a system.
- DELETE operation is used to delete the data from a system.
- The PUT operation updates the data if it exists; otherwise, it creates a new entry.
- PATCH operation is used to update the data.

Here, we will take the GET method example to understand the details. This Example uses the get method to get all the information about the car. We pass a query parameter named status to get the car's information with a specific status. This query parameter is not a required field. It is an option field. If we do not pass any value, it will return all the car information irrespective of the status. Query parameters and URI parameters are used to filter out the specific data.

We can define the method's request structure so that consumers can understand what format to follow while calling this endpoint and what kind of different responses this endpoint or method will give with different HTTP status codes.

```
  get:
    displayName: Get the list of available cars
    description: |
      Get all the cars that are currently available in all the inventory for AllDrive Dealers
    queryParameters:
      status:
        required: false
        enum:
          - Booked
          - Arrived
          - Delivered
          - In-transit
      dealer:
        required: false
        enum:
          - StarWorldCars
          - NewBharat
          - ReadyGo
```

Fig 2.11 Passing Query Parameters

The below Example is for sending URI parameters to the get method. Here, we are sending the vehicle identification number as a URI parameter for the resource cars and applying the get method to get a specific car's details instead of all the car details.

```
/cars:
  description: |
    Working with cars available in the inventory:
    * Retrieving all cars
    * Retrieving any specific car

  /{vin}:
    get:
      displayName: Get a car details by vin number
      description: |
        Working with cars using VIN:
        * Get a car details by it's Vehicle Identification Number(VIN)
```

Fig 2.12 Passing URI Parameters

baseUri: baseUri defines the URL for all the resources defined in the RAML specification. It serves as the foundation for all the complete URLs for all the endpoints.

```
#%RAML 1.0
title: AllDriveMobile Experience API
description: This is the experience API for the alldrive car company for mobile users.
version: v1
baseUri: https://alldrivemobile.com/exp/api/v1
```

Fig 2.13 baseUri

Here, v1 is the version. This is the URL that is going to be used by all the endpoints of this API specification.

For Example, their resource inventories below are the URL
https://alldrivemobile.com/exp/api/v1/inventories

Data Types: Data Types define the request and response of payloads. They are also helpful for validating the data.

To create a datatype, click the '+' button next to Files and select the option New Folder, as shown in the image below. A popup will appear, where you can enter the folder name as dataTypes.

Fig 2.14 Creating Folder

Once the folder is created, click the '+' button next to the folder name, as shown in the picture below. Select the New File option.

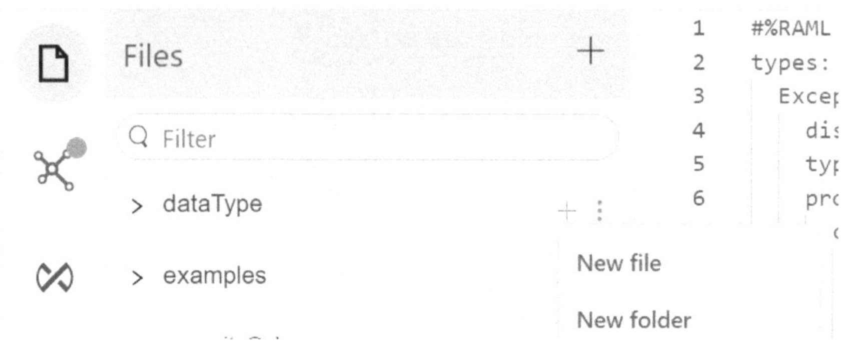

Fig 2.15 Creating a File inside the folder of a Specification.

Once the new file is selected, we can see a popup where you can select the file type as Data Type and enter the file name as shown below:

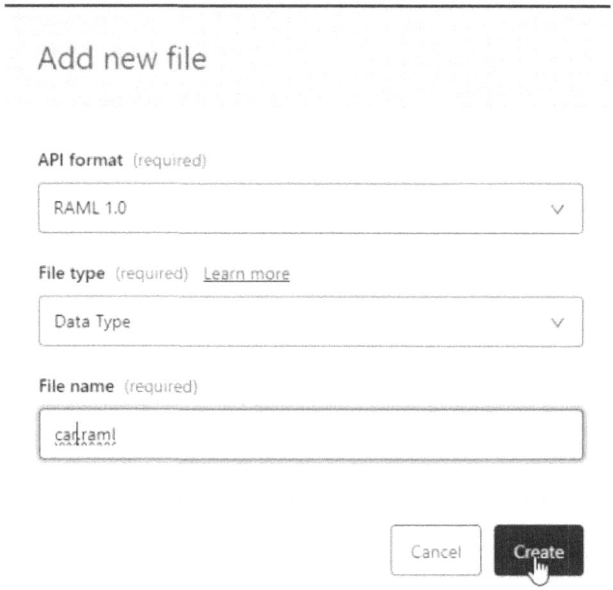

Fig 2.16 Create DataType

Once we click the Create button, a datatype file with the name car.raml will be created. Once the datatype is created, we can define the variables with the required datatype and whether the variables are required or optional. We can also define enum variables with the respective values. The documentation of the fields and the details is on the right side.

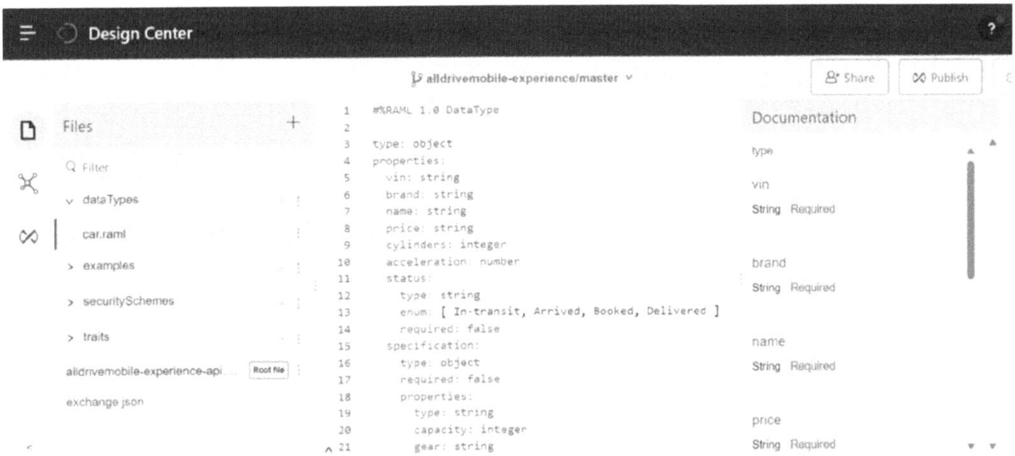

Fig 2.17 DataType Specification

Datatypes can be included in RAML using the keyword "include" under types and using them in the request and response wherever required.

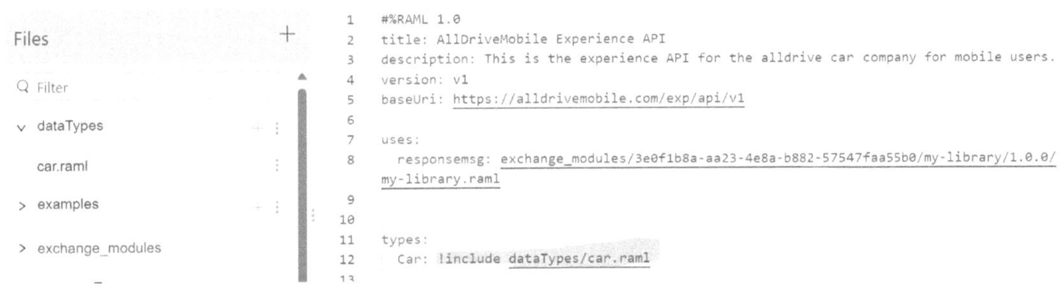

Fig 2.18 Adding DataType in API Specification.

Security Scheme: Securing an API is very important. Security is required to access the different parts of the API. This includes authentication methods, OAuth tokens, etc. Security Schemes can be created using the Anypoint Platform API Designer and used in the respective APIs.

To create a security scheme, click on the '+' button next to Files and select the option New Folder. A popup will appear, where you can enter the folder name as securityScheme. Once the folder is created, click the '+' button next to the securityScheme folder's name. Select the New File option. The Add New File popup will appear. Select the type of security scheme and enter the file name. Click on the Create button.

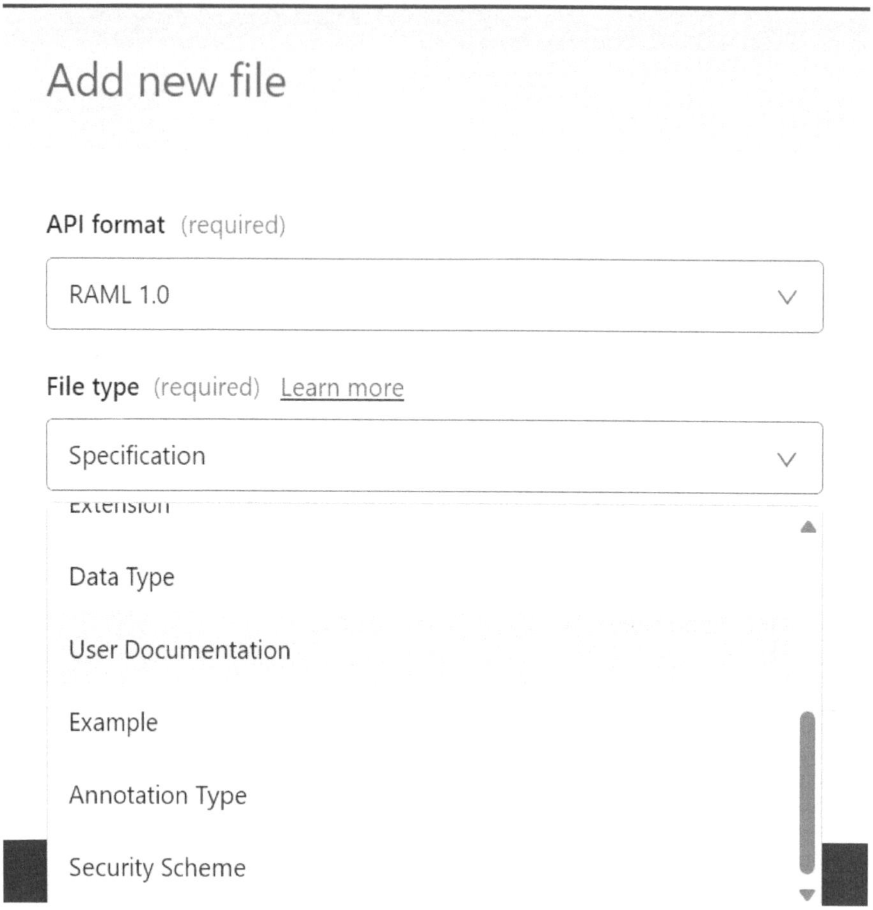

Fig 2.19 Creating Security Scheme

Security Scheme can be included in the API specification as shown below:

```
securitySchemes:
  BasicAuthentication: !include securitySchemes/basic-auth.raml
```

Fig 2.20 Defining Security Scheme in Specification

A Security Scheme can be applied to the API using the keyword secured, as shown below.

```
securedBy:
  - BasicAuthentication
```

Fig 2.21 Applying Security Scheme

Traits: Traits are a set of reusable properties that can be applied to multiple methods of multiple resources. Traits can be defined at the application level or as an API specification fragment. If we create the traits as an API specification fragment, we must publish them in the exchange to use multiple API specifications. We have seen the creation of Fragments in the above section of RAML Fragments.

Now, we will create the Traits at the API specification level. Create a folder named traits, like dataTypes or securityScheme. Once the folder is created, create a file for it.

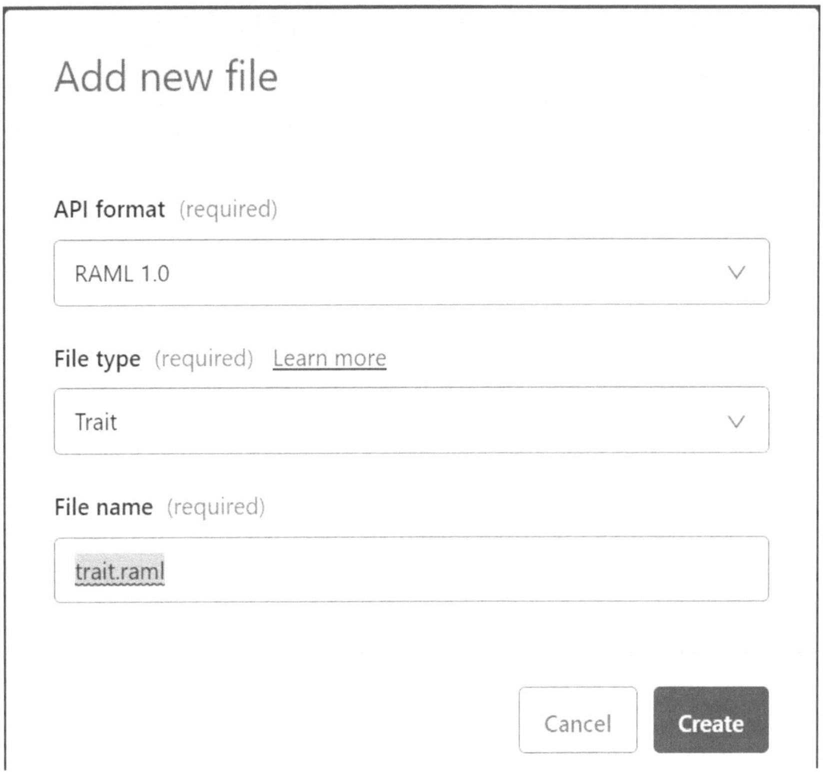

Fig 2.22 Creating Trait

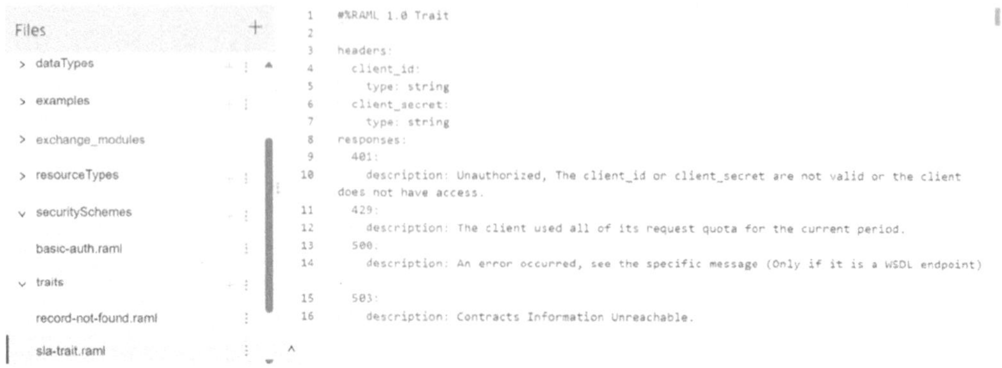

Fig 2.23 Trait Definition

Traits are defined at the Root level of RAML like below:

```
traits:
  SLA: !include traits/sla-trait.raml
```

Fig 2.24 Defining Traits in Specification

Traits can be applied to resources and HTTP methods using the keyword "is" like below:

```
/payments:
  post:
    displayName: Process a new payment
    description: |
      Process and record a new payment
    is: SLA
```

Fig 2.25 Applying Trait

ResourceType: Resource Types are reusable resource definitions used in multiple resources. In a Resource Type, we define a set of properties, examples, and methods that can be applied to multiple resources in an API.

ResourceTypes can also be created, as we have created datatypes, traits, and security schemes in the above topics.

Create a folder with resourceType and add a file by selecting the file type as Resource Type, as shown below.

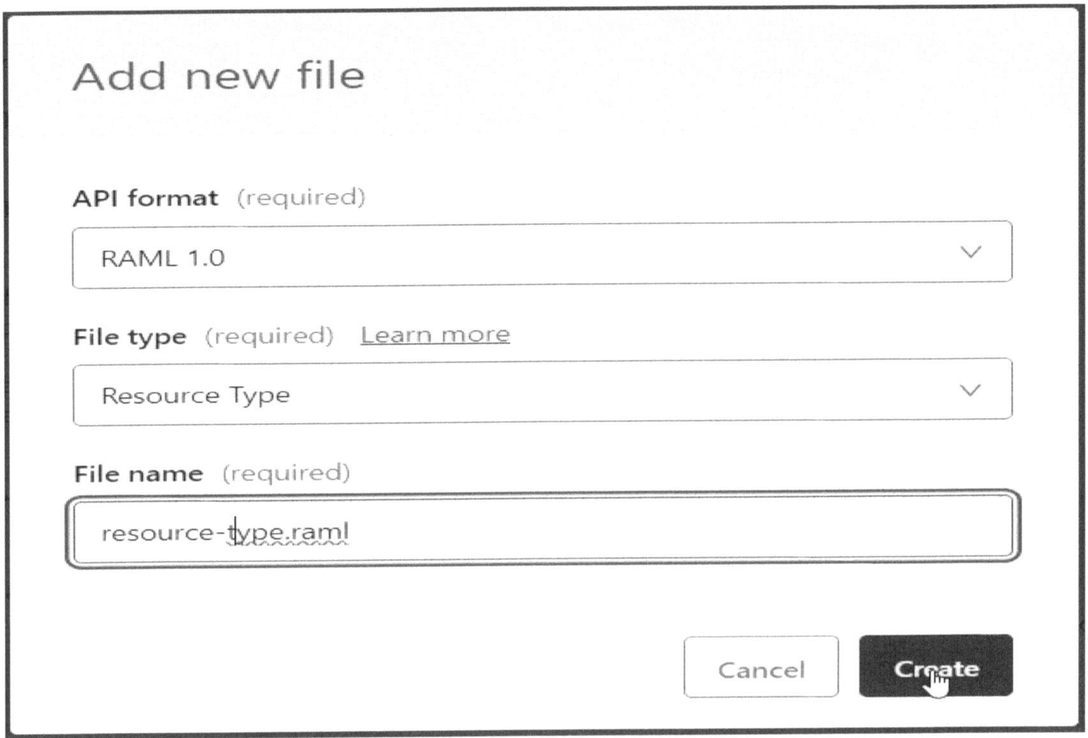

Fig 2.26 Creating ResourceType File

Once the file is created, add the definition as shown below. Here, we are adding the response for the get call, which will be standard for all the API endpoints.

```
#%RAML 1.0 ResourceType

get:
  responses:
    200:
      body:
        application/json:
          examples: <<successExampleReference1>>
```

Fig 2.27 ResourceType Definition

Define these resource types in API specification using the keyword "**resource types,**" as shown below.

```
resourceTypes:
  carresponseType: !include resourceTypes/object.raml

```

Fig 2.28 Defining the Resource Type in API Specification

Use them at the resource level once they are defined at the specification level.

```
/cars:
  description: |
    Working with cars available in the inventory:
    * Retrieving all cars
    * Retrieving any specific car

  is:
    - commonLib.recordNotFoundTrait

  type:
      carresponseType:
        successExampleReference1: !include examples/get-all-cars-example.raml

  get:
```

Fig 2.29 Applying Resource Type

Named Example:
While applying the Resource Type, examples can be used as references, as shown in the above Example.

For this, we will create an example folder like the other folders and create a file by selecting the file type as Example, such as Data Type, Trait, Security Scheme, and Resource Type.

Fig 2.30 Example Definition

These examples can be referenced from the Resource Type.

Documentation: The documentation node provides a concise, human-friendly API description. All documentation should be formatted as a separate file using GitHub-Flavored Markdown [https://help.github.com/categories/writing-on-github/] and included under the documentation tag.

This can be done by creating the fragment or File type as User Documentation and describing the API. The DocumentItem can be defined as shown in the screen below.

Fig 2.31 Documentation Definition

Once the documentation file is generated, it can be used in the API specification using the documentation type shown below:

```
#%RAML 1.0
title: AllDriveMobile Experience API
version: v1
baseUri: /alldrivemobile/exp/api/v1

documentation:
  - !include documentation/documentation.raml

```

Fig 2.32 Defining documentation in API Specification

Advantages of RAML

RAML is a language used to design RESTful API specifications. Writing API specifications using RAML has the following advantages.

Descriptive: RAML is self-descriptive. By reading it, one can understand the API, the points it will support, and the API's Request and Response structure.

Validation: I can understand what validations are available on the request. For Example, does the field accept strings, numeric, or alpha numbers? Also, the field's length, whether the field is required or optional, etc.

Code Generation: By importing the RAML specification, MulSoft API flows can be generated automatically for every endpoint, including the methods supported by each endpoint, such as GET, POST, DELETE, etc. As part of the code generation process, we get the flows of each resource with an HTTPith global error handling the main flow with HTTP l is responsible for routingmponent. API Kit component is responsible for routing the requests.

Documentation: RAML provides clear, human-readable documentation of APIs. This helps developers understand the API's purpose, all supported methods, and sample requests and responses.

Mocking and Testing: RAML provides mocking of APIs before implementation. This can be done using API specifications. We can share the mock API with consumers and stakeholders to go through the mock API request and response, validation of the fields, etc. Consumers can also understand how the API works. For Example, what security will be there to access the API? To access the API, stakeholders can get a glimpse of the username and password. This way, stakeholders can get a glimpse of the API before implementation. If changes require red, we could update the specification and get approval from the stakeholders. Once we get the stakeholders' approval, the API implementation can be started to avoid any rework.

Versioning: RAML also supports versioning. This will help you understand the changes and updates that have occurred over time in an API specification.

Consistency: We can reduce the inconsistencies and errors in the API's implementation by defining the API specification in a structured way and presenting the API as a mocking service to consumers and all other stakeholders.

Interoperability: RAML is not tied up with any specific programming language. Describe the API structure that can be implemented in various technology stacks.

Security: The RAML API specification can also define security requirements to control API access and follow best practices.

Tooling: RAML has active tools, including editors, validators, code generators, and testing frameworks, which make API specification development and maintenance easy.

Code Reusability: RAML supports reusable components like datatypes, security schemes, and raits across different APIs. , enabling consistency in the APIs.

Easy to Read and Write: RAML is easy to read, write, and understand. The syntax of writing the RAML is straightforward. The code is in human-readable format.

Easy to Learn: RAML syntax is straightforward to learn and use as it is straightforward. The

Anypoint Designer helps to correct syntax-related errors immediately and automatically adjusts the indentation of the code. It also provides information about the kinds of fields and attributes supported by the various concepts of the RAML.

Conclusion

RAML has many advantages, including streamlined API design. The documentation generated from the RAML API specification enhances communication and can be easily understood by developers, consumers, and stakeholders. The ability to generate mock APIs gives consumers an advantage by allowing them to get a glimpse of the API's purpose and provide feedback on it before its implementation. RAML supports versioning, enabling the APIs' evolution over time while maintaining backward compatibility. RAML is a valuable tool for developing API specifications; however, which API specification tool can be used based on specific IC needs and workflows depends on factors. We will also discuss SOAP APIs and their purposes. Finally, we will describe implementing a MuleSoft API using the RAML API specification.

Exercise: Test Your Understanding

Answer the following questions and test your understanding of learning from `Chapter 2`:

`Q. 1.` What is RAML?

`Q. 2.` Which Anypoint Platform component is used to develop RAML API specification?

`Q. 3.` What are fragments?

`Q. 4.` Provide some examples for RAML fragments.

`Q. 5.` What is the use of creating the Datatypes?

3

APIs - At a glance

An API, Application Programming Interface, is a set of rules and protocols that allows different applications, services, and systems to communicate. It defines the resources, methods, and data formats that can be exchanged between various applications or systems. In software development, an API acts as a mediator between different application systems. It allows developers to access the application systems' functionality or data without knowing the API's implementation and internal details. Overall, APIs play a crucial role in today's software development world by enabling integration, automation, and collaboration between applications and systems. They empower developers to build complex and innovative solutions by leveraging the capabilities of existing software services and platforms.

In this chapter, we will cover

- An Introduction to Rest APIs
- An Introduction to SOAP APIs
- Implementing Mule API using RAML in Anypoint Studio IDE

Rest APIs

Rest stands for Representational State Transfer Application Programming Interface. It is a style of architecture for building APIs or services. It uses the HTTP protocol. Rest APIs are flexible and easy ways to expose services. Some of the characteristics of the Rest APIs are:

Stateless Communication: The request from a client to a server is independent. There is no state maintained for each request on the server side. For example, if the client requests customer information, the Server returns it with the requested information. In the subsequent request, if the client requests to find out all the orders of the same customer, the Server will provide the order information based on the customer ID provided in the request by the client. The Server does not maintain the first request response or provide the order information.

Client-Server Architecture: The client and Server are independent of each other and developed separately. Generally, the client is the user interface or mobile app, and the Server manages the data and business logic. Communication between the client and Server happens over HTTP.

Resource-Based: A resource is a specific piece of data or collection of data that can be accessed through an API. The resource is uniquely identified by URI (Uniform Resource Identifier). In the URI, the client interacts with the resource using the endpoint.

e.g. https://alldrivemobile/exp/api/v1/inventories

inventories are the resource names in the above example.

HTTP Methods: As Rest APIs work on the HTTP protocol, they use the below HTTP methods to interact with the resources.

- **GET**: Retrieve the information of a resource.
- **POST**: Create a new resource.
- **Delete**: Delete a resource.
- **PUT**: Update a resource. If it does not exist, create the resource
- **PATCH**: Partial update of a resource.
- **OPTIONS**: Used to find out what a particular resource supports all methods.

Cacheable: Responses from the Server can be cacheable. This allows clients to reuse the data instead of going to the Server every time. This can apply to static data or data that does not change frequently. Some of the benefits of the Rest APIs are:

Simplicity: Rest APIs are easy to develop and understand. Using these APIs is also easy.

Flexibility: It accepts different data formats, such as JSON, XML, Text, etc. It can be built using multiple technologies, such as Mule, Spring Boot, IIB, etc.

Interoperability: These APIs can be used by any client who can understand HTTP, such as web and mobile applications.

SOAP APIs

SOAP APIs are web services that run on Simple Object Access Protocol (SOAP). Some of the characteristics of SOAP APIs are:

- **XML-Based:** SOAP APIs use XML, a markup language that can be readable by humans and machines. XML is a complex data representation. SOAP APIs do not allow the use of other data formats.
- **Protocol Independence:** Unlike REST APIs, which are bound to the HTTP protocol,

SOAP services can work on any protocol, including HTTP, TCP, etc.

- **Web Services Description Language:** SOAP services use Web Services Description Language (WSDL) to define data types and operations. WSDL is an XML language. Here, we define how the client and Server can interact to access the services.
- **Complexity:** SOAP services are more complex than REST services. This is due to the strict rules for formatting messages and processing them.
- **Tight Coupling:** SOAP services are tightly coupled with the underlying systems due to their strict contract definitions with WSDL.

Implementing Mule API using RAML

From **Chapter 2**, we learned how to implement RAML and fragments using Anypoint Designer from the Anypoint Platform. Once the RAML definition is approved by the stakeholders, one can start implementing the Mule API. Anypoint Studio is the IDE commonly used to develop Mule applications. It comes with a built-in Java Mule Runtime so that we can deploy our Mule applications and run them locally before deploying them to the Server.

Now, we will see how to implement a Mule application using RAML.

1. Open the Anypoint Studio.
2. Provide the workspace location where the applications are getting created.
3. Go to File -> New Mule Project

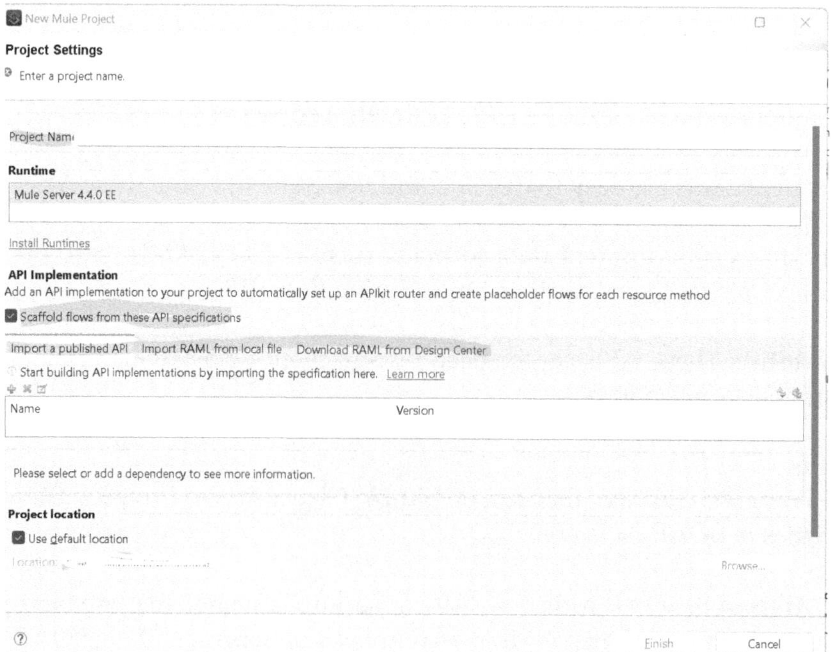

Fig 3.1 Selecting RAML for API Implementation

- Enter the Project name.
- Check the checkbox Scaffold flows from these API specifications. This option creates the APIKit router and the flows for the resource methods defined in the RAML specification.
- There are three ways to add the RAML: from local, from Anypoint Designer, and from the RAML specification published in Anypoint Exchange.
- In order to Download RAML from Anypoint Designer or Import it from Published API, you need to log in to Anypoint Platform and select the RAML. In this case, we are going to select the RAML from Anypoint Designer.
- After selecting the Download RAML from the Designer tab, it will ask for the location.
- Click on the three dots in the text box.
- The dialog box will appear as shown below. If the Anypoint account is already configured in your Studio, it will show the username and the available business groups in the drop-down. If the Account is not configured, click on Add Account and add the Anypoint Platform Account where the RAML is created. You can see all the RAML definitions available in that business group.

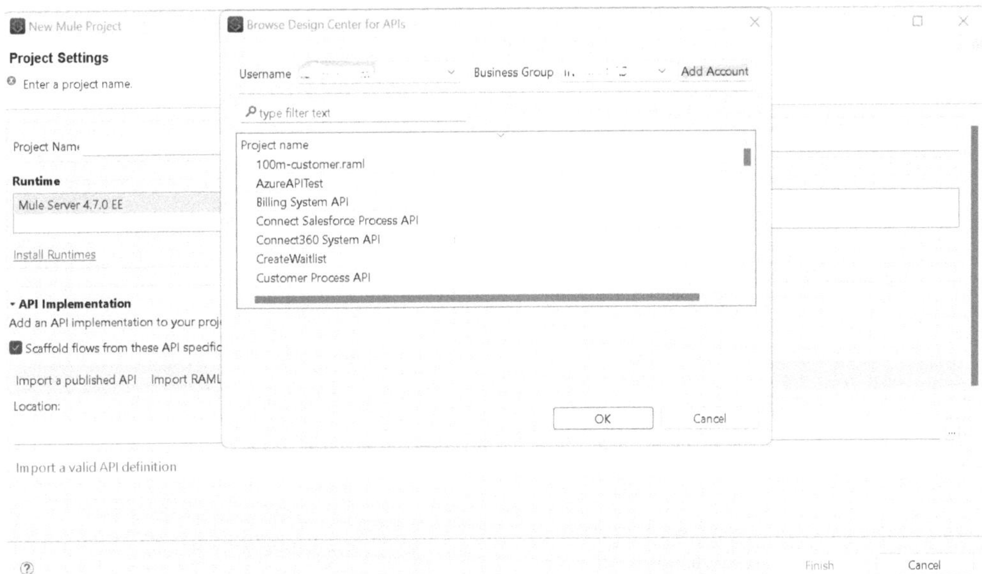

Fig 3.2 Selecting RAML for Anypoint Platform

- Select the RAML you want to create the implementation and click the "OK" button.
- The location field will be updated with the path of the RAML
- Change the Project location if the project needs to be created in another location instead of the workspace.

- Click on the "Finish" button.
- Mule Project is created in the package explorer. All the RAML-related files will be present under the src/main/ resources.

Fig 3.3 Mule Project in Package Explorer

The skeleton of the Mule application is created by reading the RAML. The application contains the APIKit router to route the requests to the respective endpoints/resources with

appropriate methods. This flow also handles generic errors like resource not found, method not found, bad requests, unsupported media type, API not implemented, etc.
The advantage of the APIKit router is that it validates the request before calling the implementation itself. It works in this way because of the RAML API specification, where we have already written how the API should accept a request and what methods the API is going to support, including what kind of request is accepted by the API and the data validations.
Below are some of the errors by default generated in the APIKit router flow and handled by the APIKit router

- **APIKIT:NOT_FOUND:** This error occurs when a request is sent to an endpoint/resource that is not defined in the RAML. It is thrown with the HTTP status code 404 Not Found.
- **APIKIT:METHOD_NOT_ALLOWED:** This error occurs when a request is sent to an endpoint/resource using an HTTP method not defined in the RAML. An error is thrown with HTTP status code 405: Method Not Allowed.
- **APIKIT:NOT_IMPLEMENTED:** This error occurs when a request is sent to an endpoint/resource with an HTTP method defined in the RAML, but the implementation is unavailable in Mule flow. An error is thrown with HTTP status code 501, "Not Implemented."
- **APIKIT:UNSUPPORTED_MEDIA_TYPE:** This error occurs when a request is sent with Content-Type as header and a media type that is not supported by the API requested endpoint method in the RAML. For example, in the RAML, the content type is defined as application/XML, and while sending the request, the content type is passed as text/plain. An error is thrown with HTTP status code 415, "Unsupported Media Type."
- **APIKIT:BAD_REQUEST:** This error occurs when a request has missing fields or invalid parameters defined in the RAML specification. It is thrown with HTTP status code 400, Bad Request.
- **APIKIT:UNAUTHORIZED:** This error occurs when a client does not provide valid credentials to access the endpoint or resource. It is thrown with HTTP status code 401 Unauthorized.
- **APIKIT:FORBIDDEN:** This error occurs when a client is able to authenticate but doesn't have the permissions to access the endpoint or resource. An error is thrown with HTTP status code 403 Forbidden.
- **APIKIT:NOT_ACCEPTABLE:** This error occurs when a client using the Accept header requests a media type that is not supported by the API as per the RAML specification. For example, the client is expecting the response in application/XML, but the API can provide the response in application/JSON. An error is thrown with HTTP status code 406, "Not Acceptable."

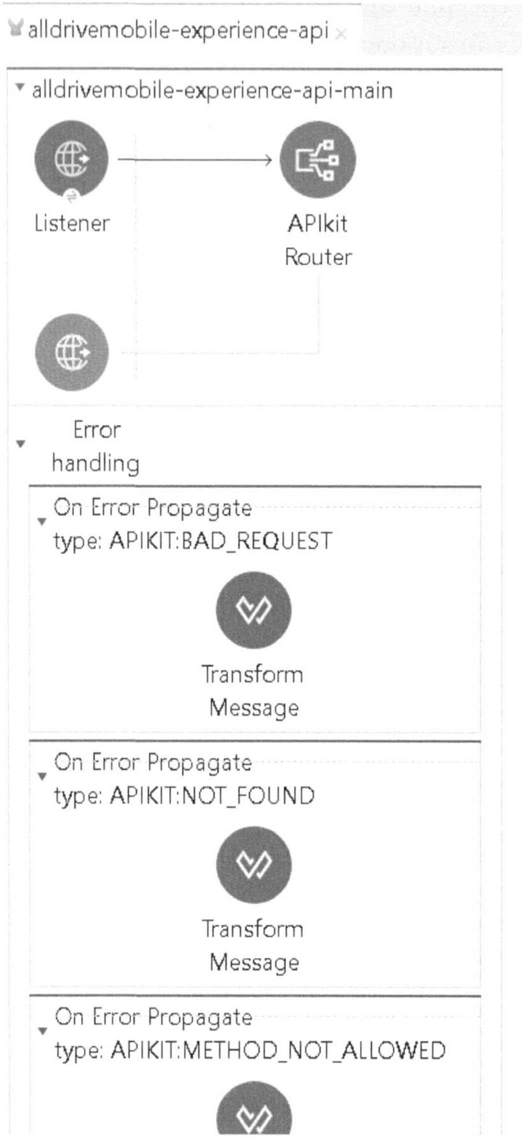

Fig 3.4 APIKit Router

Once we import the RAML from the Design Center, the APIKit Router configuration is automatically created in global configurations. We can add new resources through this configuration window if necessary.

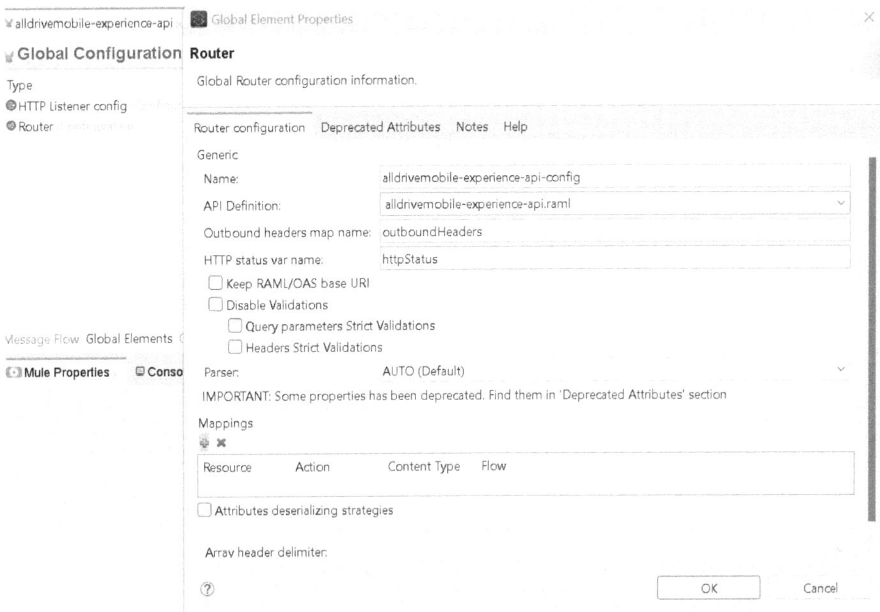

Fig 3.5 APIKit Router Configuration

The APIKit Router flow error handling is also generated with the respective error transformation message inside the On Error Propagate scope. This means the process's execution will be stopped if any of the error conditions match.

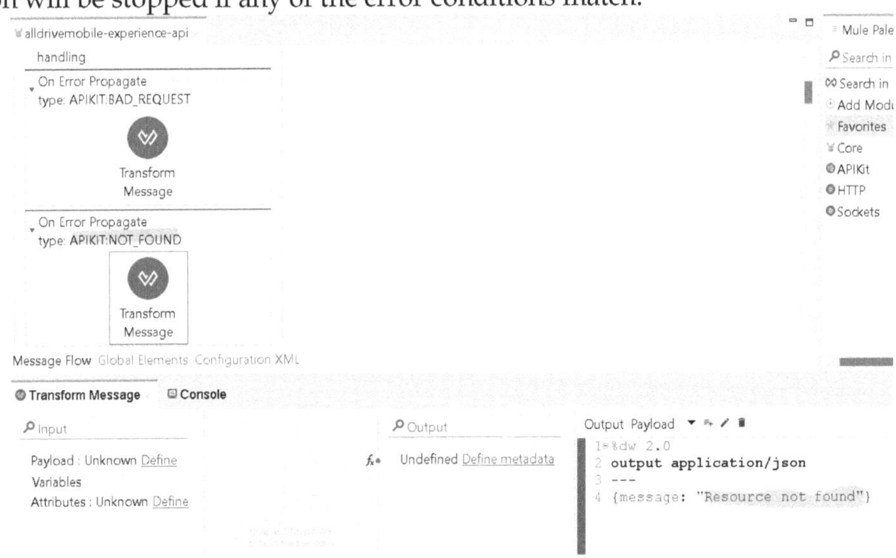

Fig 3.6 APIKit Router Error Configuration

Now, we will see how to update the APIKit Router if RAML changes after the API Implementation starts or if any enhancement comes in the same API where RAML is modified. Possible ways that the RAML can be changed

- Change it in Anypoint Studio and then upload it to Anypoint Designer.
- Update in the Anypoint Designer and download the RAML changes in Studio.

In both cases, the APIKit router must be updated to accommodate the changes. If the RAML file is changed in Studio or locally, update the RAML file present in the src/resources/api folder. Once the RAML file is updated, right-click on the Mule Project, select Mule, and then Generate Flows from Local REST API.

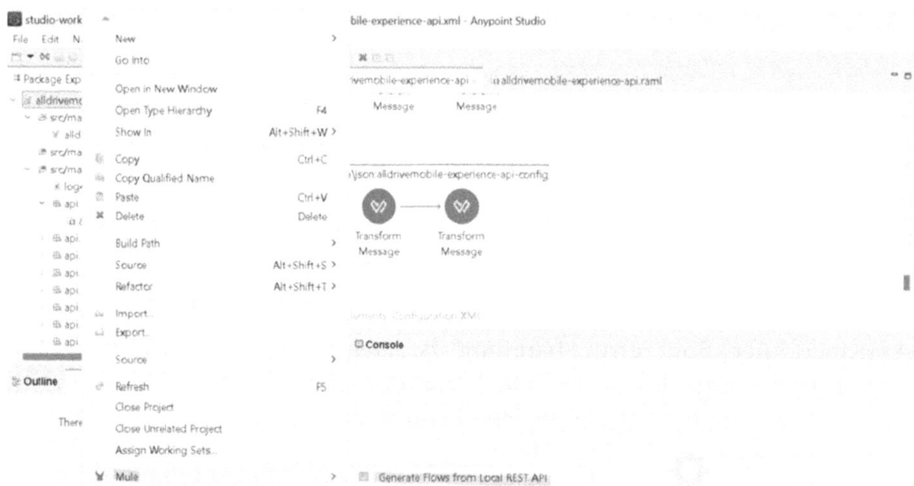

Fig 3.7 Updating the RAML From Local

Once the processing is completed successfully, you can see that the Scaffold Execution Succeeded No errors Found message if the RAML changes are successfully completed.

Fig 3.8 Scaffold Execution Success

If the RAML is updated in the Anypoint Designer, the changes can be accommodated by right-clicking the project, selecting the Anypoint Platform, and Downloading the RAML from the Design Center.

Fig 3.9 Updating RAML From Anypoint Designer

It also contains the APIConsole, which is generated through RAML for interactive representation of the API. Using this, one can see the available endpoints and the supported HTTP methods of each endpoint. This is a visual representation of the API. It is useful for testers, developers, and mainly API Consumers to understand the API structure and how they need to use it when the API implementation is available.

Fig 3.10 APIKit Console

When we deploy the Mule application, an automatic console endpoint is also created in Anypoint Studio or the platform wherever we deploy the API. The deployment might be cloud hub, on-premises, hybrid, etc.

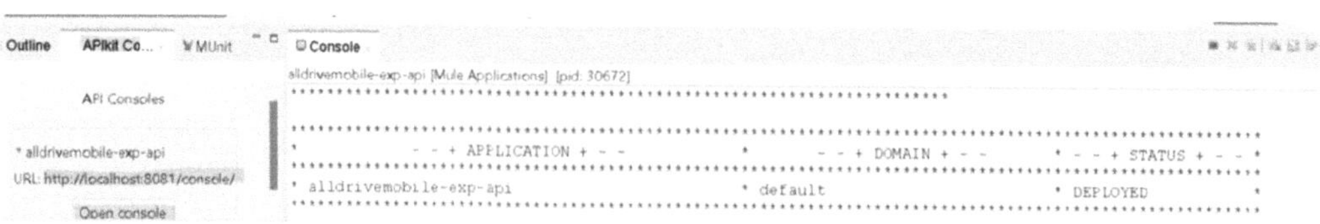

Fig 3.11 APIKit Console URL

Click on Open Console. It will open in a browser with the default HTTP port 8081 and display a summary of all the available resources and supported methods.

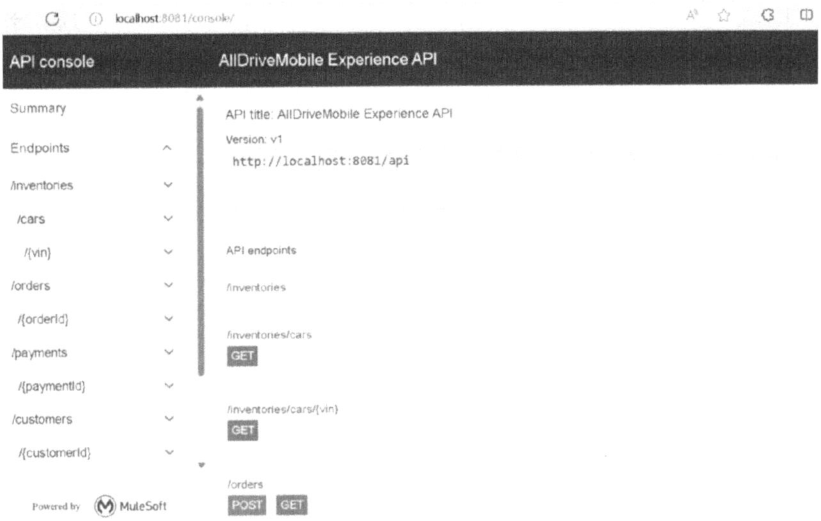

Fig 3.12 API Console

From the console, by clicking on the resource name, we can see the description details added in RAML to understand the purpose of the endpoint, what methods it supports, what each method will do, etc.

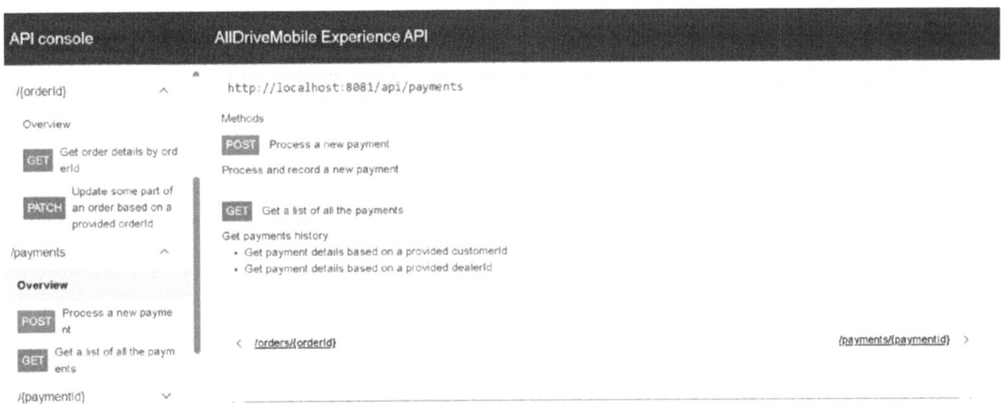

Fig 3.13 Summary of endpoints from the console

By clicking on the method, we can get details like how we can access the endpoint with the method and what kind of request the endpoint provides a response. What security will be applied if we add the RAML specification? It gives the Try it option to try the endpoint. The request and response are mocked examples and not the actual output. All this information can be available if you define them properly in RAML specification. These details can be shown to the consumer once the consumer confirms and gives the go-ahead. Once the consumers receive confirmation, developers can start the API implementation to avoid the rework. If the consumer asks for any changes before API implementation, we can update the RAML and get approval from the consumer before implementing the API.

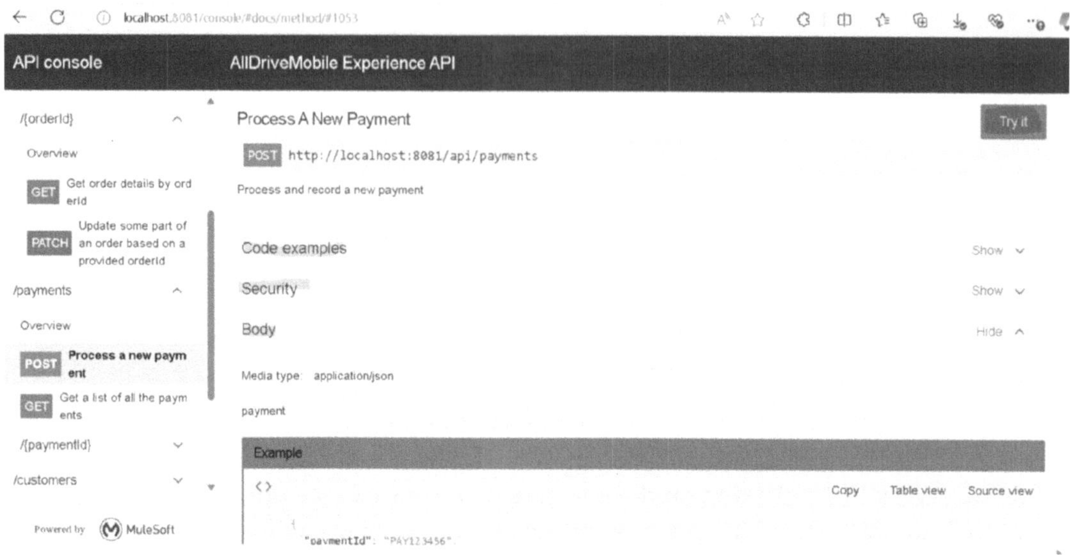

Fig 3.14 Try the API from the console.

Once you click the Try it button, you can enter the fields and send the request. However, this request is not connected to the backend system and provides the response. It provides the data from the mocked examples. A validation error is displayed if you do not pass the required fields. This will give the API consumer an idea of what are required fields and what are option fields, what fields need to be passed as part of the request, and what fields are getting in response.

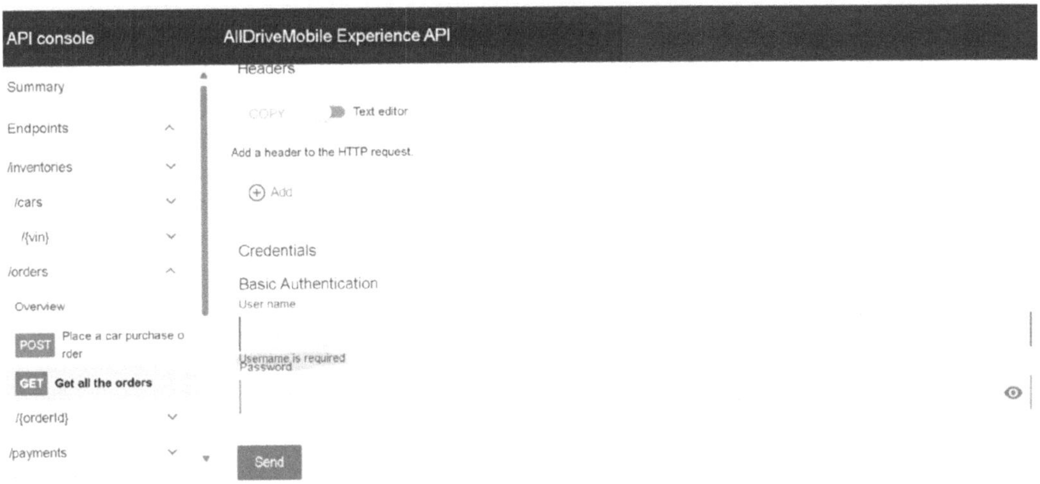

Fig 3.15 Mock API

Now, we will see some of the generated flows by RAML. Here, the example is considered from the orders endpoint. We have a get method to get all the order information and a get method that takes the order ID as a URI parameter and displays the details of a particular order ID. First, we see how to get all the order information. The transformation automatically maps the fields based on our RAML examples and the response structure defined in the RAML. In this flow, developers need to add the logic to connect the backend systems, get the order information, and provide the payload to this transformation as part of the implementation. Also, implement the error handling mechanism. If errors are not handled correctly, the error is thrown from the APIKit Router. If errors are handled correctly, the APIKit Router will throw the error received from the flow.

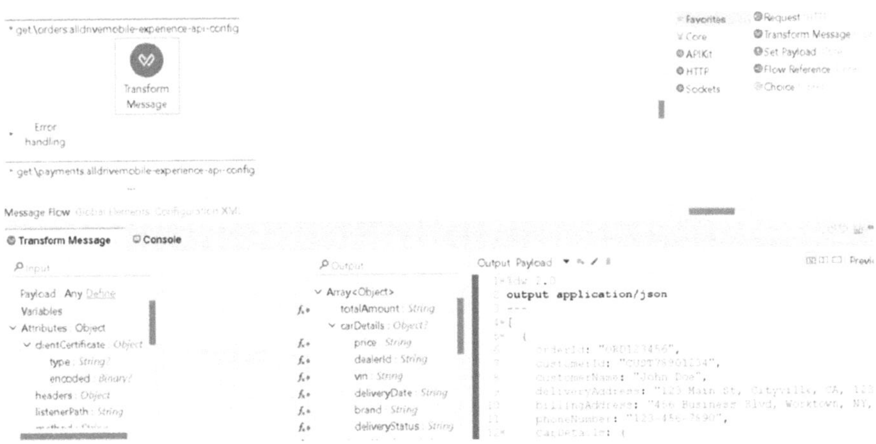

Fig 3.16 Get Orders Flow

Now, we will see Get Order details for a particular order ID. The transformation is generated by reading the order ID from the URI parameters and passing it to the next transformation. So, the flow is generated smartly based on the RAML specification. Here, the orderId variable is created, and the orderId is captured. So, the implementation can be done using this variable and by calling the backend system to get the required information and pass through the next transformation.

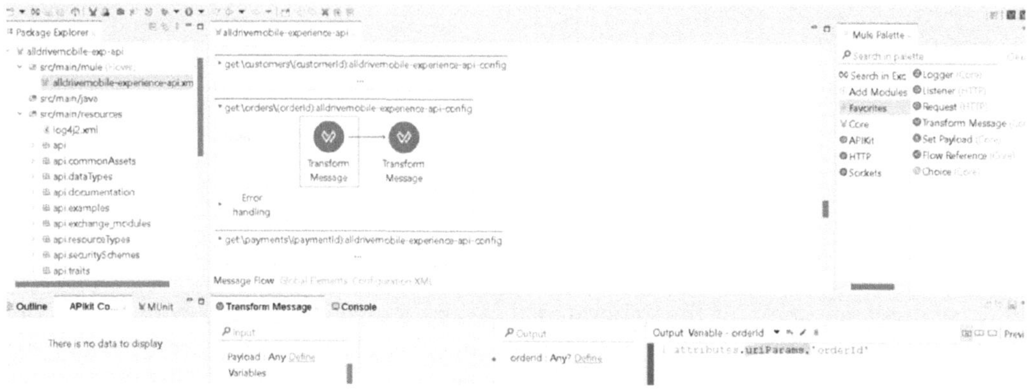

Fig 3.17 Get Orders by Order ID Flow

Similarly, flows and corresponding validations can be generated based on the resources and methods defined in each resource. Minimum transformations are generated when you create the Mule API using the RAML specification. As part of the implementation, we can start using the required connectors, validators, scopes, loggers, and error-handling components to complete the implementation. The other option for creating a Mule project is importing a published API.

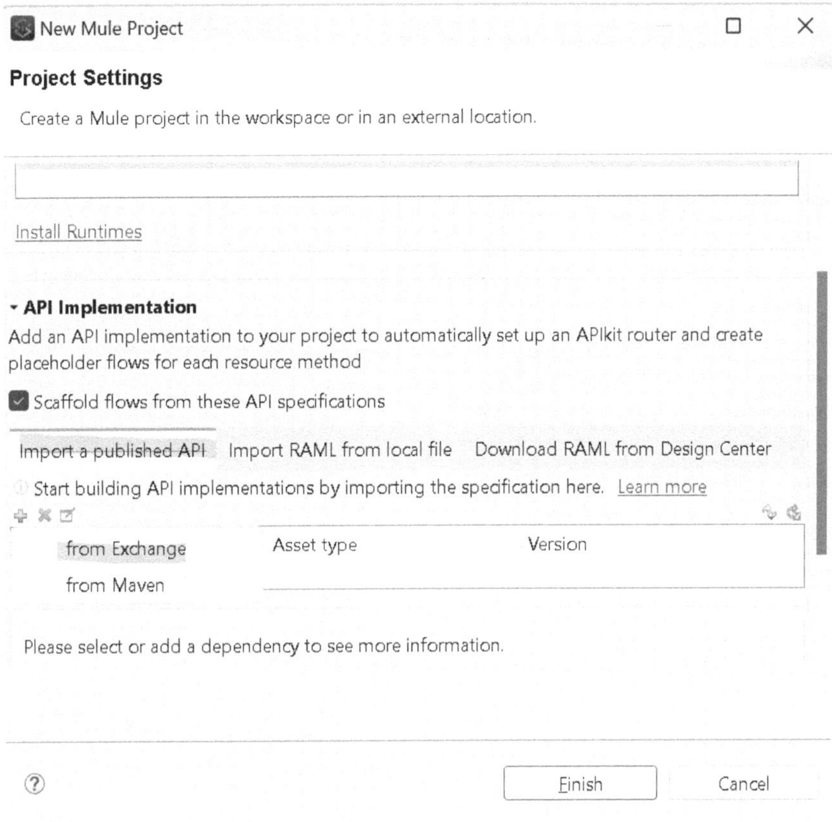

Fig 3.18 Mule Project with Published API

If the Anypoint Platform account is configured, a dialog to add the dependencies opens, from where you can select the published APIs from Exchange. If the Account is not configured, it will prompt the login screen. Once logged in, add the dependencies. Search for the published API specification you want to add as a dependency. Select the published API, click the Add button, and then click the Finish button.

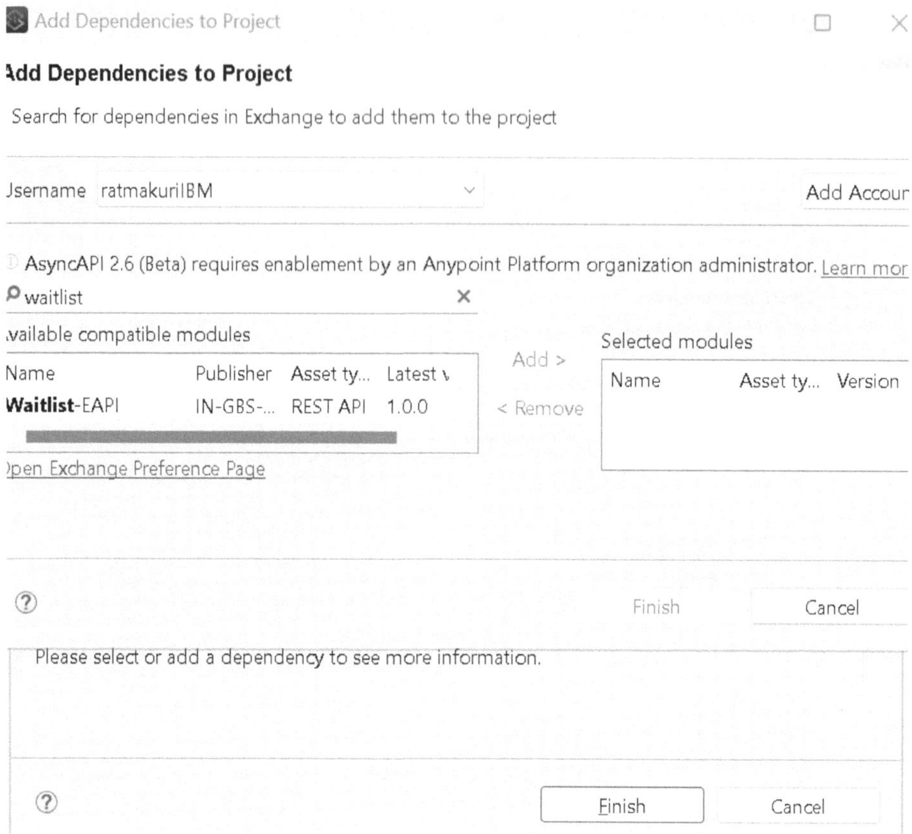

Fig 3.19 Adding Published API from Exchange

It will be added to the New Mule Project window. Then click Finish again. The Mule project is created in the Studio with APIKit Router, APIKit Console, and the flows of respective resources/endpoints with the corresponding methods. The other option you can see under Import a published API is from Maven. We need to download the published API as RAML from Exchange to create a Mule Project using this option. It gets downloaded as a zip file. If you extract the zip file under exchange.json, you can see the pom dependency information.

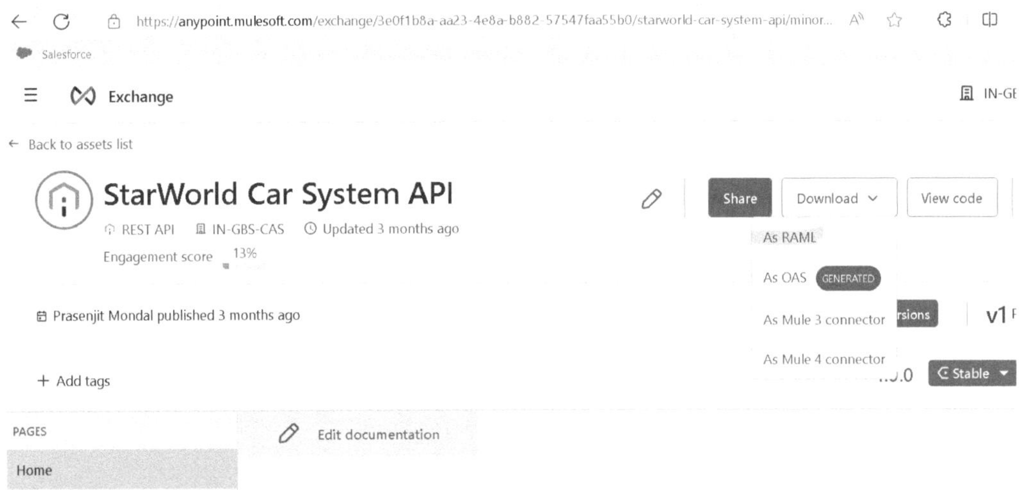

Fig 3.20 Downloading the RAML from Exchange

From the Mule Project dialog box, select the Maven option under Import a published API, as shown in the image below.

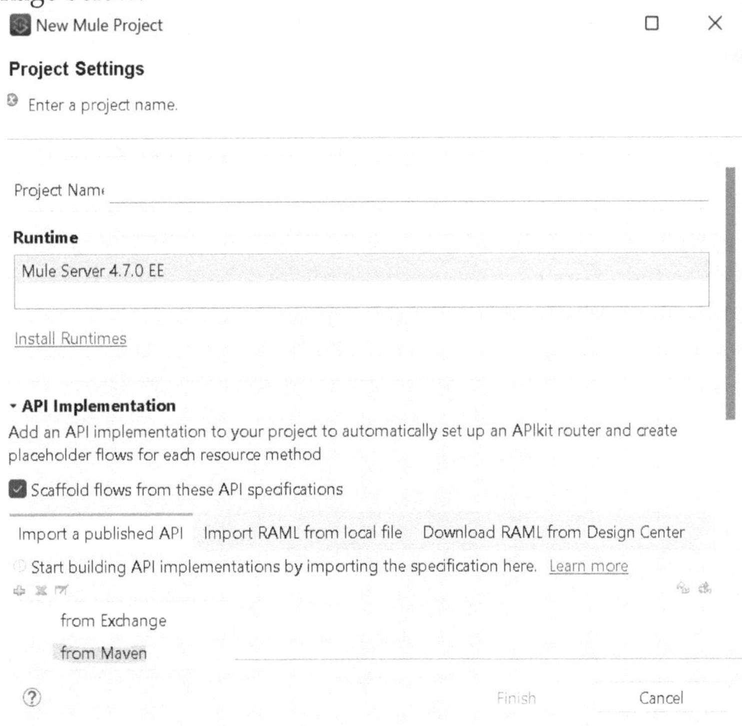

Fig 3.21 Adding Published API from Maven

Once you click on Maven, a dialog opens where you can add Maven dependency information or use the option to install a local dependency.

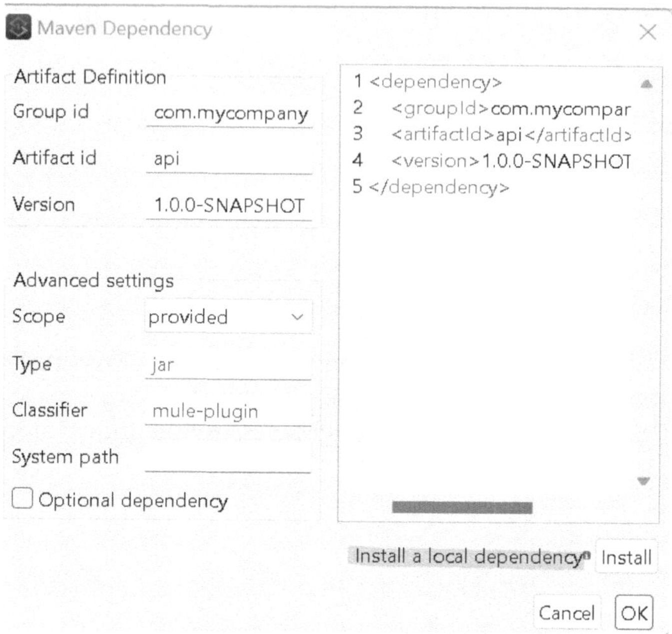

Fig 3.22 Adding Maven Dependency

Click the install button to add the downloaded rail zip file from the exchange. Once the install button is clicked, a dialog opens. Browse to the folder where the zip file is present. The artifact ID is populated automatically based on the zip file. Add rail as classified, and click on the install button.

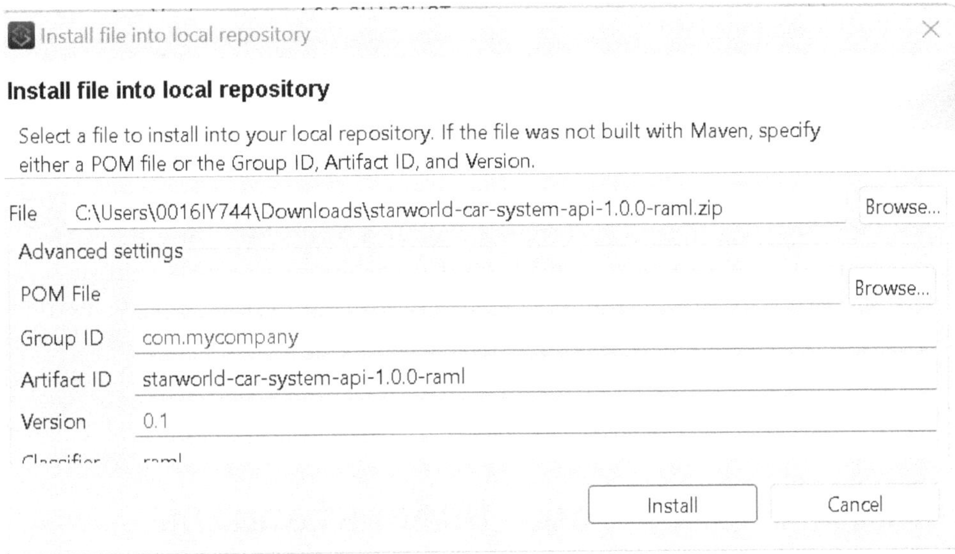

Fig 3.23 Selecting the RAML zip file

Once the successfully installed message comes up, click on OK. The dependency is successfully added.

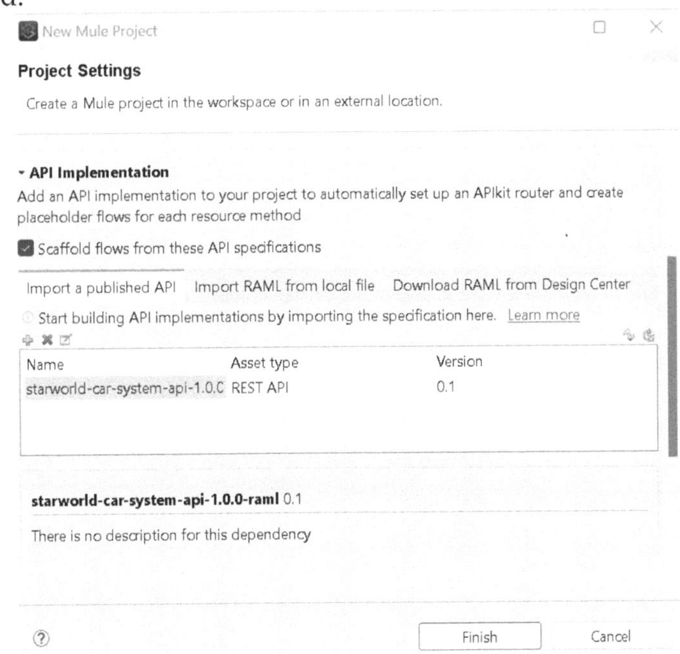

Fig 3.24 Installed Maven Dependency

Click on the Finish button. The Mule project is successfully created with the APIKit Router, APIKit Console, and the default flows for the resources and the respective methods.

Conclusion

In this chapter, we learned about REST APIs and their supported methods and protocols, as well as SOAP APIs. We also learned how to create a Mule API using the RAML definition, the purpose of the APIKit router, and how it functions. We understood how the package structure of a Mule API gets created once the RAML is imported, and we learned about the advantages of the APIKit console and how it is useful for various teams. In the next chapter, we will cover the best practices for creating and implementing Mule applications and the naming conventions for working on the APIs.

Exercise: Test Your Understanding

Answer the following questions and test your understanding of learning from **Chapter 3**:

Q. 1. What are the methods supported by Rest APIs?

Q. 2. On which protocol do SOAP services work?

Q. 3. What is the purpose of checking Scaffold flows from these API specifications while importing the RAML?

Q. 4. SOAP services use which language.

Q. 5. What are the different ways of creating a Mule project?

Q. 6. What is the use of selecting the option Scaffold flows from the API specifications while creating the Mule project?

4

Mule APIs – Best Practices

Every technology has recommendations and guidelines that should be followed as best practices. This chapter discusses the standards that must be followed while developing Mule applications. By following these recommendations and standards, your organization will have a consistent code base, making it easier to maintain quality and enabling collaboration between development teams. If no such standards are defined and followed, this can lead to negative consequences and challenges.

In this chapter, we will cover

- What is the C4E team, and what are the responsibilities of the C4E team?
- Guidelines to define API specifications
- Guidelines to implement APIs using API specifications.

Creation of C4E Team:
MuleSoft suggests creating a Center for Enablement(C4E) team by adding employees from different Line of Business (LOB) teams.

The responsibilities of the C4E team are:

Define API Design and Standards:

- Develop and promote API design best practices and standards at the organizational level. This ensures consistency in the design and implementation of APIs.
- Accelerate software project delivery by setting application standards and providing immediate guidance through the software development lifecycle.

Reusable Assets:

- Reducing development costs by offering highly reusable APIs and integrations for consumption.
- Identify the common assets that can be used across the organization, such as a common error handler, a common logger framework, notification-related APIs, etc.
- Identify the reusable fragments, templates, and connectors to streamline project development.

API Strategy and Governance:

- Communicate the overall API strategy to the organization.
- Provide a stable, scalable, and secure platform that enables innovations throughout IT organizations.
- Identify the Key Performance Identifiers.
- Identify the Data Models
- Identify the API performance, such as throughput, latency, etc.

Coaching and Support:

- Provide guidance and support to development teams, helping them design, implement, and troubleshoot the Mule APIs through the Anypoint Platform.

Monitoring and Analytics:

- Implement monitoring and analytics solutions to track the APIs' performance using key metrics.
- Using these analytics, optimize the API implementations and troubleshoot the issues.

Versioning and Lifecycle Management:

- Establish guidelines for API versioning and follow API lifecycle management by controlling API changes, updates, and deprecation.

Quality Assurance:

- Ensure the reliability and functionality of the APIs developed in MuleSoft by implementing quality assurance processes.

C4E Practice Benefits

- **Alignment with the Business Strategies and Goals:** The C4E team collaborates closely with the IT and business teams to ensure that the solutions align with the business strategies and goals.
- **Expedite Delivery:** Using existing reusable assets will accelerate development and delivery, reduce the cost of the development and deployment effort, and avoid creating duplicate integrations.
- **Maintaining Consistency:** As the C4E team's consistency and quality define the design principles, standards will be maintained across the development of integrations.
- **Governance and Security:** The C4E team ensures that the integrations are secure due to the centralized governance, which mitigates the risks associated with integrations.
- **Progressive Optimization:** The C4E team continuously works to collect feedback, improve the quality of reusable assets, and update practices based on business changes and lessons learned. This team also supports continuous learning by

adapting the latest tools and practices based on industry changes.

Center for Enablement plays an important role in the success of MuleSoft API initiatives by providing centralized governance, guidance, and support at the organization level.

API Specification Practices
The below practices are for RAML specifications and fragments.

Project Naming Conventions:
MuleSoft suggests that the API specification name should follow a pattern.

{context}-{name}[-{layer} | {identifier}]

Where:

- {context}: short code that is unique to the domain that this API belongs to, e.g. car
- {name}: logical name of the application, e.g., employee. The {name} value can also be broken into multiple components; each separated with "-," e.g., car-customer-benefits
- {layer}: the API layer, one of eapi, papi, or sapi; not relevant for interface fragment projects
- {identifier}: interface fragment project identifier can be blank; typical values include common traits and types, e.g., car-types; not relevant for interface specification projects.

Other Naming Conventions:

- Project name components are always separated by hyphens ("-")
- Folder names should use camelCase, e.g., dataTypes, examples
- The main RAML file should have the same name as the project, e.g., car-customer-benefits-eapi.raml
- All other API specification files should use TitleCase, e.g., example JSON payloads, RAML named examples
- Resource names should:
    - be plural when they represent collections (e.g. /customers); otherwise singular (e.g. /cart);
    - use kebab-case when there are multiple components.
- Query and URI parameter names should use camelCase.
- Data type names should use Title Case
- Data attribute names should use camelCase.
- Use kebab-case namespace definitions when importing libraries and other resources via the API specification's uses declaration (e.g., product types, global responses).

API Implementation Practices
The practices below are for API Implementation purposes.

Anypoint Studio Project Structure
The Anypoint Studio project layout will adopt the following structure:

- /src/main/mule (lower-kebab-case)
    - {application-name}-main.XML
    - common
        - z-global-config.xml
            - (Nonsecured connector configuration)
        - z-global-secured-config.xml
            - (Secured connector configuration and the key name must be added in the mule-artifact.json for obfuscating the value)
        - z-common-error.xml
            - A place for API Kit errors, common error handling
        - z-common-config.xml
            - A place for common or utility flows for reusability (i.e., code translation, calculation, etc.)

> ***Note** that the "z-" prefix is used for template-generated files and to distinguish them from other common files.*

    - implementation
        - [get | put | post | delete | patch]-{domain-context}.xml (e.g. post-account-benefits.xml)
- src/main/resources
    - dwl (lower-kebab-case)
        - p-<dataweave-payload-transformation>.dwl (for Payload)
        - v-<dataweave-variable-transformation>.dwl (for Variables)
        - c-<dataweave-common-utility>.dwl (for Common or Utility)
    - examples (TitleCase)
        - {EntityName}[Input | Output].[json | xml | csv]
    - properties (lower-kebab-case)
        - config[-secure][-{env}].[properties | yaml]

Project Naming Conventions
The names of API Implementation projects will adopt the following pattern:
{domain}-{app}-{layer}

Where:
- {domain}: short code unique to the domain that this API belongs to, e.g., car

- {app}: logical name of the application, e.g., employee. The {app} value can also be broken into multiple components; each separated with "-," e.g., customer-benefits
- {layer}: the API layer, one of eapi, papi or sapi.

Complete example: **car-employee-benefits-papi.**

Mule naming conventions Flow files

- Must be named using all lowercase names separated by hyphens (dashes). No underscores are to be used.
- The "main" flow file (either generated by APIKit or a main entry point) must exactly match the name of the interface specification (e.g., customer-benefits-papi.xml for customer-benefits-papi.raml). However, if the project implements multiple interface specifications, there can be multiple "main" flow files.
- The "implementation" flow must have the following pattern:
    - [get | post | put | delete | patch]-{context}.xml (e.g. get-employee-benefits.xml)

Flows and sub-flow names

- Must be named as {method}-yyyy, where {method} is the flow file name (excluding the .xml extension) and yyyy is the actual flow or sub-flow name, with name components separated by hyphens (e.g. get-employee-benefits). This causes flows to be grouped in the dropdown and autocomplete menus, making them easier to navigate.
- Flow names must be descriptive and concise and cannot contain embedded underscores or special characters (e.g., get-employee-benefits).
- The flow name in the main XML file must exactly match the root file name (e.g., car-employee-benefits.raml) of the API specs from RAML (again, excluding the .raml extension) and have the term—central appended to it (e.g., car-employee-benefits-main).
- Use the Notes tab to describe the flow or sub-flow briefly.

> **Note**: *The names of flows generated by APIKit scaffolding must not be modified; otherwise, the router will fail to find the flow implementing a particular endpoint.*

Message Processors and scopes

- Do not keep the default names as Anypoint Studio defines.

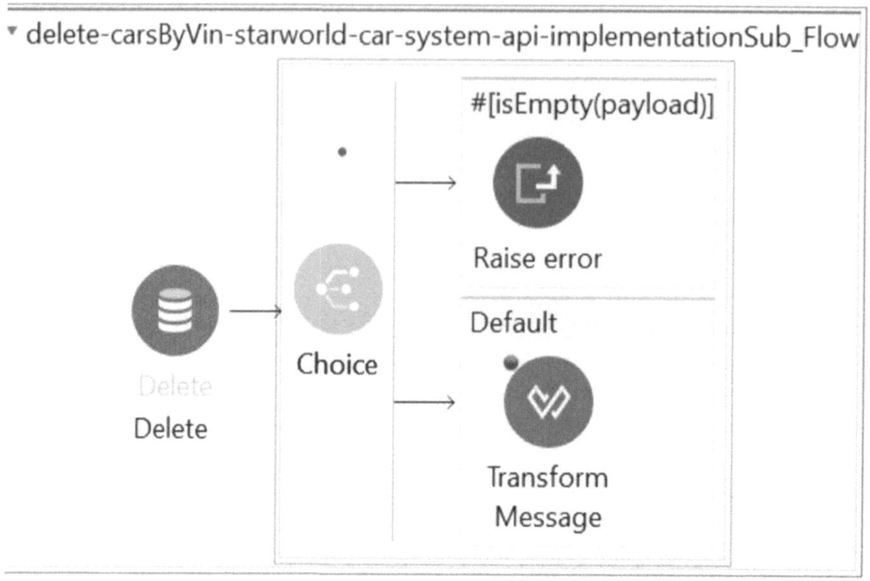

Fig 4.1 Mule Flow with default names

- In the above flow, we cannot understand which table it gets deleted from when we see the DB delete operation. Similarly, in the failure scenario, the error is raised. The Transform Message component is used for an unknown purpose. Since the processor type remains visible, the display name should be added to the overall description. For example, the display name for a Set Variable processor should indicate the actual variable being set (e.g., Response Status). In contrast, for a Transform Message processor, it should be the type of transform being done (e.g., DB Success Response).

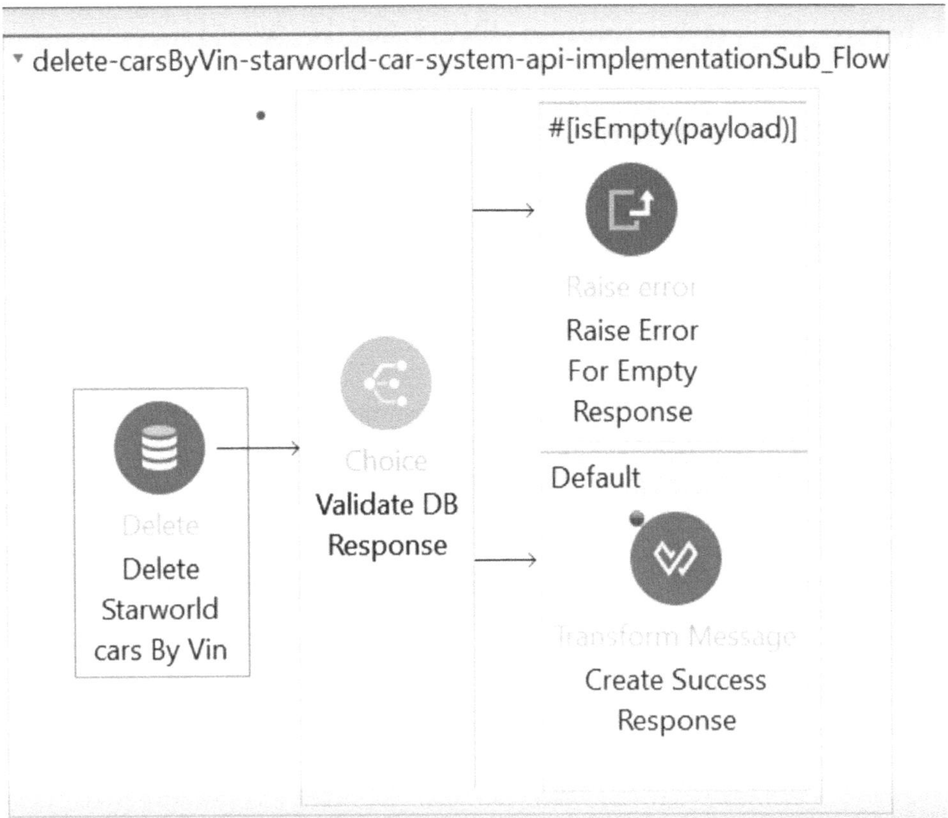

Fig 4.2 Mule Flow with description

- Keep the scope name for scopes but add an underscore and a brief description of the scope (e.g., "For Each Customer Entry")—name components following the same convention as for flows above.
- For a more complete example, the names in the following image are undesirable because they are all left at their studio default values:

Global Configurations

- All global configuration elements in applications must be defined in the flow src/main/mule/common/z-global-config.xml. This includes all configuration items such as HTTP listeners, ObjectStore references, connector configs, etc. There should be no configuration elements in any other flow files within the project. This means that after generating a skeleton flow from an API, the HTTP connector and Router definitions must be moved out of the default location and into the global config file.

- For libraries, the global configuration file should be called global-{library}.xml, where {library} is the short name of the library. For example, if the org-common-core library requires some global resources, they would be defined in a file named global-common.xml.

Configuration and Properties Files

All deployment-specific properties, such as hosts, ports, access keys, etc., will be externalized in properties files located under the src/primary/resources/properties folder. This is useful if any changes in these values do not require code changes in all places. For Mule properties, use .yaml files; for Java properties only, use .properties files.

At a minimum, each project should contain the following files:

- Config.yaml: Unsecured properties common to all environments
- config-{env}.yaml: Unsecured properties specific to individual environments
- config-secure-{env}.yaml: Secured properties specific to those environments.

The deployment environment identifier {env} represents the target environment in CloudHub (typically one of dev, test, or prod) used for application deployments. Note that it does not need to match the exact name of the CloudHub environment, e.g., test rather than test. For local workstation deployments, use local; config-local files are typically not checked into source code. Note that there are generally no common secured properties.

If additional organization of properties files is required because there are separate files for mapping or translating values in each environment, group them under sub-folders by environment identifier (e.g., src/primary/resources/properties/dev). This makes referencing using the same property as the file names easy.

User-defined property keys should use camelCase and be stored in a hierarchical structure rather than a flat one, e.g., retry. Account and retry.interval rather than retryMaxCount and retryInterval.

Configuration Element Names

Configuration elements in an API can be defined as description_type, where the description can be any name that describes the purpose for which the configuration is created. Type is the type of configuration it is.

Below are some examples:

- oracle_db-configuration
- weather_http-listener

Example Project Structure

The diagram below depicts the structure of the Anypoint Studio project.

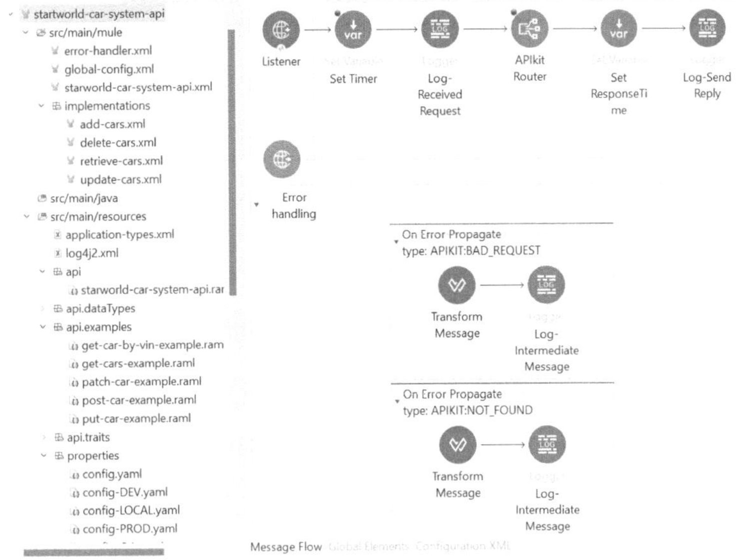

Fig 4.3 Project Structure

Case option descriptions

- kebab-case
- snake_case
- SNAKE_CASE_CAPS
- camelCase
- TitleCase (aka PascalCase)

Case	Description	Example
Kebab	All lowercase with words separated by "-"	customer-name
Snake	All lowercase with words separated by "_"	customer_name
Snake (Caps)	All uppercase with words separated by "_"	CUSTOMER_NAME

Case	Description	Example
Camel	The first word is all lowercase, and the first letter of subsequent words is capitalized with no separator character between words	customers name
Title / Pascal	The first letter of all words is capitalized, and all other characters are lowercase with no separator character between words.	CustomerName

Table 4.1: various Cases

Event-based API best practices

Event-based APIs are important integrations where systems require asynchronous real-time processing. When implementing these integrations, we must consider that they are reliable, scalable, and easily maintainable.

Points to be considered while developing the event-based API integrations are:

- Design so that the consumers and producers are loosely coupled so that they can evolve independently and are easily scalable.
- Design consumers to handle duplicate events. This is important because events in distributed systems might be delivered more than once. Use unique IDs to represent the events.
- Implement dead letter queues and retry mechanisms for events that fail for various reasons and process them to avoid data loss. If the events fail after multiple retries, make sure those are appropriately handled.
- Design the topics carefully to ensure scalability and balanced load distribution.
- Use batching wherever it is applicable and manage the queues efficiently.
- Use Data Encryption to encrypt the sensitive data in transit and rest to protect from unauthorized access.

Conclusion

The best practices mentioned in this chapter are just guidelines. You should follow these guidelines to build your standards based on the organizational needs. The standards you define might change as the organization grows or changes its internal structure. It is important to publish these standards organization-wide and review them periodically. Keep these factors in mind when you publish new versions of your standards:

1. Identify the key stakeholders who will be impacted.
2. Assess the current processes and identify the gaps
3. Define development goals.
4. Assess the current technology stack.
5. Prioritize continuous development - incentivize teams to come up with improvements.
6. Create systems to measure the impact of standards.

In the next chapter, we will learn the importance of securing properties and the different mechanisms available to secure properties in MuleSoft.

Exercise: Test Your Understanding

Answer the following questions and test your understanding of learning from `Chapter 4`:

`Q. 1.` What is a C4E team?

`Q. 2.` What are the responsibilities of the C4E team?

`Q. 3.` What is the importance of Global configuration files?

`Q. 4.` Which Case can user-defined properties be in.

a) Upper Case
b) Lower Case
c) Camel Case

`Q. 5.` What is the format to define flow and subflow names in MuleSoft?

5

Secure Properties

Application Programming Interfaces play a crucial role in today's communication between various systems. They enable data exchange between various systems, access to various systems, integration between various platforms. All these services come with the responsibility of security and integrity of the data exchange between various systems. The main aspects of the API security are protecting the properties which can include a system credentials, secrets, data. Securing properties implementation can be done by using various algorithms to safeguard the assets from unauthorized access and not expose them publicly. In this chapter we will talk about how properties can be secured in a Mule API using various options. Securing configuration properties by encrypting as another security level for your applications.

In this chapter, we will cover:

- How to Secure properties in Mule
- Different ways of Securing properties in Mule API.
- Use of Securing properties in Mule Application

Need of Secured Properties

Securing the properties in an API is essential for various reasons which are described as below:

- **Protecting Sensitive Data:** In the APIs we define sensitive data like user credentials, credentials of a system, some data which can be used as business logic needs to be secured and protected from unauthorized access and tampering.
- For example, we define the properties to connect a DB system like username and password to connect the Database and perform various operations. The username, password credentials need to be encrypted as a best practice.
- **Maintaining Trust and Compliance:** Clients, partners and users are relying on APIs to exchange the data between various systems. By securing the properties Organizations can demonstrate how they are ensuring the data privacy by following various security compliances.
- For example, the credit card information of the user exchanging between the APIs

and the payment gateways etc...

- **Preventing Security Breaches:** APIs are exposed to various vulnerable attacks like injection attacks, data breaches, denial of service attacks and unauthorized access. Securing properties mitigates such attacks and breaches. [Accidental source code access should not disclose system credentials.]

Various ways to Secure Properties in an API

Securing properties in an API involves implementing a combination of security mechanisms and following best practices.

- **Authentication:** Verifying the identity of the users, systems who are accessing the APIs. This can be achieved by using client credentials, Oauth tokens, JSON Web Tokens.
- **Authorization:** Controlling the access of API resources based on the permissions, privileges granted to the specific users, systems. This can be done by adding the scopes, role-based access control.
- **Encryption:** Protecting the sensitive data by encrypting using various algorithms. Also following some kind of logic or masking of the data while printing the data in the logs. Transport Layer Security ensures encrypted communication between clients and API server.
- **Input Validation:** Validating user input while accessing the API to avoid injection attacks. This helps to ensure the security of data processed by API.
- **Logging and Monitoring:** Logging the API activities and monitoring helps to identify any security threats in timely manner. It also helps to track the security regulations and policies.
- **Rate Limiting and Throttling:** Implementing rate limiting and throttling policies to prevent DoS attacks and excessive usage of APIs. This will help the leverage of the APIs use, maintain the API availability and performance.

Securing Properties in a Mule API

Though there are various ways to secure the application properties in Mule, we will discuss most widely used 4 ways to secure mule Application/API properties.

Create a file with a proper name under **src/main/resources** of the project folder in Anypoint Studio. The file extension can be **.yaml** or **.properties**.

In our example we will use the name of the file as secured-application.properties. In this file define those properties which needs to be secured based on the application requirements.

Generally, we define the credentials of the systems which we are going to connect in the API will be encrypted and stored in this file. These files also need to be created for environment specific as every environment the credentials are different.

e.g **secured-application-dev.properties, secured-application-qa.properties, secured-application-prod.properties**

Here, securing properties refers to encrypting critical information in the mule application. Though we are using multiple ways to encrypt the property key values for mule application. But the decryption method is same for all of them. Also, we might have scenarios where we need to encrypt the whole file or just some key-values in a **.yaml/.properties** file.

Mule Secure Properties tool require an algorithm as a parameter to encrypt the data. The tool allows below algorithms to encrypt the data.

- **AES (Advanced Encryption Standard):** This is the default algorithm if no algorithm is specified explicitly while running the tool. This is most used symmetric encryption algorithm which comes with different key sizes like 128, 192 and 256 bits.
- **Blowfish:** This is also a symmetric encryption algorithm. It comes with key lengths from 32 to 448 bits.
- **DES (Data Encryption Standard):** This is an old symmetric algorithm with a 56-bit key size.
- **DESede:** This symmetric encryption algorithm is an advanced version of DES. It provides higher level security than DES by applying the DES algorithm 3 times to each block.
- **RC2:** This is also a symmetric encryption algorithm works on a variable key size from 8 bits to 1024 bits. It operates on fixed size blocks.

Mule Secure Properties tool require the mode as a parameter to encrypt the data. Mode refers the specific way in which the encryption algorithm processes the data.

The tool supports below modes:

- **CBC:** Cipher Block Chaining is the commonly used mode. The process creates each block of plain text combined with the previous ciphertext block
- **CFB:** Cipher Feedback encrypts the plain text in smaller increments.
- **ECB:** Electronic Codebook is a simple mode operation which divides the plain text into fixed size blocks and encrypts them independently using the same encryption key.
- **OFB**: Output Feedback is a mode which generates a keystream block and then combines with plaintext to generate the ciphertext.

Let's talk about various ways to achieve encryption in a mule application –

Using Secure Properties Generator Online Tool: MuleSoft is having an online tool to generate encrypted values for the properties which we want to secure:

- Go To https://secure-properties-api.us-e1.cloudhub.io/
- Below screen gets displayed.

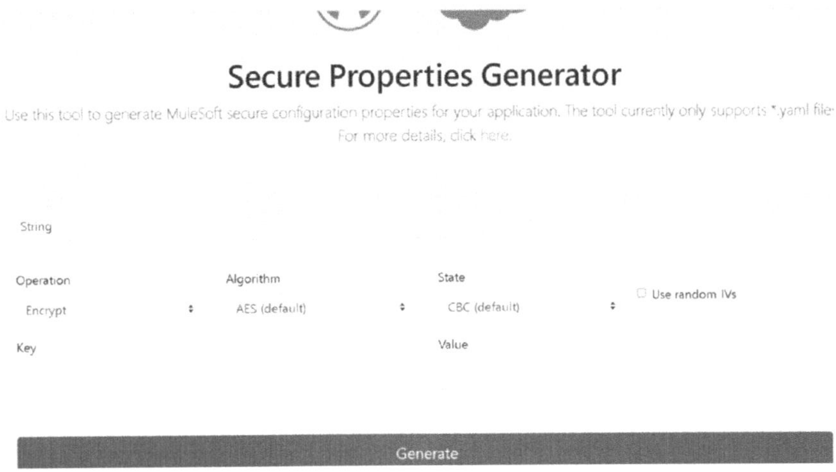

Fig 5.1 Secure Properties Generator Tool

- Choose the operation as encrypt as we are encrypting the value. Choose the algorithm and state. State is nothing but the mode which is the procedure which allows the Mule runtime to repeatedly use a block cipher with a single key. Also, set the attribute Use random initialize vectors (IVs) value as true or false. If this value is set as true, the decryption algorithm assumes IVs are prepended to the cipher text during the decryption process.
- Enter the Key and Value and click on Generate button to get the encrypted value. Key is the value which is used by the selected algorithm to encrypt the value. Value is the value which needs to be encrypted.

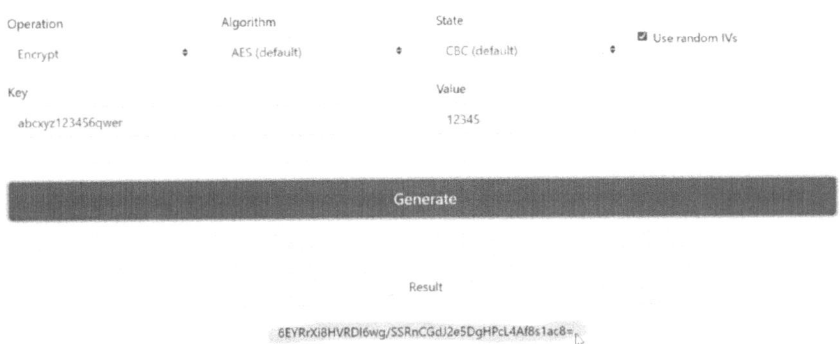

Fig 5.2 Secured Properties Tool Configurations

- Copy the generated encrypted value and define the encrypted value in the Secured Properties Configuration file of the project as shown in the below screen.

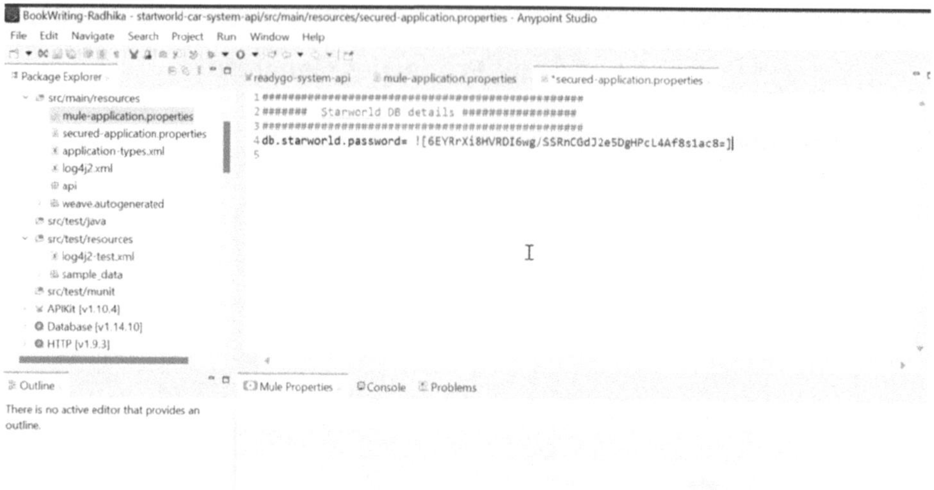

Fig 5.3 Define the encrypted value in Secured Properties Configuration File

- Right click on the API name in package explorer and select Run As and then select the Runtime Configuration option.

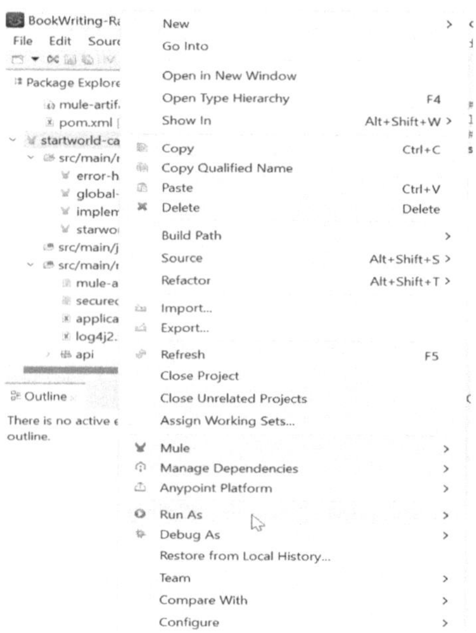

Fig 5.4 Runtime Configuration Window

- Configure the Key as VM arguments in Runtime Configuration window. Select the api name for which the VM arguments need to be applied as shown below.

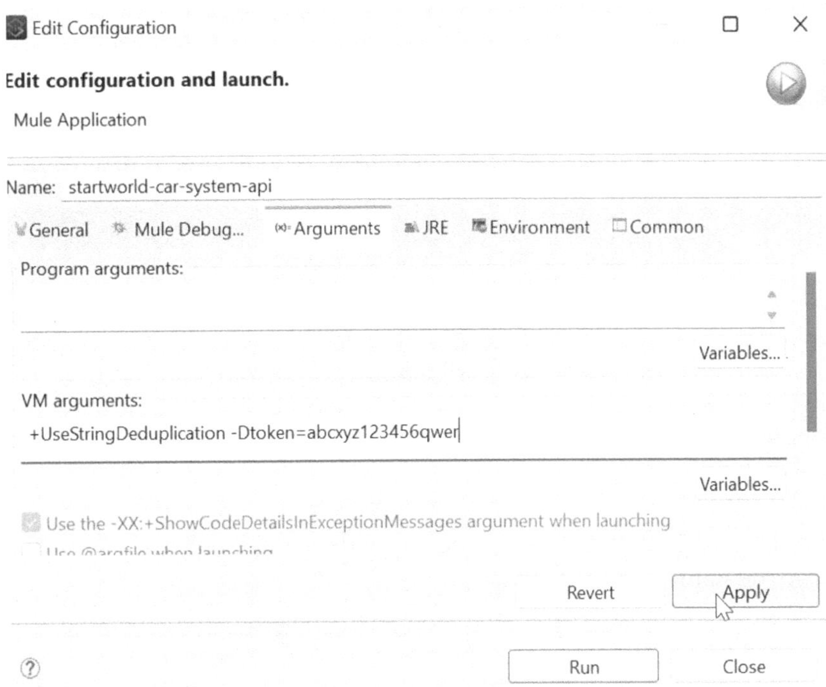

Fig 5.5 Configuring the key

Using Anypoint Enterprise Security Module: Anypoint Enterprise Security is a suite of security features provided by MuleSoft Anypoint Platform. It offers various tools and features. One of the features is to encrypt the data to protect from unauthorized access.

To use Anypoint Enterprise Security Module, first we need to install the software in Anypoint Studio by going through Help and Install Software

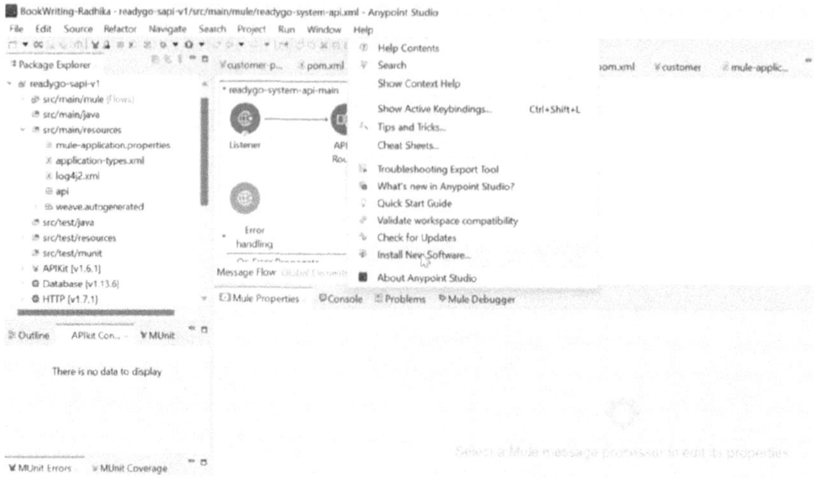

Fig 5.6 Installing New Software

Once Install New Software selected, popup window will be displayed to add the software as shown below:

- Click on add button. One more popup window will appear.
- Enter the name of the software and the location of the software for download.

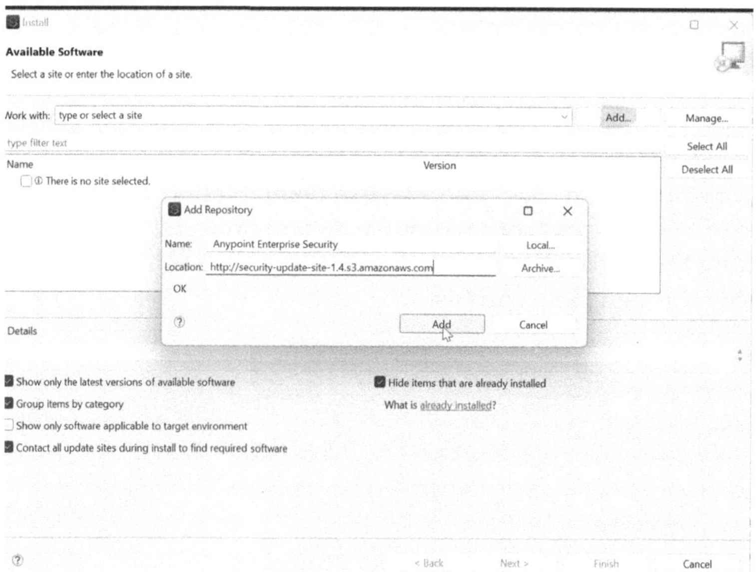

Fig 5.7 Adding the Software

- Once you click on Add button on the above window, it will show the availability of software. Select the software and click next button. It will show the installation details in the next window and click next button.

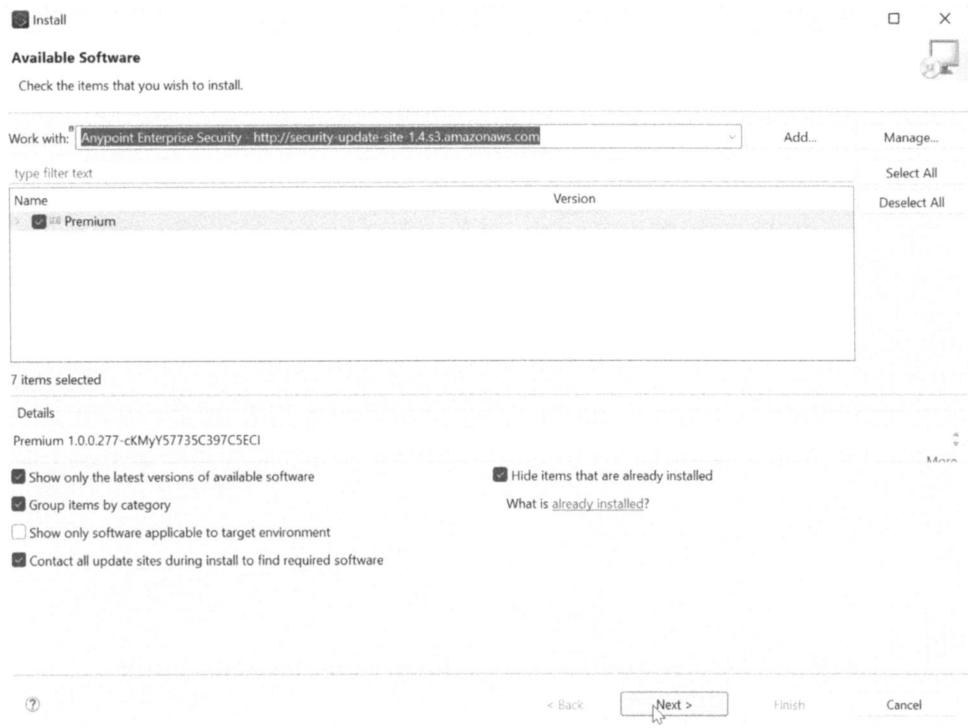

Fig 5.8 Available Software

After clicking the next button in installation details window, it gives the details to accept the license. Select the option to accept the terms and license agreement and click on Finish button.

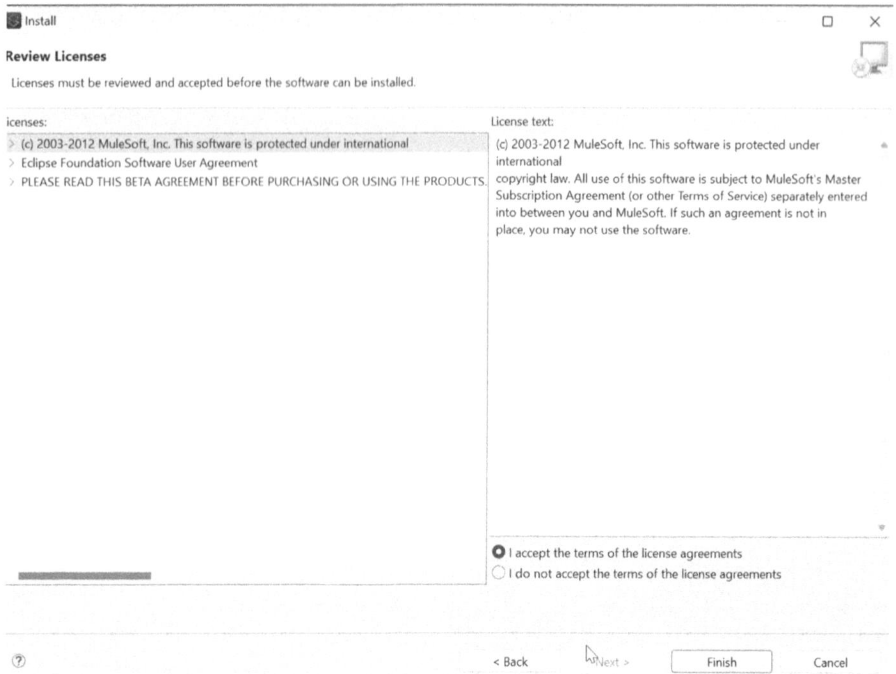

Fig 5.9 Terms and License

After this Anypoint Studio restart is required. Restart the Anypoint Studio.

Using Secure Configuration Property Extension:

MuleSoft Secure Configuration Property Extension is another way to encrypt the properties. We can add the extension by clicking the exchange button in the Mule Palette as shown below:

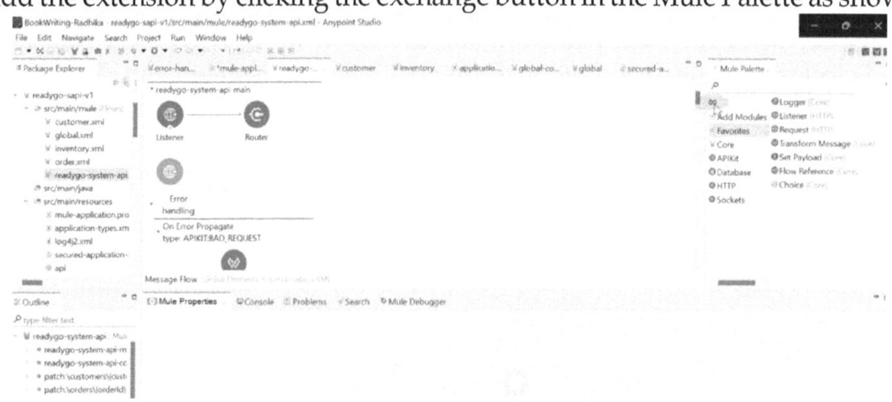

Fig 5.10 Adding the extension

The below popup will be displayed where we can add the modules. To add the modules we need to login in our Anypoint Platform account. As shown in the below screen if the account is not added already add the account by clicking Add Account or if we already added an account in Anypoint Studio click on Please login to login in case the session expired. Once the module selected from the available modules click on Add button and the dependency will move to selected modules. Once done click on Finish button.

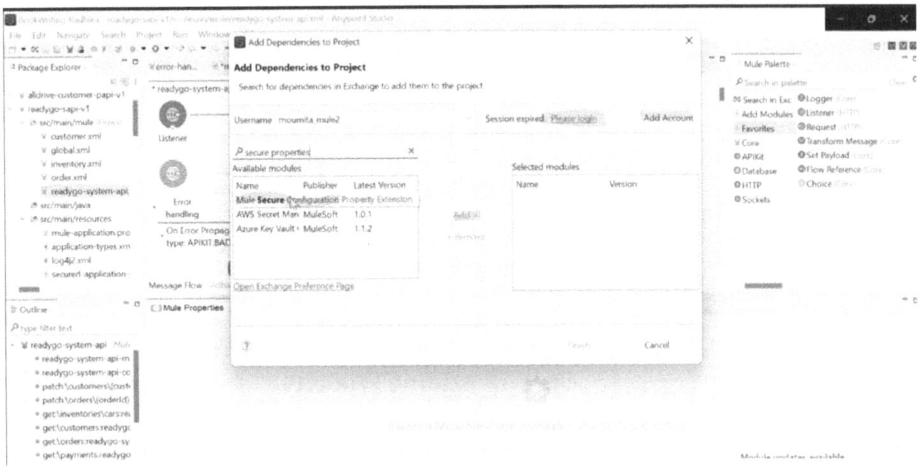

Fig 5.11 Adding the Dependencies

Once the dependency is added, we can encrypt the properties using Mule Properties Editor

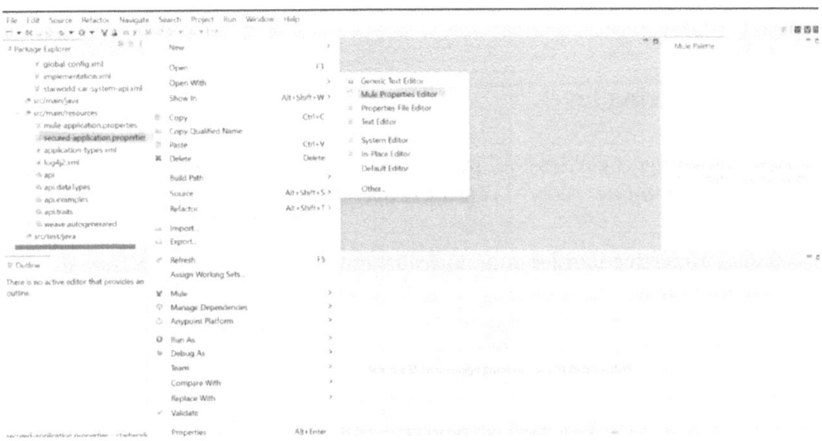

Fig 5.12 Mule Properties Editor

Then create a property to encrypt.

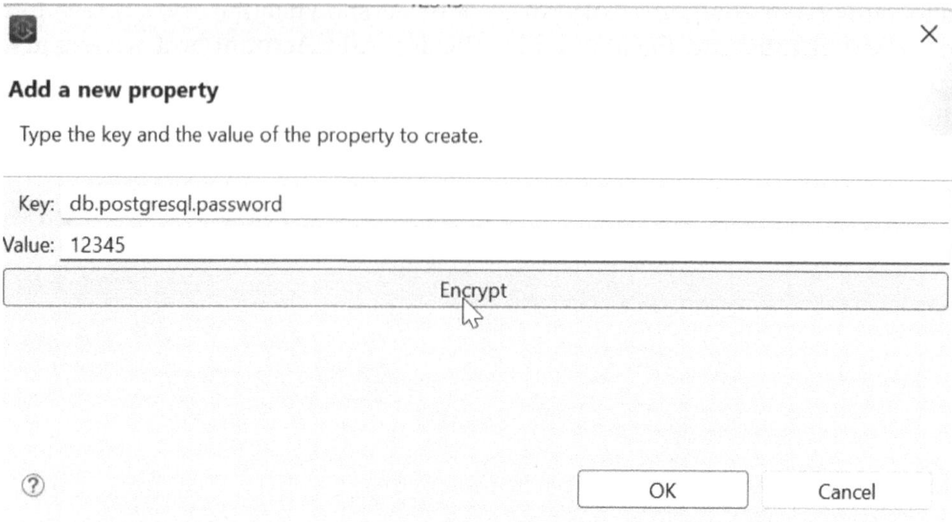

Fig 5.13 Adding Property

Using Secure Properties Tool Jar file: MuleSoft Secure Properties Tool jar can be downloaded from the below link.
https://docs.mulesoft.com/mule-runtime/latest/_attachments/secure-properties-tool.jar

Once the jar file is downloaded open the command prompt and go to the location where the jar file is downloaded or located. Here we can encrypt the properties at individual key level or at the entire file level:

Syntax to encrypt at string level.

java -cp secure-properties-tool.jar com.mulesoft.tools.SecurePropertiesTool string <operation><algorithm><mode><key><input property>

e.g. **java -cp secure-properties-tool.jar com.mulesoft.tools.SecurePropertiesTool string encrypt AES CBC mule123 dbpasswordadmin**

Here operation is either encrypt or decrypt, key is the value by which the algorithm encrypts the input property. After running the above command, you will get the encrypted value for dbpasswordadmin input property. Copy the encrypted value and paste it in our secured-application.properties file of the Mule Project.

Syntax to encrypt at file level.
Java -cp secure-properties-tool.jar com.mulesoft.tools.SecurePropertiesTool <method><operation><algorithm><mode><key><input file><output file>

Here input file has the values without encrypting and output file is going to be produced with the encrypted values. In our example we will encrypt the entire file and replace the file in our Mule project as shown below:

First define all the properties in a file which needs to be encrypted.

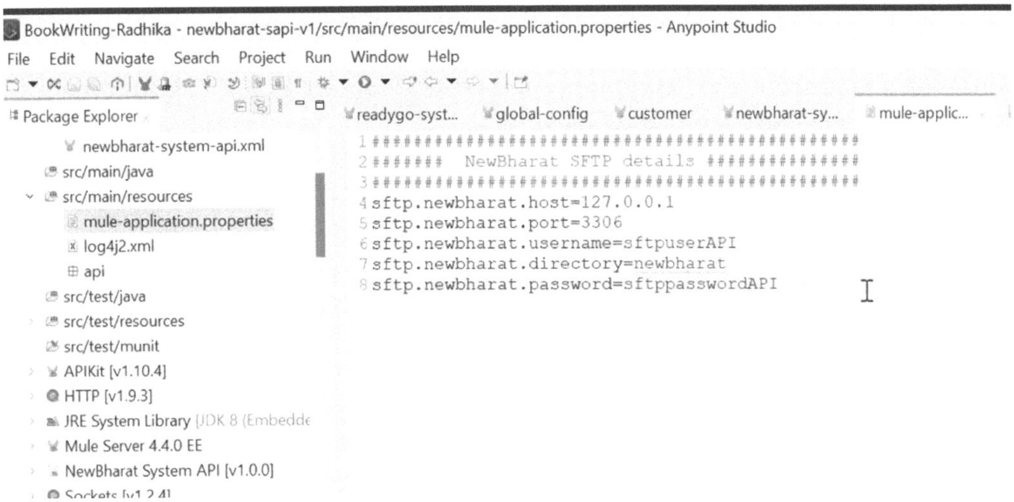

Fig 5.14 Properties File

Go to the folder where the jar file is placed and ran the below command to encrypt the entire file. Provide the entire path of the file. The encrypted file gets generated in the mentioned path.

Fig 5.15 Encrypting Property File

After generating the encrypted file place, the file in src/main/resources if it is not created in the specified location.

> **Note:** In the above examples, we have used separate files to place the encrypted properties to keep it easy to understand. However, you can use the same file as the output file/to have both the encrypted and unencrypted values based on your own requirements.

So far, we have encrypted the critical application property key-values. However, we should let the mule runtime know the key as well. So that it can decrypt the encrypted values to let our mule application access the actual value to communicate with the respective systems that it wants to connect during processing the API requests. Otherwise, application won't work. Hence, let's talk about the decryption method that we are going to use to help our mule application unlock the encrypted values.

We need to use the mule-secure-configuration-property-module to achieve this. Add the below dependency in your mule API/application pom.xml file:

```
<dependency>
    <groupId>com.mulesoft.modules</groupId>
    <artifactId>mule-secure-configuration-property-module</artifactId>
    <version>1.2.7</version>
    <classifier>mule-plugin</classifier>
</dependency>
```

Fig 5.16 POM Dependency

Any method which described above, we follow to secure the properties we need to create a global configuration in the Mule project as shown below:

In **global.xml** click on create button and search for Secure Property Config

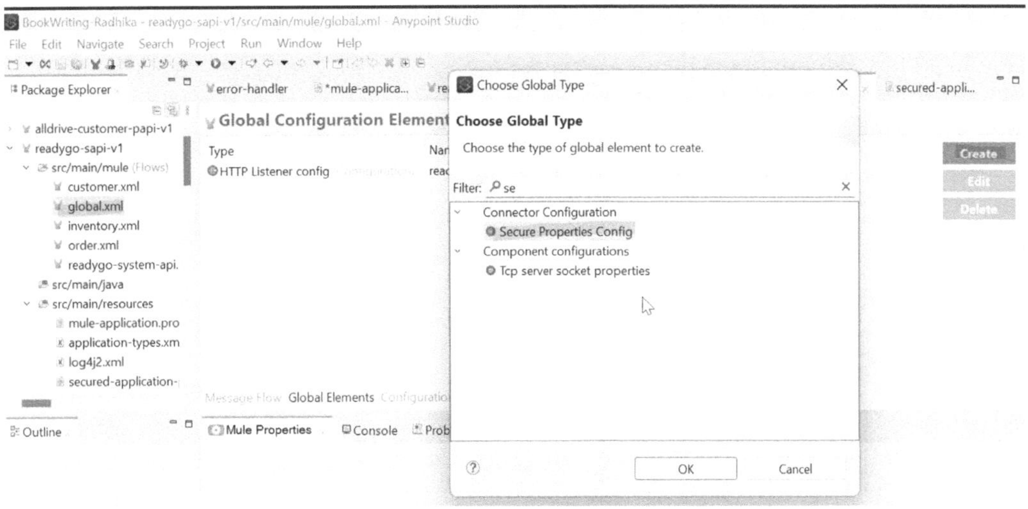

Fig 5.17 Creating Secure Global Configuration

Secure Properties Config popup window gets open to define the values for algorithm, mode and key. Provide the values for the configuration as shown below:

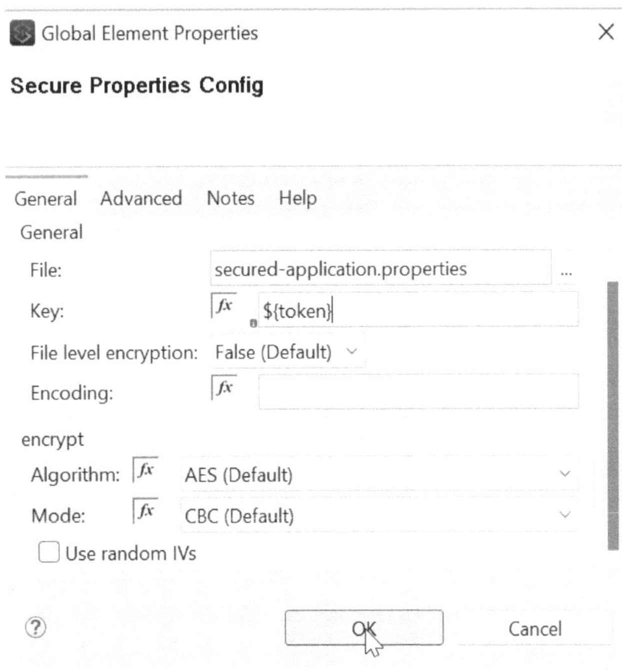

Fig 5.18 Secure Properties Configuration

In the above screenshot, look at the 'Key' field. Here we need to pass the key that we used

throughout all our encryption process. Here, we are passing the key dynamically. Hence, we have used the key reference by using **${ }** syntax.

To access any secured property in your application, you need to use ***secure::*** keyword -

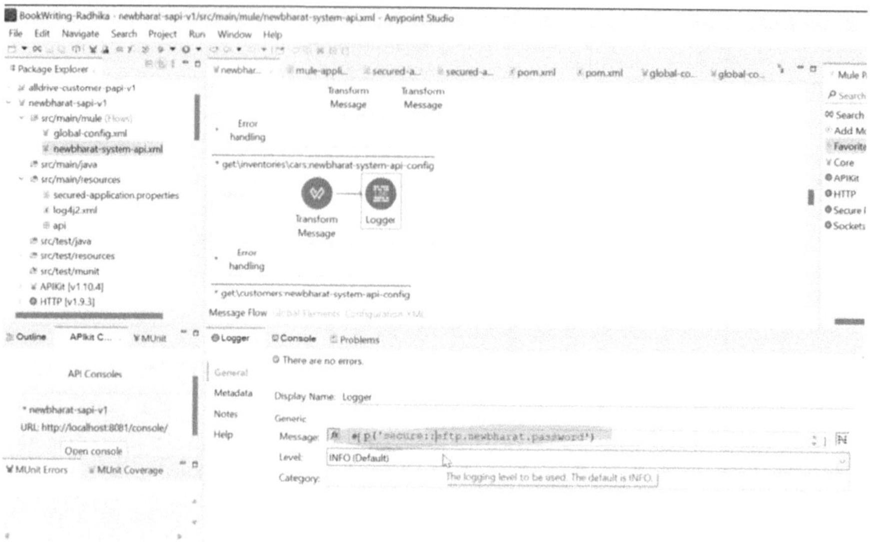

Fig 5.19 Using Secure Properties

Now, the actual token value can be configured in runtime configuration properties by clicking **Run As** and **Mule Application (configure)** as shown below:

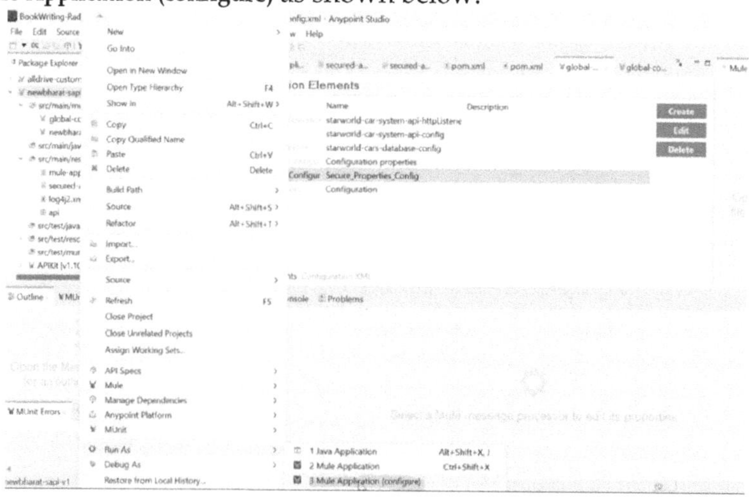

Fig 5.20 Runtime Configuration

Edit configuration popup will be displayed as shown below. Using -Dtoken vm argument pass the key value. This is used for decrypting the values during deployment. This way the deployed application will only have the actual decrypted values.

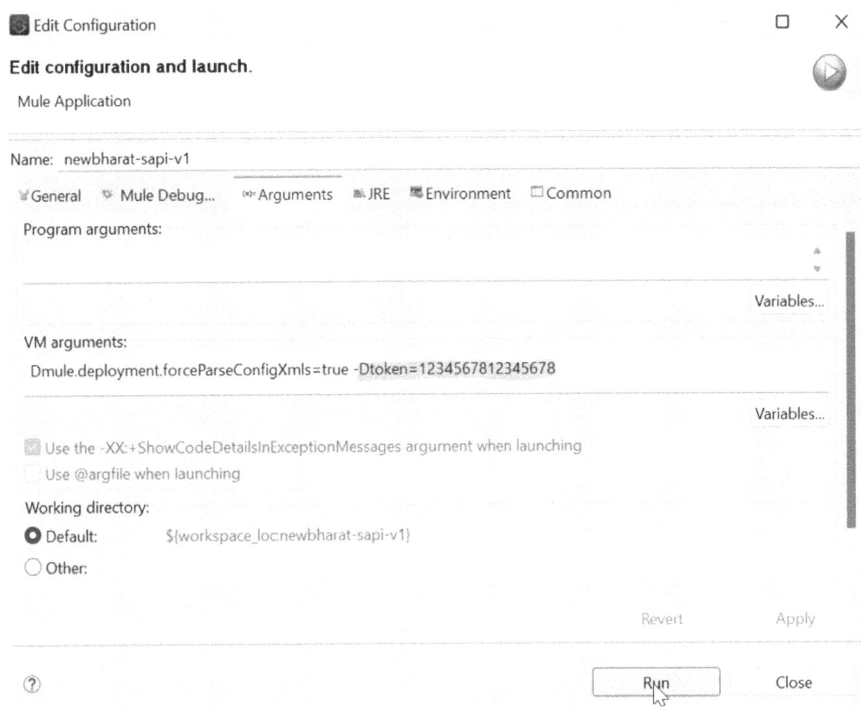

Fig 5.21 Passing token argument

Note: For the deployment, you can configure this same token value in Anypoint Runtime Manager as well. In case of on-premise mule enterprise runtime, you can mention the token in the wrapper.config as vm argument or you can pass the same as jvm argument while starting the mule runtime.

Conclusion

Securing important properties in an API implementation is an important aspect to protect the sensitive data to maintain the compliance with the regulatory requirements. It also helps in preventing security breaches and maintaining the trust with stakeholders. Securing the API from unauthorized access is another important aspect where the API cannot be accessed by unauthorized sources. Implementing various combinations of security mechanisms, measurements and best practices organizations can mitigate various risks and build secure, reliable APIs for the seamless integrations. In next chapter, we will learn about DataWeave. DataWeave is a powerful data transformation language used in MuleSoft.

Exercise: Test Your Understanding

Answer the following questions and test your understanding of learning from `Chapter 5`:

`Q. 1.` What is the need for securing properties?

`Q. 2.` What are the different ways to secure the properties?

`Q. 3.` What is the keyword to be used to access the Secured property?

`Q. 4.` Where to pass the token to decrypt the secured property?

`Q. 5.` Where to define Security Property Config?

6

DataWeave – Part 1

DataWeave is the powerful data transformation language used in MuleSoft to map, query, and transform data between different formats, such as **JSON**, **XML**, **CSV**, **Java** objects, and more. Introduced in **Mule 3.x** and significantly enhanced in **Mule 4.x**, **DataWeave 2.0** is designed to handle complex data integration tasks easily. This chapter will mainly discuss **DataWeave 2.0 as Mule 4** uses it.

In this chapter, we will cover

- How do you use DataWeave, and what are the different editors available to write DataWeave?
- DataWeave Code Structure
- DataWeave Expression and Supported Data Types

Why Use DataWeave?

- Unified Language: Every system wants to be unique and define its data format. DataWeave supports multiple formats in a single language.
- Declarative Syntax: DataWeave provides a simple, JSON-like functional programming language to help quickly transform and query data. The language is designed to be declarative, allowing you to focus on what you want, not how to achieve it.
- High Performance: Optimized for performance, making it suitable for both simple and complex data transformations.

How DataWeave Fits into MuleSoft

DataWeave is an integral part of the MuleSoft runtime, allowing developers to transform data seamlessly within Mule applications. It is used everywhere in Mule 4. DataWeave can be directly typed into most Mule flow component attributes or placed in a separate (.dwl) file and referred from a Mule flow.

DataWeave Editors

Using Anypoint Studio: Anypoint Studio has a Transform Message component where we can write our transformation code.

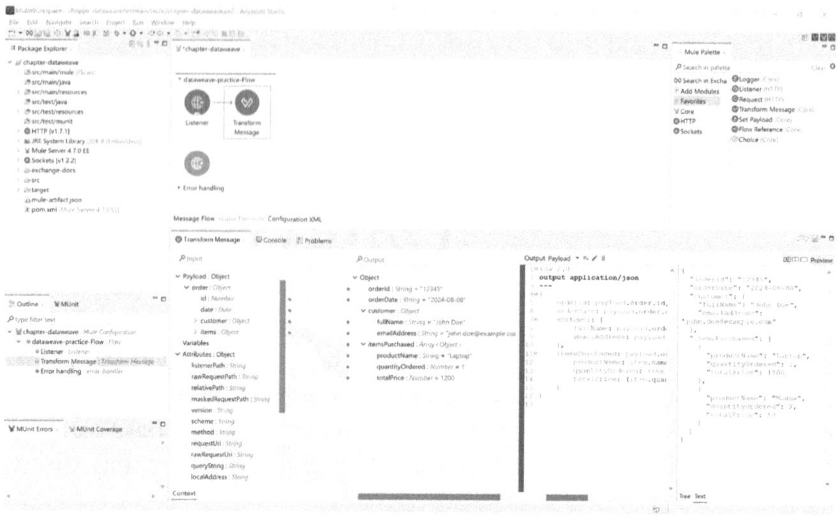

Fig 6.1 DataWeave editor in Studio

Using DataWeave Playground: MuleSoft provided an online tool where DataWeave code can be written to check how the code provides the output.

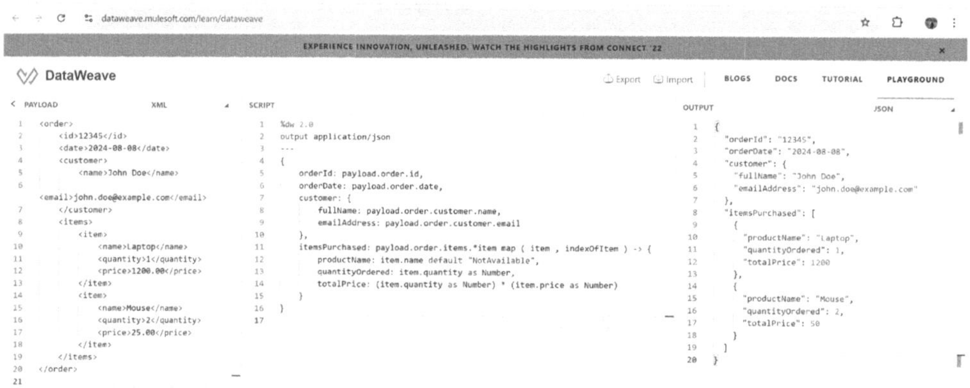

Fig 6.2 DataWeave Playground

Almost every component in Mule has DataWeave expression support in Mule 4 –

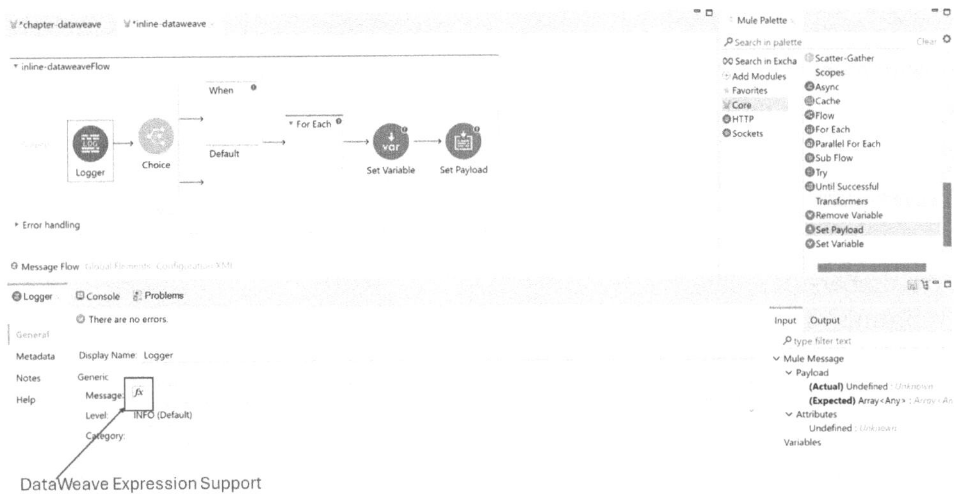

Fig 6.3 DataWeave Expression Support

Basic Concepts of DataWeave

DataWeave Code Structure: DataWeave code is divided into a header and body:

- **Header:** Defines metadata, such as namespaces, input types, and functions.
- **Payload Section:** The core transformation logic.
- **Output Section:** Specifies the format of the output data.
-

DataWeave Expression: DataWeave expressions allow you to extract, filter, map, and transform data from one format to another.

Basics of the type of system

A type system defines a set of type constraints to a set of constructs. For DataWeave, these constructs are:

- Variables [Syntax: var <varName>: TypeContraint = <varValue>]
- Functions [Syntax: fun <functionName>(arg1: TypeContraint1, arg2: TypeContraint2): functionReturnType = <functionBody>]

The possible type constraints are:

- Simple types:
  - String, Number, Boolean, Regex, Temporal Types, Null
- Composite types:
  - Array, Object, Function
- Complex types:
  - Any, Nothing, Union Type, Literal Types, Intersection Type

- Type declaration:
    - Also, you can declare custom types to reuse them as a constraint

Literal type and values in DataWeave
Think of a type as a set of values, like the type Number represents all the possible numbers. For Type Strings, we have values for all the possible sequences of characters.

A literal type is a set of just one value; it represents only one literal value:
- Numbers: 123, 4.56
- Strings: "Hello"
- Booleans: true, false

Variables
Variables temporarily store values that can be reused in a DataWeave script or inline snippet. DataWeave variables are immutable. A variable is assigned a value, which is either a constant (such as var msg = "mule") or a lambda expression such as () → "mule." This way, a variable can behave like a function as well.

Syntax - var <varName> = <varValue>

Example:
var name = "Prasenjit"

> **Note:** If we do not mention any type constraint while declaring the variable, the variable type would be automatically set as per the value type. In this case, the variable 'name' type is a String.

Variable Scopes:
- Global Variables - Accessible anywhere in a single DataWeave script.
- Local Variables - Accessible only within a specified scope by '{' and '}'.

Example DataWeave Script:

```
%dw 2.0
output application/XML
var name1: String="Radhika"   //Global variable
var name2="Prasenjit" //Global variable
var myVar = do {
  var language = "DataWeave 2.0" //Local variable
  ---
  "Hello " ++ language //Local variable 'language' is accessible in this scope '{' '}' only
}
---
{
```

```
  XML: {
    message: myVar, //Local variable 'language' is not accessible here
    authors: name1 ++ " and " ++ name2
  }
}
```

Output:

```
<?xml version='1.0' encoding='UTF-8'?>
<xml>
  <message>Hello DataWeave 2.0</message>
  <authors>Radhika and Prasenjit</authors>
</xml>
```

DataWeave variables should not be confused with mule flow level variables that are set using **Set Variable** components

Predefined Variables

Variables	Description	Fields and Examples
app	The Mule artifact in context.	• Fields: ○ encoding: Encoding used by the Mule message processor. ○ Name: Name of your project and Mule app. ○ Standalone: Returns true or false. ○ workDir: Working directory for the Mule app. For Studio, this is an Eclipse plugin directory. ○ Registry: Map of Mule registry entries. • Example: #[app.encoding] might return UTF-8.
attributes	Attributes (metadata) of a Mule Message object (message).	• Fields: Depends on the message type, such as HTTP request attributes. • Example: #[attributes] returns message attributes. For an HTTP request, #[attributes.header] returns HTTP header metadata, and #[attributes.version] might return HTTP/1.1.
authentication	Provides access to the authentication information.	• Fields: ○ Principal: The main part of the authentication, such as the user or subject. ○ Credentials: The credentials for the authentication. ○ Properties: A map of properties for the authentication. • Example: #[authentication.principal]

Variables	Description	Fields and Examples
correlation	The correlation of the message being processed.	• Fields: No fields. • Example: #[correlationId] might return 0-f77404d0-e699-11e7-a217-38c9864c2f8f.
dataType	The data type of the message payload.	• Fields: No fields. • Example: #[dataType] might return SimpleDataType.

error	The error is associated with a Mule message object.	• Fields:
		  ○ Description: Concise description of the error.
		  ○ Detailed description: Can provide a more thorough description.
		  ○ failingComponent: The component where the error occurred.
		  ○ errorType: The type of error. The error type is composed of an identifier and Namespace.
		  ○ Cause: The internal Java Throwable that caused the error.
		  ○ errorMessage: An optional Mule Message provided by the failing component (used by components like HTTP when a response is invalid).
		  ○ childErrors: An optional list of internal errors (provided by components that aggregate errors, such as scatter-gather).
		• Example: #[error.description]

flow	Deprecated: The name of the current flow. Because flow names are static, this field is deprecated and only available through the Logger component.	• Fields: ○ name • Example: #[flow.name] returns testFlow in the Studio console when executed within a Flow with the name testFlow.

message	The package (payload and attributes) is being processed.	• Fields:
		  ○ Payload: The message payload, or null if the payload is null.
		  ○ dataType: The message payload's data type.
		  ○ Attributes: The message attributes are null if the attributes are null.
		• Example: #[message]

mule	The Mule instance on which the application is currently running.	• Fields:
		  ○ clusterId: The ID of the cluster when the Mule runtime is part of a high-availability cluster.
		  ○ Home: Home directory.
		  ○ nodeId: Cluster Node ID.
		  ○ Version: Mule version.
		• Example: #[mule.version] might return 4.0.0.

Variables	Description	Fields and Examples
payload	The body of the current Mule message object (message) is being processed.	• Fields: Depends on the current payload. • Example: #[payload] returns the body of the message.
server	The operating system on which the Mule instance is running. Exposes information about the physical server and the JVM on which Mule runs. • Note that the ability to select system properties, like user.name, depends on the behavior of the JVM on your operating system.	• Fields: ○ env: Map of operating system environment variables. ○ file separator: Character that separates components of a file path, which is / on UNIX and \ on Windows. ○ host: A fully qualified domain name is required for the server. ○ ip: IP address of the server. ○ locale: Default locale (java.util.Locale) of the JRE. Language (locale.language), country (locale.country) can be used. ○ javaVendor: JRE vendor name ○ javaVersion: JRE version ○ osArch: Operating system architecture. ○ osName: Operating system name. ○ osVersion: Operating system version. ○ systemProperties: Map of Java system properties. ○ timeZone: Default time zone (java.util.TimeZone) of the JRE. ○ tmpDir: Temporary directory for use by the JRE. ○ userDir: User directory. ○ userHome: User home directory. ○ userName: User name. • Example: #[server.osName] might return Mac OS X.
vars	All variables currently set on the current Mule event being processed.	• Fields: No fields. • Example: #[vars.myVar] returns the value of myVar.

Table 6.1 Predefined Variables

Functions

DataWeave 2.0 provides a wide set of ready-to-use functions that can be used in writing transformations. Here is a comprehensive list of functions that are commonly used:

Function	Description	Example	Output
map	Transforms each element of an array by applying a function.	%dw 2.0 output application/json var numbers = [1, 2, 3] --- numbers map ((num) -> num * 2)	[2, 4, 6]
filter	Filters elements in an array based on a condition.	%dw 2.0 output application/json var numbers = [1, 2, 3, 4, 5] --- numbers filter ((num) -> num % 2 == 0)	[2, 4]

Function	Description	Example	Output
reduce	Reduces an array to a single value by applying a function iteratively.	%dw 2.0 output application/json var numbers = [1, 2, 3, 4] --- numbers reduce ((acc, num) -> acc + num)	10
pluck	Extracts a specified field from each element in an array of objects.	%dw 2.0 output application/json var people = [{name: "John", age: 30}, {name: "Jane", age: 25}] --- people pluck "name"	["John", "Jane"]
groupBy	Groups elements of an array based on a key or condition.	%dw 2.0 output application/json var people = [{name: "John", age: 30}, {name: "Jane", age: 25}, {name: "Joe", age: 30}] --- people groupBy ((p) -> p.age)	{30: [{name: "John", age: 30}, {name: "Joe", age: 30}], 25: [{name: "Jane", age: 25}]}
flatten	Flattens a nested array into a single array.	%dw 2.0 output application/json var nestedArray = [[1, 2], [3, 4], [5]] --- nestedArray flatten	[1, 2, 3, 4, 5]
sizeOf	Returns the size or length of an array, String, or object.	%dw 2.0 output application/json var text = "hello" --- sizeOf(text)	5
joinBy	Joins elements of an array into a single string with a specified delimiter.	%dw 2.0 output application/json var words = ["apple," "banana," "cherry"] --- words joinBy, ""	"apple,banana,cherry"
splitBy	Splits a string into an array of substrings based on a delimiter.	dw %dw 2.0 output application/json var text = "apple,banana,cherry" --- text splitBy ","	["apple", "banana", "cherry"]
contains	Checks if an array or String contains a specific element or substring.	dw %dw 2.0 output application/json var text = "hello world" --- text contains "world"	true
upper	Converts a string to uppercase.	dw %dw 2.0 output application/json var text = "hello" --- upper(text)	"HELLO"
lower	Converts a string to lowercase.	dw %dw 2.0 output application/json var text = "HELLO" --- lower(text)	"Hello"
substring	Extracts a substring from a string based on start and end indices.	dw %dw 2.0 output application/json var text = "hello world" --- substring(text, 0, 5)	"Hello"
trim	Removes whitespace from the beginning and end of a string.	%dw 2.0 output application/json var text = " hello world " --- trim(text)	"hello world"
DateTime	Converts a string to a datetime object.	%dw 2.0 output application/json var dateStr = "2024-08-12T12:34:56" --- dateTime(dateStr)	2024-08-12T12:34:56.000Z
if	Conditionally returns values based on a Boolean expression.	%dw 2.0 output application/json var condition = true --- if (condition) "trueValue" else "falseValue"	"trueValue"
typeOf	Returns the type of a value (e.g., String, number, array).	%dw 2.0 output application/json var value = 123 --- typeOf(value)	"Number"

Function	Description	Example	Output
isEmpty	Checks if a string, array, or object is empty.	%dw 2.0 output application/json var arr = [] --- isEmpty(arr)	true
min	Returns the minimum value from an array of numbers.	%dw 2.0 output application/json var numbers = [1, 2, 3, 4] --- min(numbers)	1
max	Returns the maximum value from an array of numbers.	%dw 2.0 output application/json var numbers = [1, 2, 3, 4] --- max(numbers)	4
sum	Returns the sum of values in an array of numbers.	%dw 2.0 output application/json var numbers = [1, 2, 3, 4] --- sum(numbers)	10
indexOf	Returns the index of the first occurrence of a substring in a string.	%dw 2.0 output application/json var text = "hello world" --- indexOf(text, "world")	6
replace	Replaces all occurrences of a substring in a string with another substring.	%dw 2.0 output application/json var text = "hello world" --- replace(text, "world", "Mule")	"hello Mule"
mapObject	Transforms each key-value pair of an object by applying a function.	%dw 2.0 output application/json var obj = {a: 1, b: 2} --- obj mapObject ((value, key) -> (key ++ "_new"): value + 10)	{a_new: 11, b_new: 12}
filterObject	Filters the key-value pairs in an object based on a condition.	%dw 2.0 output application/json var obj = {a: 1, b: 2, c: 3} --- obj filterObject ((value, key) -> value > 1)	{b: 2, c: 3}

Table 6.2 Functions

Apart from the above, DataWeave 2.0 readily offers many other functions, and the collection is expanding. Also, you can define your DataWeave functions using the fun declaration in the header of a DataWeave script.

Examples: DataWeave:

```
%dw 2.0
output application/json

fun isAdult(age) = age >= 18
---
isAdult(20)
```

Output:

True

DataWeave

```
%dw 2.0
output application/json

// Function to transform JSON data
fun transformJson(data) =
    {
        fullName: data.firstName ++ " " ++ data.lastName,
        age: data.age,
        email: data.email
    }

// Sample JSON input data
var jsonData = {
    firstName: "John",
    lastName: "Doe",
    age: 30,
    email: "john.doe@example.com"
}

// Apply the function to the sample JSON data
// For practice, we can directly mention the JSON input data in the global variable
// However, it is recommended not to use hard coded input in actual DataWeave Script
---
transformJson(jsonData)
```

Output

```
{
  "fullName": "John Doe",
  "age": 30,
  "email": "john.doe@example.com"
}
```

Selectors

Selectors helps you select keys and values from Objects and item and item values from Arrays:

Selector Type	Syntax	Return Type / Result
Single Value (First value)	.<keyname>	Value of a key-value pair
Multi-Value (All values)	.*<keyname>	Array of values corresponding to each nested key matching keyname
First descendant value	..<keyname>	Array with the first matching value at each level
All descendant values	..*<keyname>	Array of all matching values
Index	[<index>]	Value at selected array index
Range	[<index> to <index>]	Array with values from selected indexes
All descendants	p ..	Array of all the values from every branch (recursive)
Single root-level values (First-root-level values)	p.keyName	First value of entries with key keyName found in each root-level object
Multiple root-level values (All root-level values)	p.*keyName	Multiple matches returned in an array; none found returns null
Multiple root-level entries (All root-level entries)	p.&keyName	Object(s) of all entries (key-value pairs) with key keyName found in each root-level object
Single descendant values (First descendant values)	p ..keyName	Array of the first value of entries with key keyName found in each object in the nested hierarchy (recursive). No results returns []. Same as (p ..).keyName
Multiple descendant values (All descendant values)	p ..*keyName	Array all values of entries with key keyName found in the nested hierarchy (recursive). No results returns []. Same as (p ..).*keyName
Multiple descendant entries (All descendant entries)	p ..&keyName	Array of Object(s) of entries (key-value pairs) with key keyName found in the nested hierarchy. Entries found in multiple objects are returned as separate objects. Same as (p ..).&keyName.
Multiple root-level attributes (All root-level attributes)	p.@attrName	All attribute value(s) for all attrName attributes found in keys of each root-level object. Multiple matches returned in an array; none found returns null
Multiple descendant attributes (All descendant attributes)	p..@attrName	All attribute value(s) for attrName attributes found in keys of each root-level object. Multiple matches returned in an array; none found returns null
Multiple root-level attributes (All root-level attributes)	p.@	Array of all attributes (as objects) found in each root-level object
Multiple descendant attributes (All descendant attributes)	p..@	Array of all attributes (as objects) found in the nested hierarchy (recursive)
Key Namespace	e.#	The Namespace of a key, as an Object of type Namespace. A Namespace has a uri key and a prefix key, that can be selected
Indexed	obj[<index>]	Value at selected object entry index. Treats an object like an array.
Range	obj[start to end]	Array with values from the start to end indexes. Treats an object like an array. Example: obj[-1 to 0] reverses the order.
Filter	p[?(condition)]	Array with values from the start to end indexes. Treats an object like an array.

Table 6.3 Selectors

DataWeave DataTypes

Simple Primitive Types

- String - Double or single quotation marks, such as "Mule", 'mule'
- Number [both Integer and Decimal] - Formats and custom types can be applied to coerce Numbers and Strings. Examples – 7, 90.10, "$900.05"
- Boolean - true, false
- Date | Time | DateTime –
  - ISO-8601 enclosed in pipes (|) - |2003-10-01T23:57:59Z|
  - These can be coerced to strings following a particular formatting pattern "1 August, 2024 – 09:48 am EST"

Complex Types

- Array [value1, value2, value3] - Indexes start at 0
- Object { key1: value1, key2: value2 } –

Example:

```
{
  "productName": "Mouse",
  "quantityOrdered": 2,
  "totalPrice": 50.00
}
```

> **Note**: An Object can have child objects

Other Types

- Regex-Regular expression enclosed in forward slashes (/), such as /(\d+)-(\d+)/
- Enum-Checks a String value against a set of defined values. Like a Java Enum class.
- CData-Extends String to identify CDATA XML blocks
- Iterator–
  - Based on the Java Iterator class
  - Often the result of a built-in connector, like a database query response
  - Used in scopes such as For Each or Batch job to break up a collection into small pieces

Type Coercion

DataWeave automatically converts data types where necessary but also provides explicit type coercion to handle more complex transformations.

Implicit Type Coercion

Implicit type coercion happens automatically when DataWeave needs to perform operations between incompatible types. For example, adding a number and a string converts the number to a string.

DW

```
%dw 2.0
output application/json
---
{
  result: 1 + "2"
}
```

Output:

JSON

```
{
  "result": "12"
}
```

In this example, the number 1 is implicitly converted to a string "1" before the concatenation.

Explicit Type Coercion

Explicit type coercion is performed by using type conversion functions provided by DataWeave, such as as, to, and is.

- as operator: Converts the value to the specified type.

DW

```
%dw 2.0
output application/json
---
{
  result: "123" as Number
}
```

Output:

JSON

```
{
  "result": 123
}
```

- to operator: Converts the value and can also be used to apply additional options.

DW

```
%dw 2.0
```

```
output application/json
---
{
  result: "2023-08-10" as Date
}
```

Output:

JSON

```
{
  "result": "2023-08-10"
}
```

- is operator: Checks if a value can be coerced to the specified type.

DW

```
%dw 2.0
output application/json
---
{
  isNumber: "123" is Number,
  isDate: "2023-08-10" is Date
}
```

Output:

JSON

```
{
  "isNumber": true,
  "isDate": true
}
```

Operators in DataWeave

Arithmetic Operators

These operators are used for mathematical operations.

Operator	Description	Example	Result
+	Addition	5 + 3	8
-	Subtraction	10 - 4	6
*	Multiplication	6 * 7	42
/	Division	20 / 4	5
mod	Modulus (Remainder)	10 mod 3	1

Table 6.4 Arithmetic Operators

Logical Operators

These operators are used to perform logical operations, returning Boolean values (true or false).

Operator	Description	Example	Result
not	Flips the value. Returns true if input is false, false if input is true	not(true)	false
!	Similar as 'not'. Introduced in DataWeave 2.2.0. Supported by Mule 4.2 and later.	!true	false
and	Returns true if all inputs' results are accurate, false if not.	true and false	false
or	Returns true if the result of any input is true, false if not.	`true or false	true

Table 6.5 Logical Operators

The logical operator 'not' works in expressions such as not<space>(value), but not(value) (without the space) does not work. You can use logical operators together.

Relational and Equality Operators

These operators compare two values and return a Boolean value based on the comparison:

Operator	Description	Example	Result
==	Equal to	5 == 5	true
!=	Not equal to	5 != 3	true
>	Greater than	7 > 3	true
<	Less than	4 < 10	true
>=	Greater than or equal	5 >= 5	true
<=	Less than or equal	8 <= 10	true
~=	Equality or "similar to" operator that tries to coerce one value to the type of the other when the types are different.	'3' ~= 3	true

Table 6.6 Relational Operators

Array and Object Operators

These operators help in working with arrays and objects:

Operator	Description	Example	Result

++	Concatenate arrays/strings	[1, 2] ++ [3, 4]
		
		{"key1": 12} ++ {"key2": 34}
			[1, 2, 3, 4]
			
			{
			"key1": 12,
			"key2": 34
			}

--	Remove elements	[1, 2, 3, 4] -- [1, 3]	[2, 4]
+	Appends data on the operator's right-hand side to	[2, 4] + 5	[2, 4, 5]

	items in the array on the left-hand side.	[2, 4] + ['5']	[2, 4, ["5"]]
-	Removes a specified element of any supported type from an array.	[2, 4, 5] - 4	[2, 5]
<<	Appends data on the operator's right-hand side to items in the array on the left-hand side.	[1, 2] << 3	[1, 2, 3]
>>	Prepends data on the left-hand side of the operator to items in the array on the right-hand side.	3 >> [1, 2]	[3, 1, 2]

Table 6.7 Array & Object Operators

Type Operators

These operators are used to check or cast data types:

Operator	Description	Example	Result
is	Check if a value is of a specific type	5 is Number	true
as	Cast a value to a specific type	"123" as Number	123

Table 6.8 Type Operators

Scope and Control Flow Operators

Operator	**Description**	**Example**	**Result**
do	Creates a scope in which new variables, functions, annotations, or namespaces can be declared and used.	5 is Number	true
using	Replaced by do. Supported for backwards compatibility only.	"123" as Number	123
if else	An if operator evaluates a conditional expression and returns the value under the if only if the conditional expression is true. Otherwise, it returns the expression under else. Every if expression must have a matching else expression.	if (1 > 2) true else false	false
else if	An else operator organizes expressions within an if-else construct by incorporating else if.	if (1 > 2) true else if (2<4) true else false	true

Table 6.9 Control Flow Operators

Update Operators

DataWeave supports the update operator. This operator updates values in objects, arrays, or specified data structure fields with new values. Introduced in DataWeave 2.3.0. Supported by Mule 4.3 and later.

Operator	**Description**	**Example**	**Result**
update	Add or update key-value pairs in an	{ "name": "Laptop", "price": 1200 }	{

	object	update {
		case price at .price -> price * 1.1
		}
			"name":
			"Laptop",
			"price": 1320
			}

Table 6.10 Update Operators

Input

```
{
 "products": [
  { "name": "Laptop", "price": 1200 },
  { "name": "Mouse", "price": 25 },
  { "name": "Keyboard", "price": 50 },
  { "name": "Monitor", "price": 300 }
 ]
}
```

Transformation

```
%dw 2.0
output application/json
---
{
 products: payload.products map (product) ->
  product update {
    case .price if (product.price > 100) -> product.price * 0.9
  }
}
```

Output

```
{
 "products": [
  {
   "name": "Laptop",
   "price": 1080
  },
  {
   "name": "Mouse",
   "price": 25
  },
  {
   "name": "Keyboard",
   "price": 50
  },
  {
   "name": "Monitor",
   "price": 270
  }
```

```
  ]
}
```

Range Operators
This operator is used to generate a sequence of numbers.

Operator	Description	Example	Result
to	Generates a sequence of numbers	1 to 5	[1, 2, 3, 4, 5]

Table 6.11 Range Operators

Grouping Operators
This operator is used to group expressions.

Operator	Description	Example	Result
()	Groups expressions	(5 + 3) * 2	16

Table 6.12 Group Operators

Example of Using Multiple Operators in DataWeave
Here is a DataWeave script that uses a combination of these operators:

```
%dw 2.0
output application/json
---
{
 isAdult: payload.age >= 18,
 fullName: payload.firstName ++ " " ++ payload.Lastname,
 discountedPrice: (payload.price - (payload.discount as Number)) * payload.quantity,
 items: payload.items map ((item, index) -> {
  productName: item.name,
  totalCost: item.price * item.quantity
 })
}
```

Explanation:

- **Relational Operator** >=: Used to determine if the age is 18 or greater.
- **String Concatenation Operator** ++: Combines first name and last name.
- **Arithmetic Operators** -, *: Used to calculate the discounted price.
- **Array Map Operator** map: Iterates over items and calculates total cost for each.

These operators are integral in transforming, querying, and manipulating data within DataWeave scripts, making it a powerful tool for data transformation in MuleSoft applications. Operators in a DataWeave expression execute in the order of their precedence level. Here is a comprehensive list of operators along with their precedence level:

Precedence Level	Operators	Description	Associativity
1 (Highest)	()	Parentheses to group expressions	Left-to-Right
2	-, !, ~	Unary operators: negation, logical NOT, bitwise NOT	Right-to-Left
3	*, /, mod	Multiplication, division, modulus	Left-to-Right
4	+, -	Addition, subtraction	Left-to-Right
5	++	String concatenation	Left-to-Right
6	>>, <<	Prepend, Append	Left-to-Right
7	<, <=, >, >=, ==, !=	Relational operators	Left-to-Right
8	~=	Equality operators	Left-to-Right
9	and, or	Logical AND, Logical OR	Left-to-Right
10	as	Type coercion	Left-to-Right
11	is, is not	Type checking	Left-to-Right
12	default	Default value operator	Left-to-Right
13	:	Key-value pair separator in objects	N/A
14	do, using, if-else, else-if	Flow control and scope operators	Left-to-Right
15	update	update operator for modifying values in objects or arrays	Left-to-Right
16 (Lowest)	=	Assignment	Right-to-Left

Table 6.13 Complete List of Operators

DataWeave Example 1:

```
%dw 2.0
output application/json

var x = 5
var y = 10
var z = "15"
var arr = ["a", "b"]

---
{
 // 1. Parentheses: () - Used to control precedence
 parentheses_example: (x + y) * 2, // 30

 // 2. Unary Operators: -, !, ~
 unary_negation: -x, // -5
 logical_not: !false, // true

 // 3. Multiplication, Division, Modulus: *, /, %
 multiplication: x * 2, // 10
 division: y / 2, // 5
 modulus: y mod 3, // 1

 // 4. Addition and Subtraction: +, -
 addition: x + y, // 15
```

```
subtraction: y - x, // 5

// 5. String Concatenation: ++
string_concat: "Hello" ++ " World", // "Hello World"

// 6. Append and Prepend: <<, >>
append_example: arr << "z", // ["z", "a", "b"]
prepend_example: "z" >> arr, // ["a", "b", "z"]

// 7. Relational Operators: <, <=, >, >=
greater_than: y > x, // true
less_than_or_equal: x <= y, // true

// 8. Equality and Pattern Matching: ==, !=, ~=
equality: x == 5, // true
inequality: x != y, // true
pattern_match: "ABC" ~= /a/, // true
pattern_not_match: "ABC" ~= /z/, // false

// 9. Logical AND and OR: and, or
logical_and: (x < y) and (y > 5), // true
logical_or: (x > y) or (y > 5), // true

// 10. Type Coercion: as
coercion_example: z as Number + x, // 20

// 11. Type Checking: is, is not
type_check: z is String, // true
type_check_not: not x is String, // true

// 12. Default Value: default
default_example: payload.name default "Unknown", // "Unknown"

// 13. Key-Value Pair Separator: :
object_example: { "key": "value" }, // { "key": "value" }

// 14. Lambda Expression: ->
lambda_example: (arr map ((item) -> item ++ "!")), // ["a!", "b!"]

// 15. Flow Control and Scope: if, else, do, var, when, otherwise
if_else_example: if (x > y) "x is greater" else "y is greater", // "y is greater"
do_example: do { var temp = 20 --- temp + 5 }, // 25
when_otherwise_example: x match { case 10 -> "Ten" else -> "Not Ten"}, // "Ten"

// 16. Update Operator: update
update_example: { "name": "Laptop", "price": 1200 } update { case .price -> 1500 }, // { "name": "Laptop",
"price": 1500 }

// 17. Assignment: =
```

```
 assignment_example: do { var a = x + y --- a } // 15
}
```

Output:

```
{
  "parentheses_example": 30,
  "unary_negation": -5,
  "logical_not": true,
  "multiplication": 10,
  "division": 5,
  "modulus": 1,
  "edition": 15,
  "subtraction": 5,
  "string_concat": "Hello World",
  "append_example": [
    "a",
    "b",
    "z"
  ],
  "prepend_example": [
    "z",
    "a",
    "b"
  ],
  "greater_than": true,
  "less_than_or_equal": true,
  "equality": true,
  "inequality": true,
  "pattern_match": false,
  "pattern_not_match": false,
  "logical_and": true,
  "logical_or": true,
  "coercion_example": 20,
  "type_check": true,
  "type_check_not": true,
  "default_example": "Unknown",
  "object_example": {
    "key": "value"
  },
  "lambda_example": [
    "a!",
    "b!"
  ],
  "if_else_example": "y is greater",
  "do_example": 25,
  "when_otherwise_example": "Not Ten",
  "update_example": {
```

```
    "name": "Laptop",
    "price": 1500
  },
  "assignment_example": 15
}
```

DataWeave Example 2:

```
%dw 2.0
output application/json

var a = 15
var b = 20
var c = 10
var d = 30
var isActive = true
var isAdmin = false

---
{
  // 1. Logical AND and OR with relational operators
  logical_and_with_relational: a < b and c <= d, // true 15 < 20 and 10 <= 30

  // 2. Logical OR with relational operators
  logical_or_with_relational: a > b or c < d, // true 15 > 20 or 10 < 30

  // 3. Combining multiple logical AND and OR
  combined_logical_operators: a < b and isActive or isAdmin, // true 15 < 20 and true or false

  // 4. Using relational operators in logical expressions
  relational_in_logical: (a < b) and (d > (c + b)), // false (15 < 20) and (30 > (10 + 20))

  // 5. Complex logical expression with mixed operators
  complex_expression: (a < b) and (c < d) or (a >= d) and not isActive, // true (15 < 20) and (10 < 30) or
(15 >= 30) and not true

  // 6. Logical NOT with relational operators
  logical_not_with_relational: not (a >= d or c < b), // false (not (15 >= 30 or 10 < 20))

  // 7. Nested logical and relational operators
  nested_operators: ((a < b) and (c <= d)) or ((d > a) and (not isAdmin)), // true ((15 < 20) and (10 <= 30))
or ((30 > 15) and (true))

  // 8. Mixed relational and logical operators with type coercion
  mixed_with_type_coercion: (a > b) or ((c as Number) <= (d as Number)), // true (15 > 20) or (10 <= 30)
}
```

Output:

```
{
  "logical_and_with_relational": true,
  "logical_or_with_relational": true,
  "combined_logical_operators": true,
  "relational_in_logical": false,
  "complex_expression": true,
  "logical_not_with_relational": false,
  "nested_operators": true,
  "mixed_with_type_coercion": true
}
```

DataWeave Readability

- **Comments**: Single-line (// comment) and multi-line (/* comment */).
- **Whitespace and Indentation**: Significant for readability but not syntactically enforced.

Conclusion

In this chapter, we learned about DataWeave and how it fits in MuleSoft. The editors write the DataWeave language. We also covered the structure of writing DataWeave scripts, supported datatypes, output formats, various operators, expressions, functions, etc. In the next chapter, we will learn how to write DataWeave code using various functions, publish DataWeave functions, and use them in various applications.

Exercise: Test Your Understanding

Answer the following questions and test your understanding of learning from `Chapter 6`:

Q. 1. Define DataWeave Structure?

Q. 2. What is DataWeave expression?

Q. 3. What are the different editors to write DataWeave language?

Q. 4. What is the use of update operator in DataWeave?

Q. 5. What is the Range operator?

7

DataWeave – Part-II

This chapter continues chapter 6 which talks about DataWeave functions and how to use them with examples.

In this chapter, we will cover

- Conversion of one data format to another
- Some of the important DataWeave libraries and their functions
- Using DataWeave various functions with examples.

Data Weave Fundamentals

Dataweave is a programming language designed for MuleSoft. It is used to transform the payload into the required output. It can transform datatype from one format to another like json to xml, xml to csv etc. DataWeave script is easy way of converting xml to json, if it is valid xml. Below is an example.

Input	DataWeave Script	Output

<users>
<user>
<id>1</id>
<name>Ram</name>
<email>aliramce@example.com</email>
</user>
<user>
<id>2</id>
<name>Laxman</name>
<email>alilaxman@example.com</email>
</user></users>
	%dw 2.0
	output
	application/json
	--- 	
	payload
		{
		"users": {
		"user": {
		"id": "1",
		"name": "Ram",
		"email":
		"aliramce@example.com"
		},
		"user": {
		"id": "2",
		"name": "Laxman",
		"email":
		"alilaxman@example.com"
		}
		}
		}

	Note - The above script is generating a key with root elements; we can	{ "users": [{ "id": "1",

	create a proper json structure with a modified data weave script as below
	
	"users": payload.users.*user
	
	Note here users is array which is repeating element like user in xml.
		"name": "Ram",
		"email": "aliramce@example.com"
		},
		{
		"id": "2",
		"name": "Laxman",
		"email": "alilaxman@example.com"
		}
		]
		}

Dataweave Functions are widely defined in many packages. Let us dive deep into them in detail.

Core (dw: core)

1. ++ - Concatenates two values.

Input	DataWeave Script	Output
[1,2,3]	%dw 2.0 output application/json var b = [4,5,6] --- payload ++ b	[1, 2, 3, 4, 5, 6]

2. -- Removes values

Input	DataWeave Script	Output
[3,4,5]	%dw 2.0 output application/json var b = [1,2,3] --- payload -- b	[4, 5]

3. Abs Returns absolute value : abs(number: Number): Number

Input	DataWeave Script	Output
	%dw 2.0 output application/json --- [abs(-3.1), abs(0.5), abs(-3.4)]	[3.1, 0.5, 3.4]

4. distinctly – Iterates over the array and returns unique elements.

Input	DataWeave Script	Output
[1,2,3,45,5,5]	%dw 2.0 output application/json --- payload distinctBy $ **Note** – Here "$" represent values **Another Syntax** – %dw 2.0 output application/json --- payload distinctBy ((item, index) -> item)	[1, 2, 3, 45, 5]

5. filter – Iterates over array and return expression matching values. Expression must return Boolean (true/false)

Input	DataWeave Script	Output

[
{
"key": " customerName",
"value": "customer",
"status" :"valid"
},
{
"key": " customerAddress",
"value": " address",
"status" :"invalid"
}
]
	%dw 2.0
	output application/json
	--- 	
	payload filter ((item, index) -> item.status != "invalid")
		[
		{
		"key": " customerName",
		"value": "customer",
		"status": "valid"
		}
		]
		]

6. Map is used to transform/iterate arrays, and output is an array.

Input	DataWeave Script	Output

[
{
"name": "Name",
"value": "customer",
"status" :"valid"
},
{
"address": "abc",
"value": " address",
"status" :"invalid"
}
]
	%dw 2.0
	output application/json
	--- 	
	(payload map ((item, index) -> {"Name" : item.name,
	"address":item.address,
	"code" :item.status}))
		[
		{
		"Name": "Name",
		"address": null,
		"code": "valid"
		},
		{
		"Name": null,
		"address": "abc",
		"code": "invalid"
		}
		]

	Note –
	
	In order to remove null values we can add syntax in dataweave as skipNullOn="everywhere"
	In header section as below-
	%dw 2.0
	output application/json skipNullOn="everywhere"
	--- 	
	(payload map ((item, index) -> {"Name" : item.name,
	"address":item.address,
	"code" :item.status}))
		[
		{
		"Name": "Name",
		"code": "valid"
		},
		{
		"address": "abc",
		"code": "invalid"
		}
		]

7. MapObject – Iterates over object and acts on keys, value and index. Output payload is object

Input	DataWeave Script	Output

{
"Car Information": {
"make": "Toyota",
"model": "Corolla",
"year": 2024,
"color": "Blue"
}
}
	%dw 2.0
	output application/json
	--- 	
	payload mapObject ((value, key, index) -> {
	
	"car" : value,
	"description" :key
	})
	Note – Here we have accessed keys and values for output array.
		{
		"car": {
		"make": "Toyota",
		"model": "Corolla",
		"year": 2024,
		"color": "Blue"
		},
		"description": "Car Information"
		}

8. Pluck – Iterates over object and acts on keys, value and index. It is same as mabobject the only difference is it returns array.

Input	DataWeave Script	Output

{
"Car Information": {
"make": "Toyota",
"model": "Corolla",
"year": 2024,
"color": "Blue"
}
}
	%dw 2.0
	output application/json
	--- 	
	payload pluck ((value, key, index) -> {
	"car" : value,
	"description" :key
	})
		[
		{
		"car": {
		"make": "Toyota",
		"model": "Corolla",
		"year": 2024,
		"color": "Blue"
		},
		"description": "Car Information" }
		]

9. Reduce – It can be applied over arrays and as the name says it reduces the lambda expression and replaces the accumulator with new result. The accumulator can be set with an initial value; if the accumulator is not set, it uses the first element of the input array

Input	DataWeave Script	Output
[1,2,3,4]	%dw 2.0 output application/json --- payload reduce ($$ ++ $)	"1234"
[1,2,3,4]	payload reduce ($$ + $) Here accumulator is not defined,hence 1 is used as accumulator now Reduce worked as 1+2=3 3+3 = 6 6+4 = 10 Item is referred to as $, and accumulator is referred to as $$	10

There are other core function too like sizeOf, splitBy, round, readURL, startsWith, trim, zip, unzip, read, write, typeOf, sum, orderBy, joinBy, groupBy, upper, lower etc.

> **Note:** All above functions come inside dw::core and imported automatically into dataweave script.

Strings (dw::core::Strings)

These modules need to be imported and need to be added in header script using import.

Example:

```
%dw 2.0
output application/json
import * from dw::core::Strings
---
```

1. **Reverse -** Reverses character in string

Input	DataWeave Script	Output
"DataWeave"	%dw 2.0 output application/json import * from dw::core::Strings --- reverse (payload)	"evaeWataD"

2. **mapString -** It is used to apply expression over input string. For example, use cases like masking fields.

Input	DataWeave Script	Output
"DataWeave"	%dw 2.0 output application/json import * from dw::core::Strings --- payload mapString if ($ == "a") "*" else $	"D*t*We*ve"

3. substring- It is used to split string from given index ranges.

Input	DataWeave Script	Output
"NameDataWeave"	%dw 2.0 output application/json import * from dw::core::Strings --- substring(payload,0,4)	"Name"

Conclusion

DataWeave is a powerful language, and we need more practice to become experts in writing functions and using the out-of-the-box functions. In this chapter, we tried to cover as many functions as possible. In the next chapter we will see the different ways of handling errors can be handled in Mule applications.

Exercise: Test Your Understanding

Answer the following questions and test your understanding of learning from `Chapter 7`:

`Q. 1.` How can we see the output of the DataWeave?

`Q. 2.` What is the use of DataWeave Library?

`Q. 3.` What is the difference between **mapObject** and Pluck?

`Q. 4.` What is the use of **map** function?

`Q. 5.` What is the use of **reduce** function in DataWeave?

8

Handling Errors

Every Application or program can encounter error-prone situations. Error handling is necessary so that the Application can work seamlessly. Effective error handling enhances reliability, debugging, and user experience. Proper error handling ensures that unexpected issues don't cause applications to crash. Providing proper errors to users will help enhance the user experience by helping them understand the mistakes they made while sending the request to the API. Proper error management and logging will reduce the developers' efforts to debug the issues and resolve them easily.

Error Handling in Mule

Mule Error occurs when any transaction fails; it can be due to runtime issues, technical issues, or any business failure. Every Mule connector has its associated ErrorError with its namespace. For HTTP, we have ErrorErrors like HTTP: BAD_REQUEST and HTTP: NOT_FOUND. We have errors like APIKIT: BAD_REQUEST and APIKIT: NOT_FOUND, etc. for the API KIT router. These are some well-defined errors. However, there are some errors that are undefined, too, and we can handle them with custom code using the Mule Error Object. When any error is raised, a Mule Error object is created. It consists of many properties, such as ErrorError.description, ErrorError.detailedDescription, ErrorError.errorType, ErrorError.cause, ErrorError.errorMessage,, etc. We can also extract the error payload with the expression error.errorMessage.payload and metadata via ErrorError.errorMessage.attributes.

key components you can use in Mule to handle errors are:

- Flow-Level Error Handler: Each flow can include its error handler that defines how errors within that flow are managed.
- Global Error Handler: You can set up a global error handling configuration to apply common ErrorError handling logic across multiple flows.
- On Error Propagate: This component catches errors and propagates them back to the caller. It is useful when you need to signal that an error has occurred and potentially stop further processing in the current flow.
- On Error Continue: Use this component when you want to catch an error, perform some custom logic (like logging or compensatory actions), and then allow the flow to continue executing.

- Raise Error: This component can define custom error types, custom error messages, and additional error details.
- Custom Error Types: Mule provides several predefined error types (such as CONNECTIVITY, VALIDATION, etc.). You can also define custom error types to handle specific scenarios uniquely.
- Logger Component (within error handlers): Although not strictly an error handler, logging within your error handling blocks is essential for debugging and monitoring, as it helps capture detailed error information.

There are multiple ways to handle ErrorError in the Mule Application like:

1. Global Error Handler.
2. Using Try Scope at the Processor level.
3. At flow using OnError Propagate, On Error Continue, or Raise ErrorError.
4. Using Default Error handler

Global Error Handling

Global Error Handler can be used to handle multiple ErrorError as per requirement. This can be referenced inside flow inside their ErrorError handling section to handle mule errors. To Create a Global handler, we need to select Error Handler palate as below and place it in the Mule message flow screen:

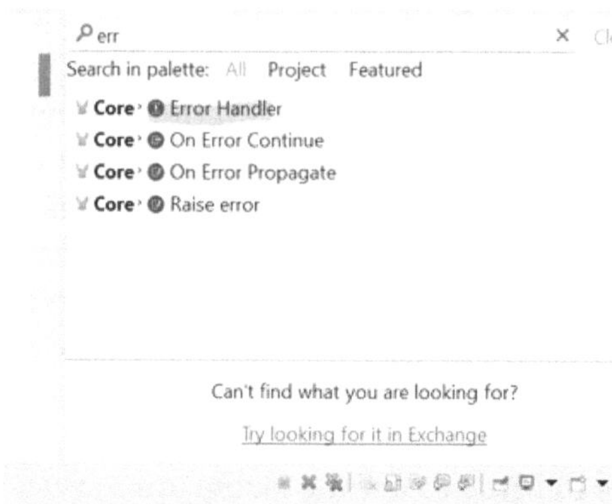

Fig 8.1 GlobalErrorHandlerFromPalette

Add the component inside the flow.

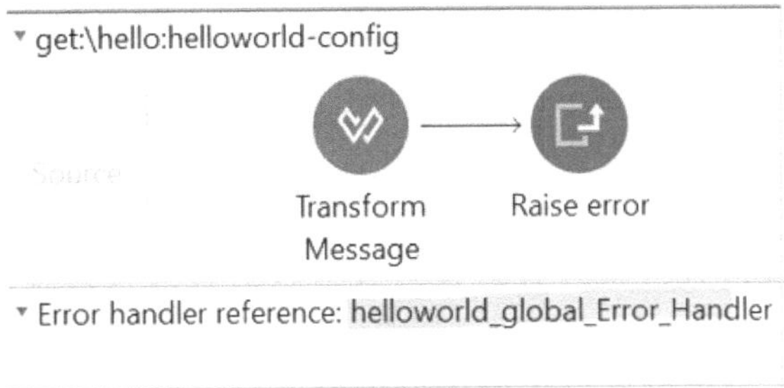

Fig 8.2 GlobalErrorHandler Inside Flow

In the Global Error handler, we can add OnErrorPropogate or OnErrorContinue as per our project requirement. Make sure the last error condition is ANY to handle an undefined exception that doesn't pass any of the error criteria. Note: It follows an error-matching sequence from top to bottom.

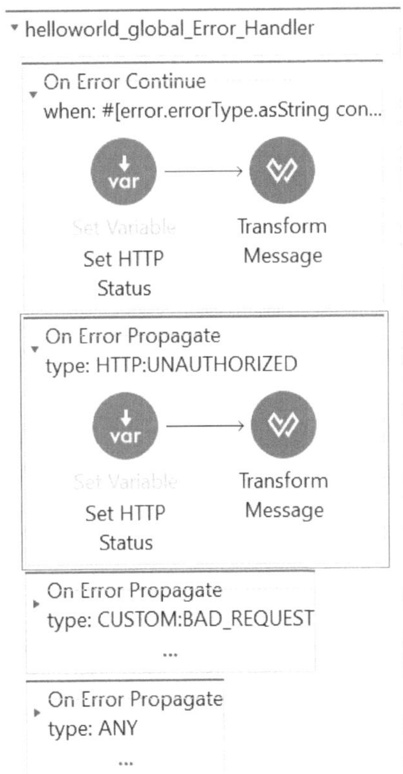

Fig 8.3 ErrorConditionsInGlobalErrorHandler

Using Try Scope at the Processor Level

Another way to handle errors is at the processor level. Mule is intelligent enough to show the

types of ErrorError related to the processor when we attach error handling.
For instance, when the try block is added to the Web Service Consumer connector consume operation, it shows all the errors associated with Consume with the namespace WSC.
The example below adds the Web Service Consumer Consume operation to the Try scope.

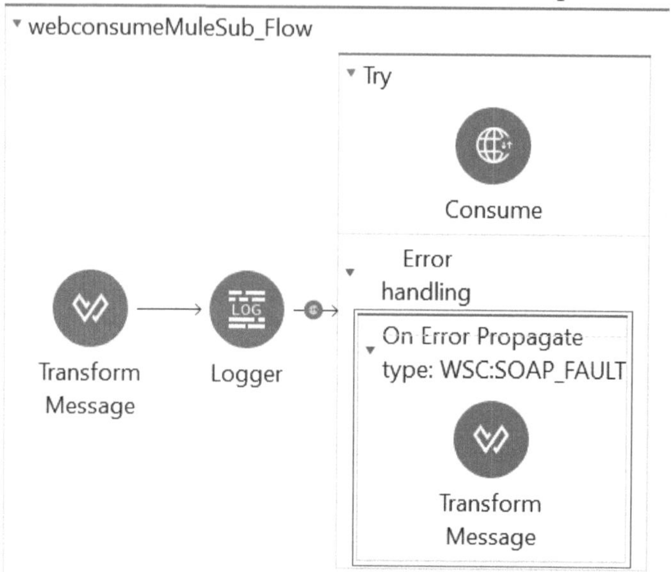

Fig 8.4 Adding Try Scope at Processor level

Inside the Try scope, we can add ErrorError handling components like On Error Propagate and Error Continue and configure the associated errors that can occur in the Consume operation, as shown below.

Fig 8.5 Configuring the errors inside the Try Scope

The Error can be handled using the mule error object, which has detailed error details using the Transform Message component.

Fig 8.6 Handling Error from Mule Error Object

Using On Error Continue

The On Error Continue component is used when an error occurs that needs to be handled and when the process wants to continue without stopping. The On Error Continue component is useful in use cases such as batch processing, integrating with multiple systems, and non-critical jobs. In the below example, we have a main flow and a subfloor. If an error occurs in the sub-flow, using On Error Continue, we handle the ErrorError, and the control goes back to the main flow to continue the process.

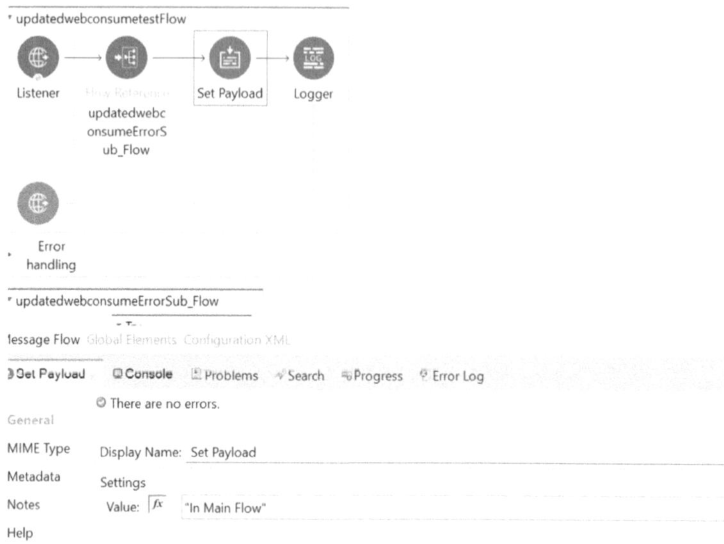

Fig 8.7 On Error Continue Main Flow

The main flow calls a sub-flow named updatedwebconsumeErrorSub_Flow, which uses the WebServiceConsumer connector to call a soap service. Since we can not add error handling to the sub-flow, we can handle the ErrorError using the Try scope, as shown below.

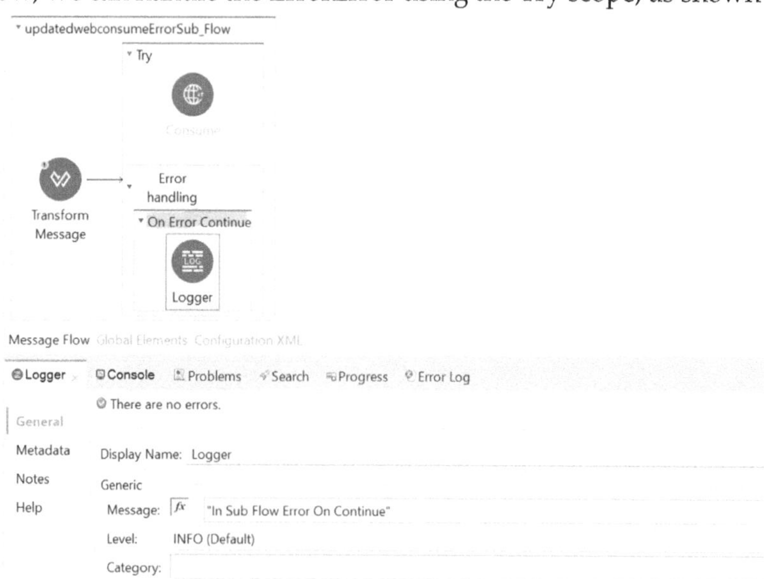

Fig 8.8 On Error Continue Sub Flow

When we run the program by providing the wrong payload as input, the API responds with an HTTP status code of 200 and provides the output as well. The output is displayed from the main flow.

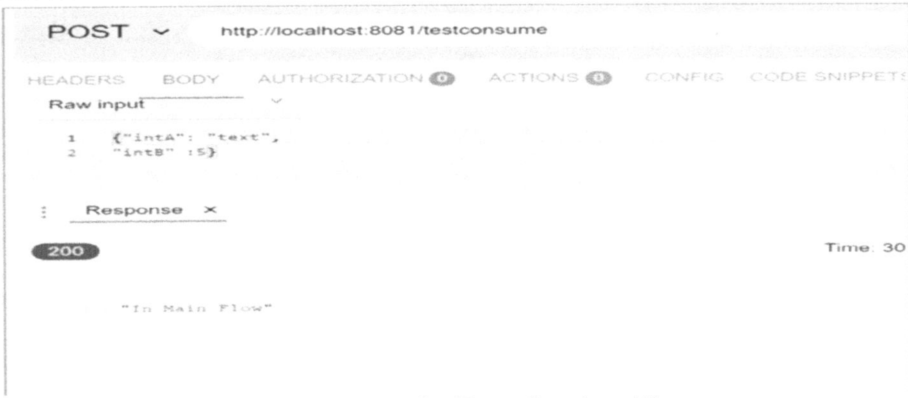

Fig 8.9 Running On Error Continue Flow

However, when you observe the console logs, you can see the error that occurred during the flow's execution. The ErrorError is logged, and the replay processing of the main flow continues.

Console Log:

Element : updatedwebconsumeErrorSub_Flow/processors/1/processors/0 @ updatedwebconsumetest:updatedwebconsumetest.xml:106 ()
Element DSL : <wsc:consume doc:id="a440796b-6788-4352-9275-b7428578819d" doc:name="" config-ref="Web_Service_Consumer_Cal_Config" operation="Add">
<wsc:message>
<wsc:body><![CDATA[#[payload.Envelope.Body]]]></wsc:body>
</wsc:message>
</wsc:consume>
Error type : WSC:SOAP_FAULT
FlowStack : at
updatedwebconsumeErrorSub_Flow(updatedwebconsumeErrorSub_Flow/processors/1/processors/0 @ updatedwebconsumetest:updatedwebconsumetest.xml:106 ())
at updatedwebconsumetestFlow(updatedwebconsumetestFlow/processors/0 @ updatedwebconsumetest:updatedwebconsumetest.xml:24 (updatedwebconsumeErrorSub_Flow))
(set debug level logging or '-Dmule.verbose.exceptions=true' for everything)

INFO 2025-03-18 16:51:46,460 [[MuleRuntime].uber.09: [updatedwebconsumetest].updatedwebconsumetestFlow.BLOCKING @2cf818b6] [processor: updatedwebconsumeErrorSub_Flow/processors/1/errorHandler/0/processors/0; event: 2bd654f0-03eb-11f0-a15d-ae675d908ecc] org. Mule.runtime.core.internal.processor.LoggerMessageProcessor: "In Sub Flow Error On Continue"
INFO 2025-03-18 16:51:46,460 [[MuleRuntime].uber.09: [updatedwebconsumetest].updatedwebconsumetestFlow.BLOCKING @2cf818b6] [processor: updatedwebconsumetestFlow/processors/2; event: 2bd654f0-03eb-11f0-a15d-ae675d908ecc] org. Mule.runtime.core.internal.processor.LoggerMessageProcessor: "In Main Flow"

Using On Error Propagate

The On Error Propagate component is used when an error occurs that needs to be handled and doesn't want to continue the process.The On Error Propogate component is useful in use cases such as APIs with request-response patterns, critical processing jobs, etc. In the same above example, we will use On Error Propagate instead of On Error Continue in the try scope of sub flow.

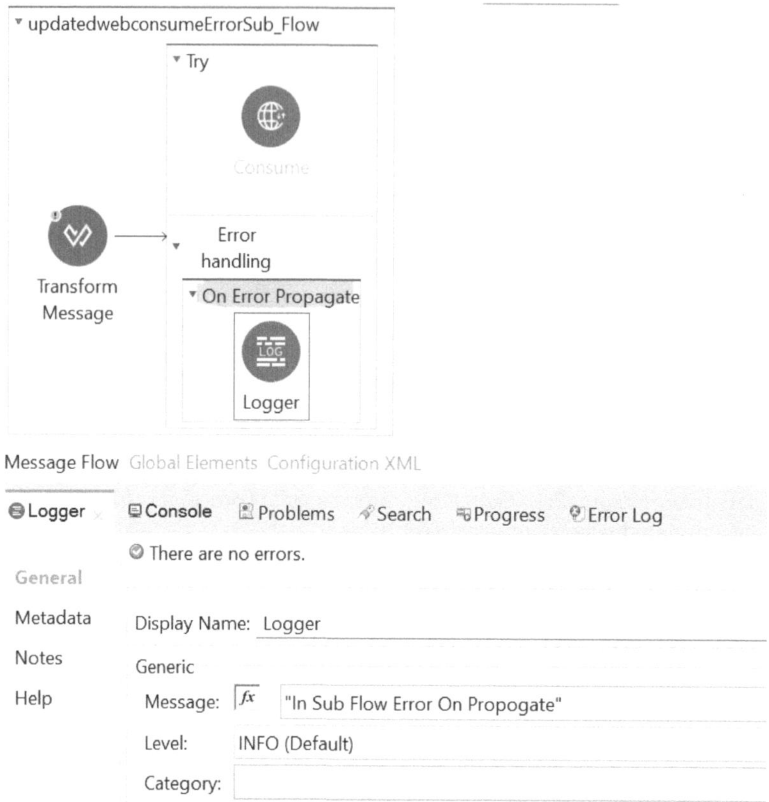

Fig 8.10 On Error Propogate Sub Flow

When we run the program by entering the wrong payload, the API responds with an ErrorError, and the processing stops in the sub flow itself.

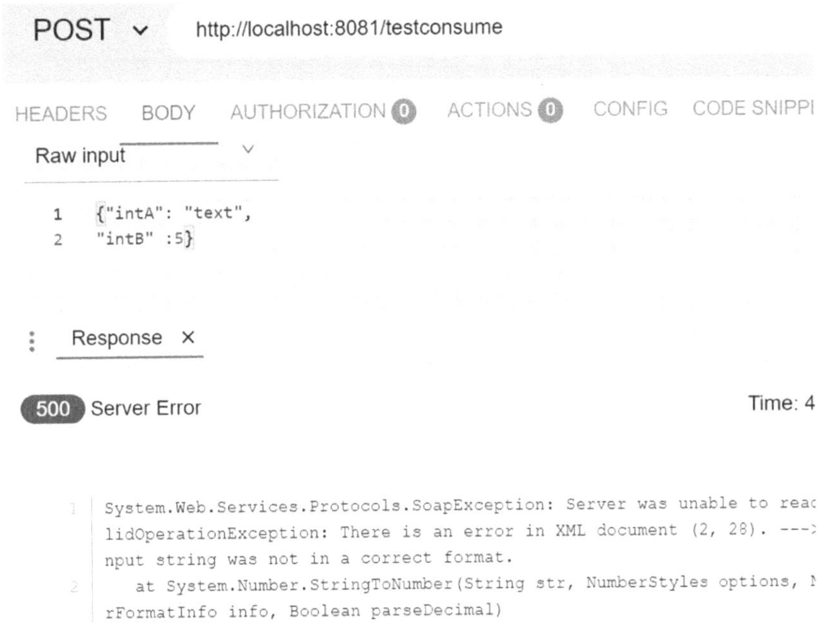

Fig 8.11 Running On Error Propagate Flow

However, when you observe the console logs, you can see the ErrorError occurred during the execution of the sub-flow. The ErrorError is logged, and the reaming processing of the main flow continues.

Console Log:

Element : updatedwebconsumeErrorSub_Flow/processors/1/processors/0 @ updatedwebconsumetest:updatedwebconsumetest.xml:106 ()
Element DSL : <wsc:consume doc:id="a440796b-6788-4352-9275-b7428578819d" doc:name="" config-ref="Web_Service_Consumer_Cal_Config" operation="Add">
<wsc:message>
<wsc:body><![CDATA[#[payload.Envelope.Body]]]></wsc:body>
</wsc:message>
</wsc:consume>
Error type : WSC:SOAP_FAULT
FlowStack : at
updatedwebconsumeErrorSub_Flow(updatedwebconsumeErrorSub_Flow/processors/1/processors/0 @ updatedwebconsumetest:updatedwebconsumetest.xml:106 ())
at updatedwebconsumetestFlow(updatedwebconsumetestFlow/processors/0 @ updatedwebconsumetest:updatedwebconsumetest.xml:24 (updatedwebconsumeErrorSub_Flow))
(set debug level logging or '-Dmule.verbose.exceptions=true' for everything)
****
INFO 2025-03-18 20:07:49,722 [[MuleRuntime].uber.07: [updatedwebconsumetest].updatedwebconsumetestFlow.BLOCKING @747c2828] [processor: updatedwebconsumeErrorSub_Flow/processors/1/errorHandler/0/processors/0; event: 8e9d3e31-0406-11f0-a85e-ae675d908ccc] org. Mule.runtime.core.internal.processor.LoggerMessageProcessor: "In Sub Flow

Error On Propogate".

Using Raise Error

The Raise Error component in MuleSoft intentionally triggers a custom error during a flow's execution. This allows you to enforce business logic or validation rules and ensure that errors are handled consistently.Some of the use cases involve scenarios where custom business logic is required, enhanced error reporting, etc.

In the below example Raise Error component is used to customize the ErrorError:

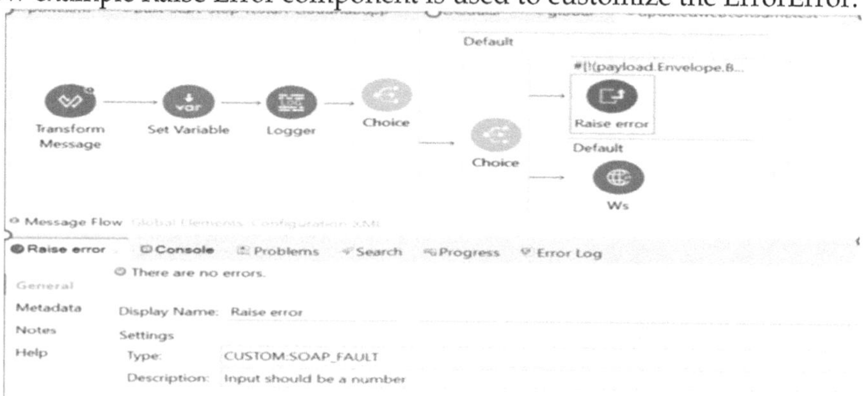

Fig 8.12 Raise Error in a Flow

If we run this program, unlike the previous example of On Error Propagate, the ErrorError can now be understood by the end user who is consuming this API.

Fig 8.13 Running Raise Error Flow

Using Default Error Handler

When errors are not, when an error occurs,flow, Mule tries to handle it via the defaults seller. This is not a best practice. In the example below, when an ErrorError occurs, the Erroit rError thrown by the respective component is sent back to the consumer. The flow's default Error handling will catch the ErrorError and send it back to the consumer.

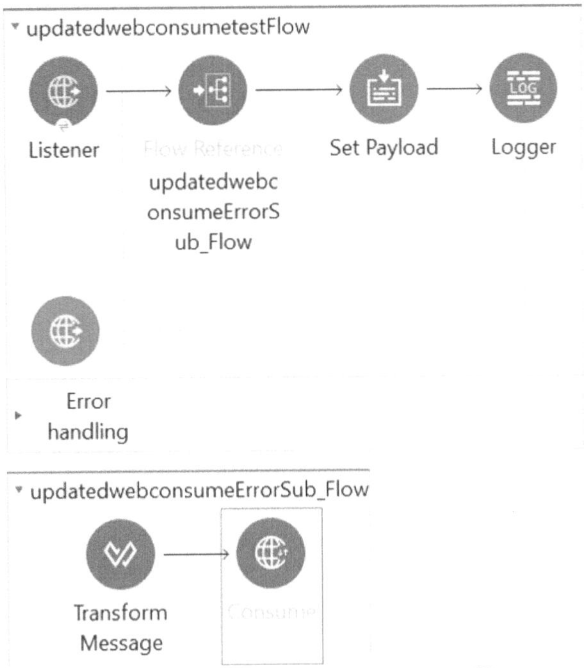

Fig 8.14 Defualt Error Handling

Using CausedBy in DataWeave

In DataWeave, the causedBy property is used to attach underlying error details when you raise or rethrow an error. This helps create an error chain, preserving the original exception information so that when the ErrorError propagates up, you have the full context for debugging.

Fig 8.15 DataWeave causedBy Property

The error object includes a message, and causedBy carries the extra context of the error object. It provides the full error stack, which makes it easy to identify the issue. In the above example, if the error object is of type SOAP_FAULT, the code will be displayed as 400; otherwise, it will display as 500.

Conclusion

In this chapter,we understood the importance of handling errors and how to handle various errors in a Mule API. We also studied the different ways to handle errors, how errors can be handled with custom messages, and the advantages of defining a global error handler. In the next chapter, we will learn about non-functional requirements and their importance. We will also learn how to apply non-functional requirements for Mule APIs using policies from API Manager. We will also see what different non-functional requirements are supported by API Manager and how to implement custom policies.

Exercise: Test Your Understanding

Answer the following questions and test your understanding of learning from **Chapter 8**:

Q. 1. What is global error handling?

Q. 2. When do we use **OnErrorContinue** component?

Q. 3. What is the use of **Try** Scope?

Q. 4. What is the use of **Raise** Error?

Q. 5. Where can we use **causedBy** property?

9

Non-Functional Requirements

Every Application or program has functional and non-functional requirements. Functional requirements define what an application needs to do. Non-functional requirements (NFRs) define how a system needs to perform in various conditions. NFRs play an important role as they define the overall quality of the system. These requirements focus on how a system should perform efficiently and effectively. Even if the system meets all the functional requirements, it may fail if the NFRs are not met effectively.NFRs are essential for a system to perform well, be easily scalable, remain secure, and be easy to maintain and use. Balancing functional and non-functional requirements is key to delivering a high-quality software solution. In this chapter, we will learn about the non-functional requirements and how to apply them using the Anypoint Platform for Mule applications. We will also learn about the different non-functional requirements that can be configured for Mule applications and the prerequisites for applying them.

Applying NFRs using Anypoint Platform

Anypoint Platform provides various tools to apply NFRs for Mule applications. The components used to apply NFRs in Anypoint Platform are:

- **Anypoint Runtime Manager:** This tool helps manage deployments and monitor API performance and health metrics. It also helps ensure that Mule applications meet performance standards through real-time performance monitoring, throughput monitoring, automatically restarting applications when they are not responsive, autoscaling horizontally or vertically, and configuring various alerts.
- **API Manager:** Allows you to apply various security, rate limiting, caching and monitoring policies.
- **Anypoint Monitoring:** Provides the insights of an application performance along with some metrices like response time, error rates and traffic patterns
- **CloudHub and On-Premises Deployment:** Depending on the deployment model, Mule runtimes will support configurations related to scaling, fault tolerance, and high availability.
- **Different NFRs configurable in Mule Applications:**
- Now we will see what the different key non-functional requirements are can be configured for Mule applications from Anypoint Platform .

Performance:

- **Throttling and Rate Limiting:** From API Manager we can apply rate limiting policies to an API to manage the processing of requests by avoiding the overload on API
- **Caching:** Analyze what data will be frequently accessed and apply caching strategies to store it instead of calling back-end systems every time to improve response time.
- **Load Balancing:** Configure load balancing in Runtime Manager to distribute the load among the servers to avoid the load on single server.

Scalability: Using Anypoint Platform Runtime Manager we can configure the scaling by adding more workers (horizontal) or by increasing the capacity of the workers (vertical)

- **Availability:** By implementing clustering on on-premises deployments and multi region deployments in CloudHub to ensure the Application are up and running in case of any failure in one worker or node.
- Ensure to configure failover strategies in the Mule applications in case of a failure in one region or node.
- **Security:** Using API Manager, apply security-related policies like Oauth 2.0, JWT, and SAML for authentication, and APIs can be accessed securely.
- Client ID enforcement, Basic Authentication can be applied to ensure the request to the API is coming from a valid client.
- Apply encryption methods to transfer the sensitive data between client and server.
- **Maintainability:** For centralized logging use Anypoint Monitoring and Anypoint logging capabilities to get the visibility on application logs.
- Configure performance-related alerts to check the response time, failure rate, and other key parameters to troubleshoot issues in real time.
- Use Anypoint Exchange and Anypoint CLI to set up CI/CD pipelines, making it easy to deploy a Mule application without downtime.

Using Anypoint API Manager and applying Policies: Mule APIs management can be done using Anypoint API Manager component and by applying the policies. This can be done

- On the level of HTTP
- Applicable to only HTTP/1.x APIs. Hence not applicable for WebSocket APIs or HTTP/2 like gRPC APIs.
- RAML defined APIs, policies can be applied at resource level instead of endpoint level.

On Anypoint Platform, API policies can always be enforced within a Mule application executing in a Mule runtime. Alternatively, policies can be enforced on an API Proxy running in front of the API Implementation. API policies are not included in the API implementation. The policies are downloaded from the API Manager into the Mule application at runtime.

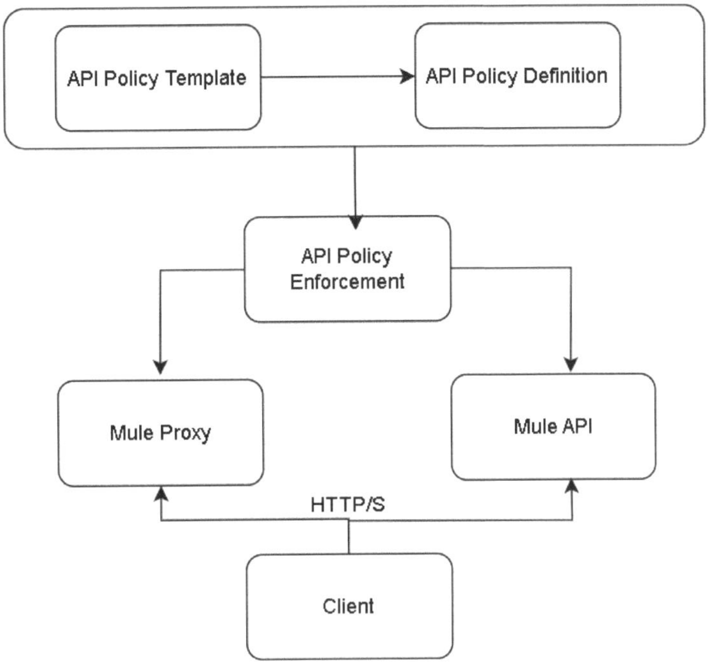

Fig 9.1 Policy Enforcement

Policies can be enforced at Mule API Proxy level in below mentioned scenarios:

- When the API Implementations are not Mule applications and not running on Mule runtime.
- API policies require special network configuration, such as access to highly secured applications that can be accessed from a particular subnet. API proxies are preferred because they can be deployed on a separate network than API Implementations.
- When the experience APIs are sensitive to expose use API proxies as they can be deployed in a DMZ so that they can shield the API Implementation

Policies can be enforced on API Implementation in below scenarios:

- API Policy enforcement preferred when resource usage must be minimized. number of nodes gets doubled if we apply the policies at API Proxy level.
- Deployment of APIs through CI/CD pipelines will be more straightforward if we follow the embedded policy enforcement.

API Policies available on Anypoint Platform:

Anypoint Platform provides following policies categories and corresponding policies as out of the box.

Compliance

- Client ID enforcement: The policy ensures that valid clients with valid IDs and client secrets can access the API.
- Cross-Orgin Resource Sharing: Controls the cross-origin requests from web browsers.

Security

- **Http Basic Authentication**
    - Basic Authentication (simple): Authenticates client credentials using predefined username and password.
    - Basic Authentication (LDAP): Authenticates the users against an active directory.
- **IP based API Policies**
    - IP whitelist: Grants the API access from the approved IP addresses.
    - IP blacklist: Blocks the API access from the specified IP addresses.
- **Threat Protection Policies**
    - JSON threat protection: Protects APIs from malformed JSON payloads.
    - XML threat protection: Protects APIs from malformed XML payloads.
- **OAuth 2.0 access token enforcement policies**
    - Using External Provider: Validates the tokens issued by an external OAuth 2.0 provider
    - OpenAM access token enforcement: Validates the tokens issued by OpenAM for API access.
    - PingFederate access token enforcement: Validates the tokens issued by PingFederate for secured API access.
    - OpenID Connect access token enforcement: Token validity based on OpenID connect standards.

Transformation

- Header Injection: Adds custom headers to API requests or responses.
- Header Removal: Removes the specified headers from the API requests or responses.

Quality Of Service (QoS)

1) **non-SLA-based API policies**
    - Rate Limiting: Restricts the number of API requests over a specified time.
    - Spike Control: Limits the number of requests in short bursts to avoid the sudden spikes.
    - HTTP Caching: Improves performance by caching the API response.
2) **SLA-based API policies**
    - Rate Limiting - SLA-based: Applies rate limiting based on service level agreements for the specific clients.

Troubleshooting

- Message Logging: Captures and logs API request and response details for monitoring and troubleshoot the issues.

Custom API Policies

One can create custom policies and publish on Anypoint exchange and utilize in the respective mule applications.Implementing and applying custom policies can be done by below steps:

- Custom API policies must be implemented very similar to Mule applications
- They must be packaged specifically as API policies and deployed to Anypoint Exchange
- This package contains the API policy template, i.e., both the code for the API policy as well as a YAML file that describes the API policy's configuration data, i.e., the parameters to be specified when the policy is applied to an API
- When applying an API policy to an API instance, Anypoint API Manager retrieves the API policy template from Anypoint Exchange and renders a configuration UI to enter the definition (parameter values)
- The API policy template and definition are then downloaded to any Mule runtime that registers as the API Instance.

Auto-Discovery

API Autodiscovery is a feature in MuleSoft that allows a deployed Mule application to connect with Anypoint Platform Api Manager to manage the API. By applying Autodiscovery, API Management can be done easily.

As part of API Management below tasks can be done

- Enforcing policies on APIs
- API Governance
- Monitoring and providing the analytics.

To enable API Auto discovery the prerequisites are

- Access To Anypoint Platform
- Access to Anypoint Platform API Manager
- Application needs to be deployed on Mule runtime
- Need client id and client secret from Anypoint Platform Organization.

Configure API in API Manager

- Go to API Manager
- Add API

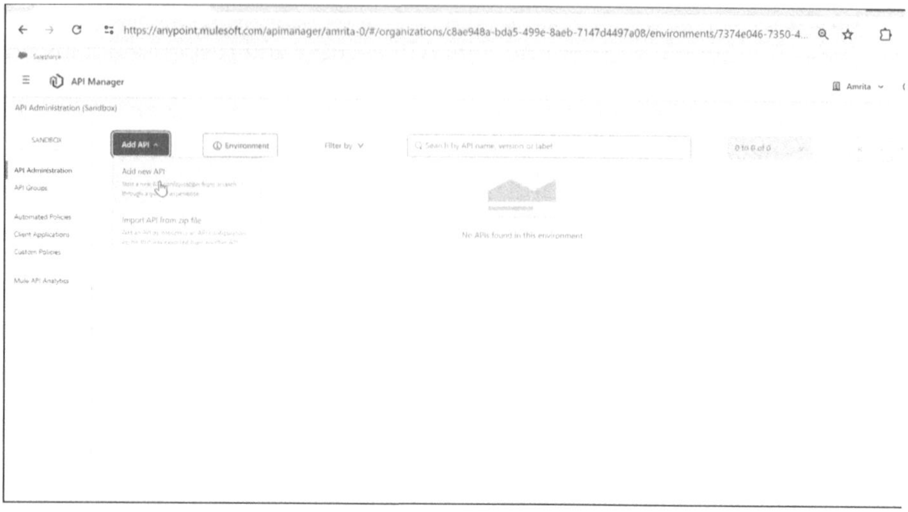

Fig 9.2 Adding API to API Manager

- Select the Mule Runtime configurations and click on Next button

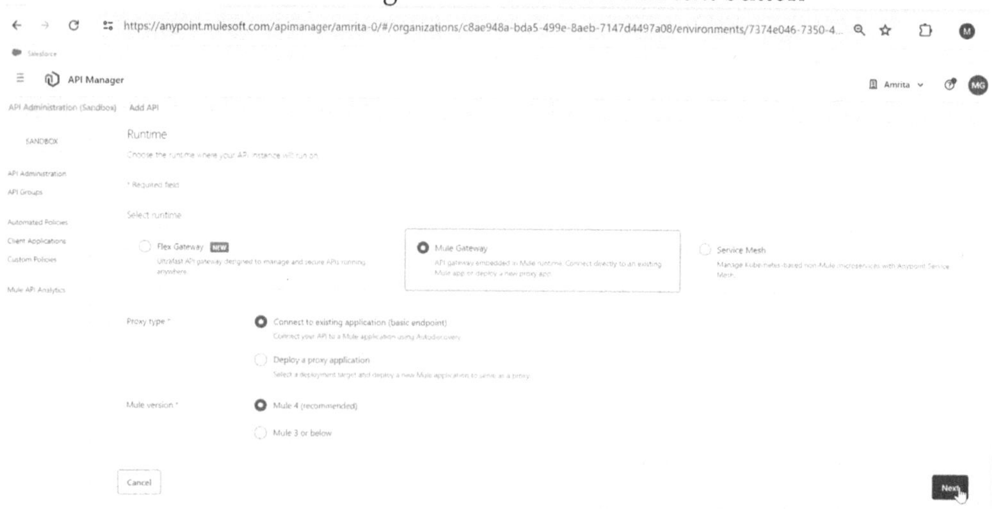

Fig 9.3 Add API Runtime Configurations

- Select the API for which auto discovery needs to be enabled and select the API version and asset type. Click on Next.

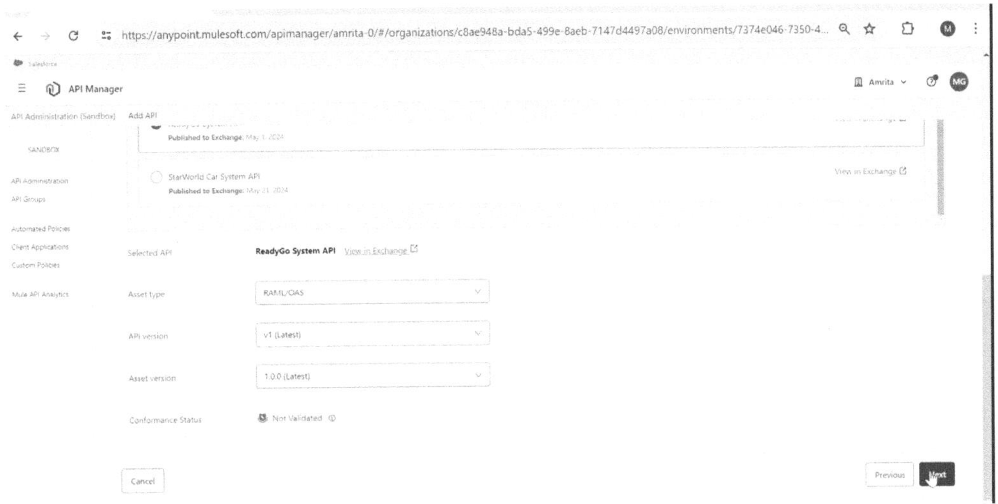

Fig 9.4 Add API Asset Configurations

- Provide required downstream and upstream details for the selected API. Click on Next. Default client provider is Anypoint, in case any external client providers added select the client provider accordingly. We can see the progress of Add API process.

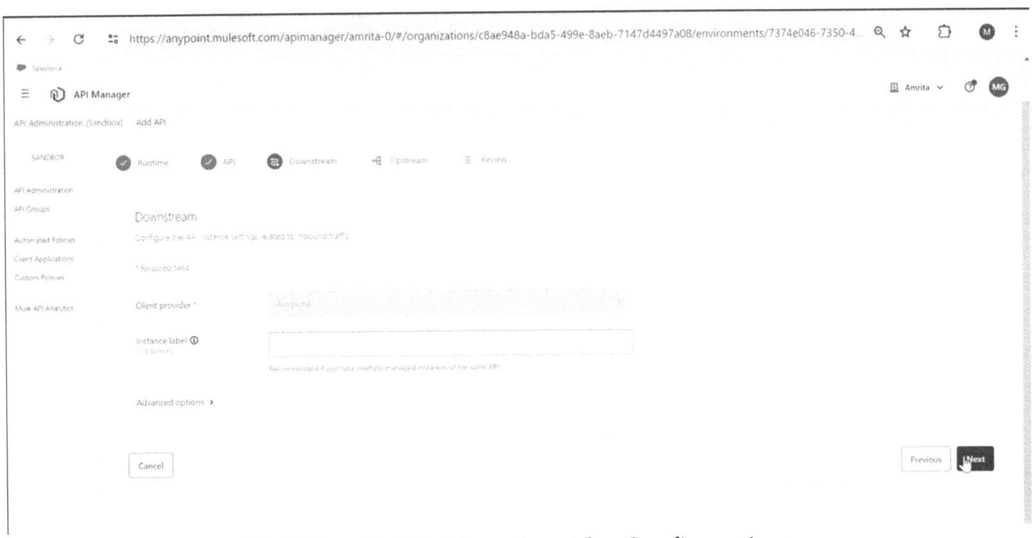

Fig 9.5 Add API Client Provider Configurations

- Once the details provided review the summary and click on save.
- API instance id gets created.

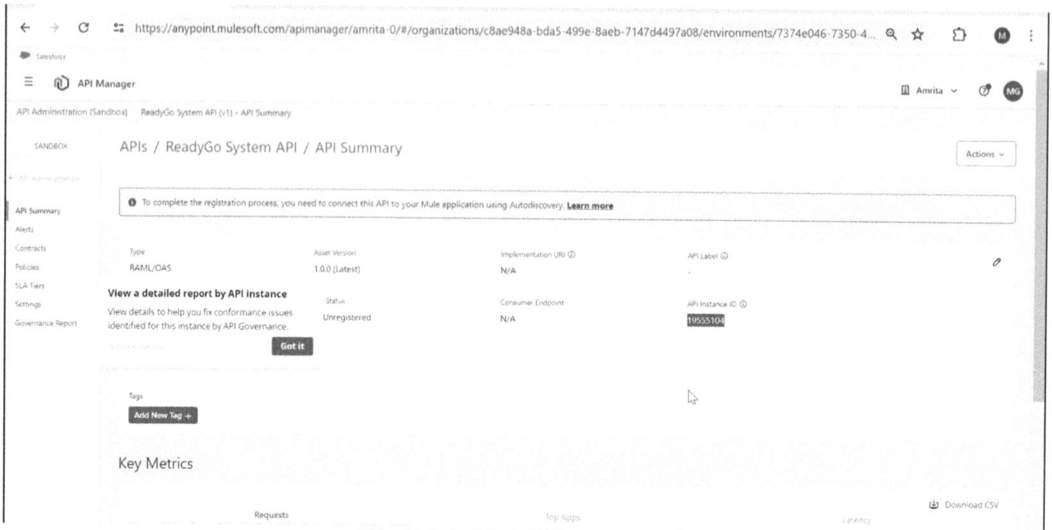

Fig 9.6 Add API Instance Id

- Note down the API Id

Configure Auto-Discovery in Mule application

- Add API instance ID in Mule application properties file.
- Create a global configuration under global elements for API Autodiscovery and click on ok

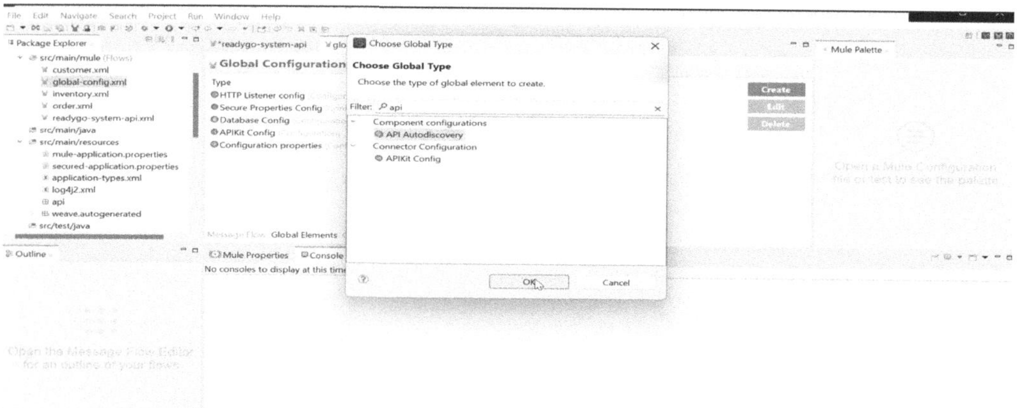

Fig 9.7 Creating api auto discovery as global element

- We can see a dialog box to select the flow we want to apply the Autodiscovery. If we select the main flow, the policies we will apply the API are applicable for all the endpoints supported by the API. If we select a flow where a particular method is defined Autodiscovery is applied to only that method.

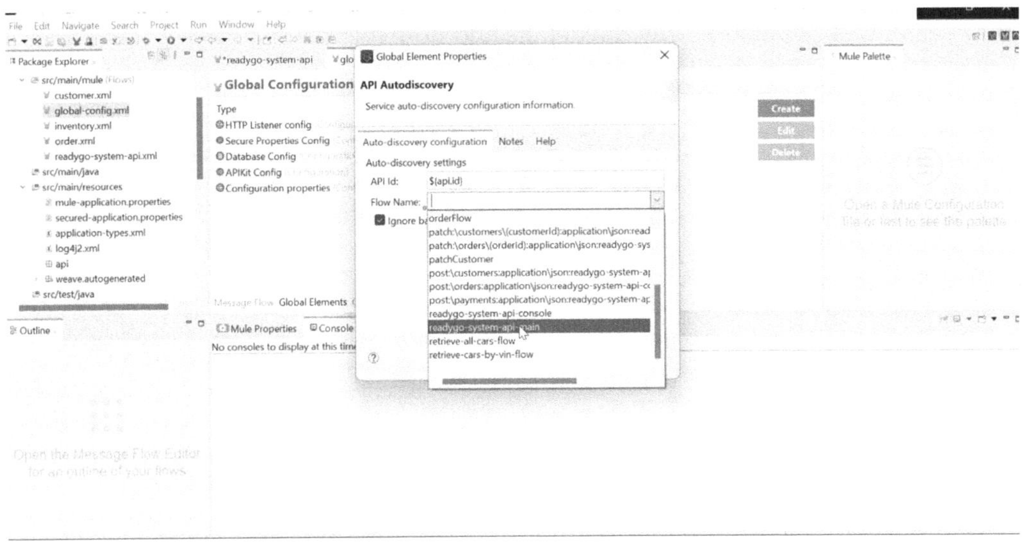

Fig 9.8 Selecting the flow to apply Autodiscovery.

- We need the client ID and client secret of the business group where we are going to deploy our Mule application. This information is available from Anypoint Platform Access Management.
- Once you select the Access Management select the Business groups and select the environment in which we are going to deploy.

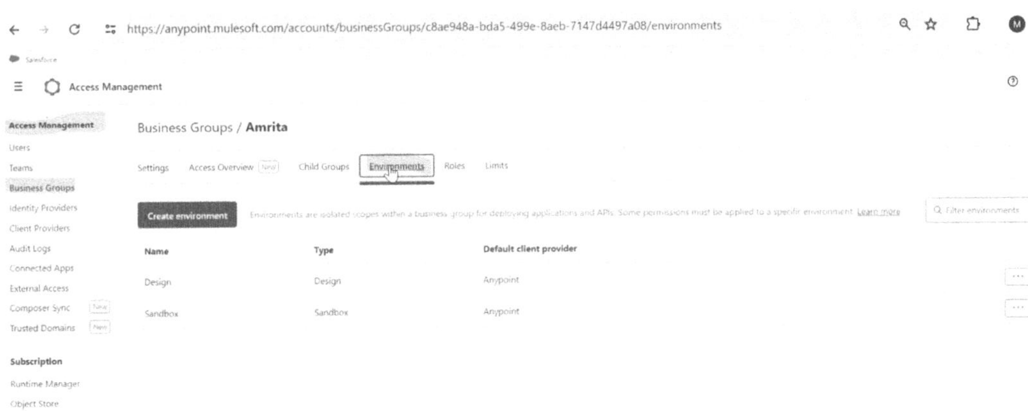

Fig 9.9 Selecting AccessManagement Environment

- Once the environment is selected, click on edit. The dialog box with client ID and client secret will populate. Copy the details and note them.

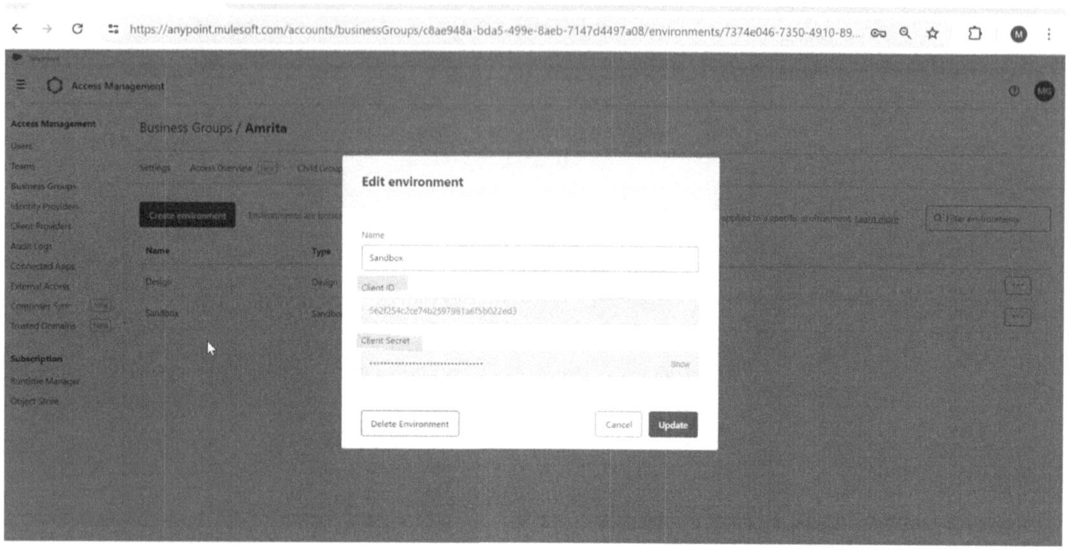

Fig 9.10 Client ID and Secret Details

- Once the client ID and secret are available, go to Anypoint Studio, click on the window on the menu bar, select the preferences, select the API Manager, provide the client ID and client secret details, and click on the Validate button.

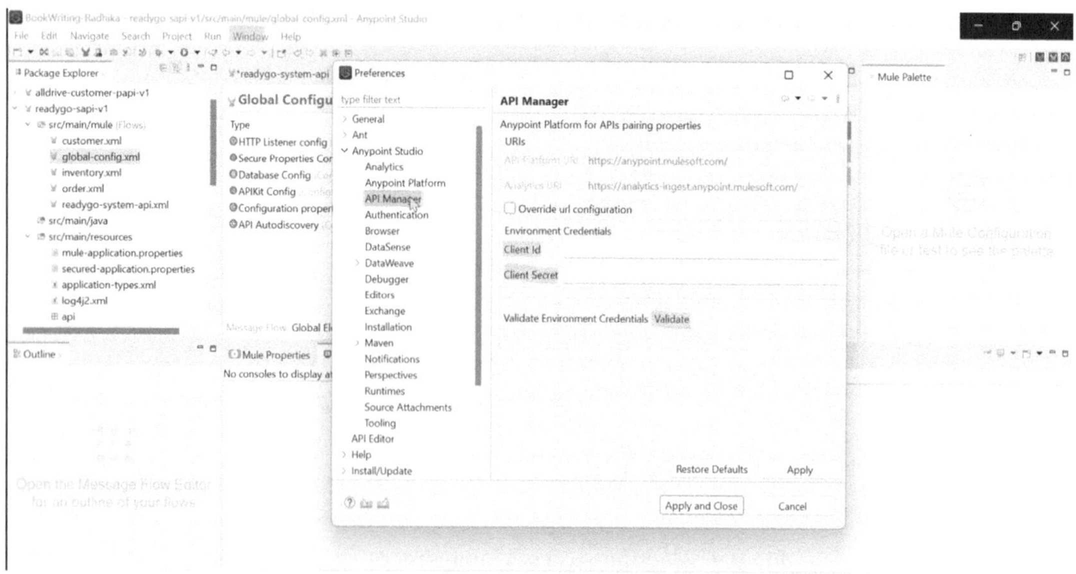

Fig 9.11 AnypointStudio APIManager Configurations

- Configure these parameters in mule-artifact.json as the secured properties.

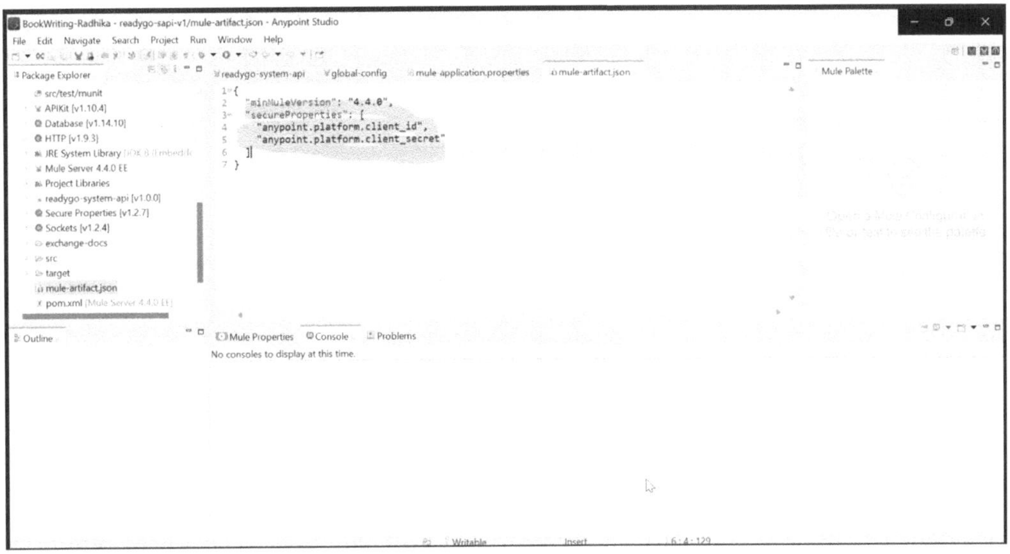

Fig 9.12 Securing Client id and secret

Deploy the Mule application

Once the configuration is completed, deploy the Mule application. While the Application is getting deployed, observe the logs to verify whether the auto discover is applied.

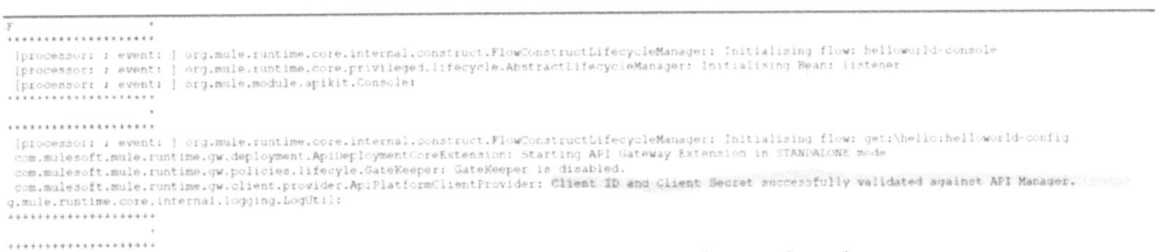

Fig 9.13 Console log for validating client id and secret

After deployment go to the API Manager and check the Application status. It should be in "Active" status.

Fig 9.14 API Status in API Manager

Applying Policies to Mule application

Once deployed and the API status is active in API Manager we can apply the required policies on the API. Policies can be applied from API Manager. From API Manager select the API for which policies must be applied and click on Policies from the left side.

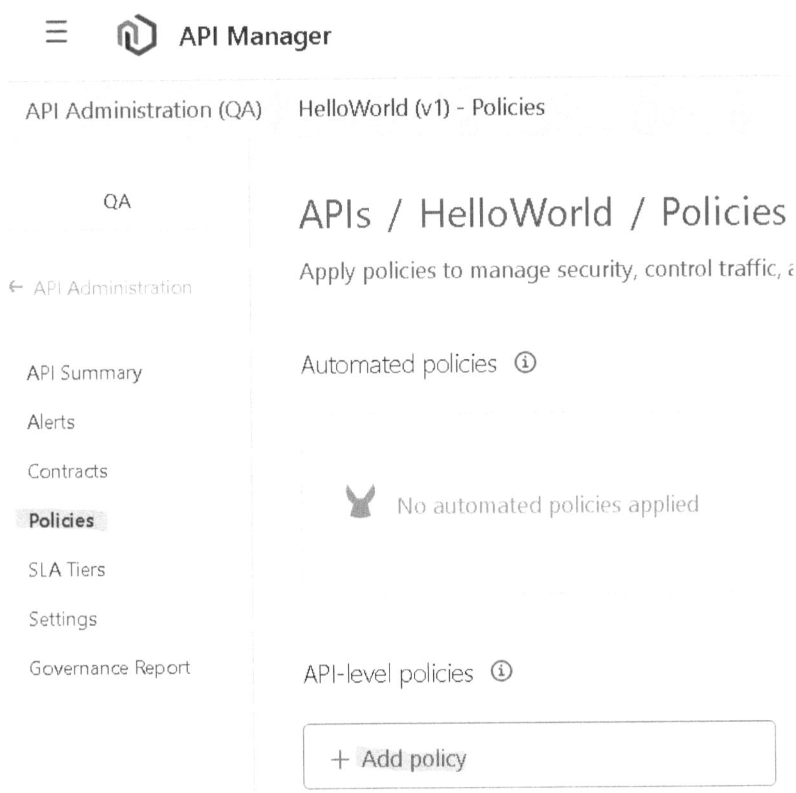

Fig 9.15 Adding Policy

Once you click on Add policy, all the available policies will be displayed. Select the policy you want to apply and click on the next button. Provide the required configurations. Here, we will see the example of a Rate-Limiting policy.

Fig 9.16 Rate Limiting Policy configuration

In this example, we allow one request per 20 seconds. If we hit more than one request in 20 seconds, we will get an error message saying the limit has been crossed.

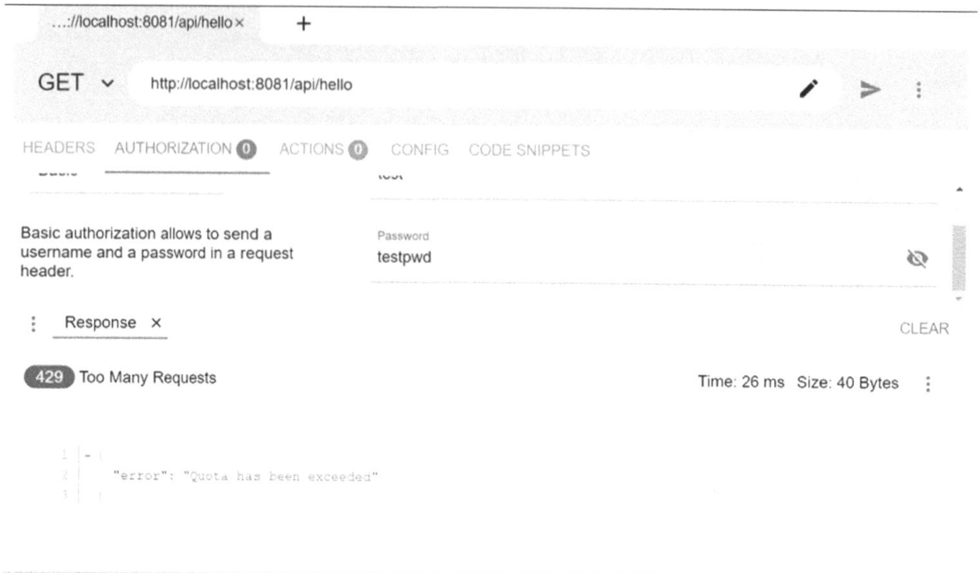

Fig 9.17 Rate Limiting Policy Execution

Once the policies are applied, you can also see the same in console logs.

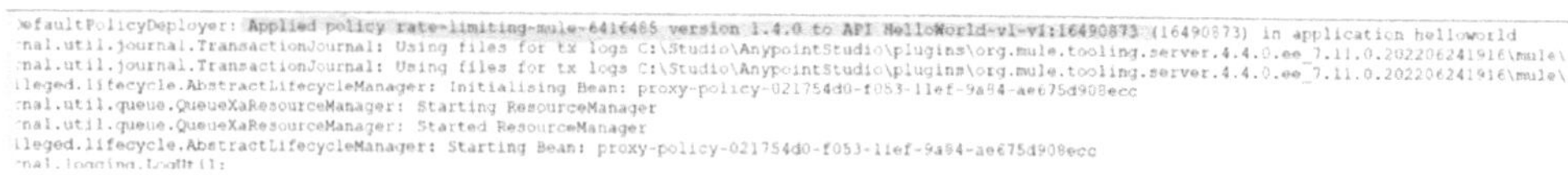

Fig 9.18 Console log for policy applied

Conclusion

This chapter taught us the importance of non-functional requirements (NFRs). We also learned the NFRs supported by the Anypoint Platform and how those can be applied using various components to Mule applications. We also understood the different categories of NFRs MuleSoft is supporting. The purpose of API-Discovery and how it can be applied to Mule applications. In the next chapter, we will learn how to deploy Mule applications and the various deployment models supported by MuleSoft. We will also understand the different ways to deploy Mule applications.

Exercise: Test Your Understanding

Answer the following questions and test your understanding of learning from **Chapter 9**:

Q. 1. How can we achieve horizontal scaling?

Q. 2. How can we achieve vertical scaling?

Q. 3. What are the Security policies available?

Q. 4. What is the difference between Rate limiting and Rate limiting with SLA?

Q. 5. What is API Auto-Discovery?

10

Deploying Mule APIs

Deploying an application is the process of packaging and distributing Mule applications to run on various environments so that they can integrate with various systems and applications and process data across the enterprise ecosystem. MuleSoft offers various ways to deploy applications based on organizational needs. Every deployment option has advantages like managing the servers, applying the patches, scalability, security, CPU, and Memory distribution. Choosing a deployment option depends on the constraints and requirements of the business, such as the organization's security policies, budget constraints, infrastructure preferences, etc. Successful deployment ensures that the Mule applications can integrate with the systems, applications following the security policies, handle real-time data exchange without interruption, handle the load within limits, etc. The deployment begins only after the Mule APIs are designed and developed by building the flows using Anypoint Platform and Anypoint Studio. Once the API implementation is complete, APIs are packaged as deployable archive files and deployed on platforms like CloudHub, Runtime Fabric (RTF), and on-premises servers. In this chapter, we will learn about the different deployment options supported by MuleSoft and how to deploy the Mule applications.

MuleSoft Deployment Options

Below are some of the significant deployment options offered by MuleSoft:

- On-prem deployment needs to be referred to as 'Hybrid.' Also, the Private Cloud Edition (PCE) deployment option is missing.
- CloudHub 2.0 vCore sizing information is missing.

CloudHub

CloudHub is a fully managed integration platform as a service (iPass) by MuleSoft. This means that MuleSoft manages the underlying Infrastructure. This is the choice for organizations that want no infrastructure maintenance and prefer a fast go-to-market strategy for their integration requirements. CloudHub has two versions. CloudHub 1.0 and CloudHub 2.0. CloudHub 2.0 was recently launched by MuleSoft.

Benefits:

- MuleSoft manages the Infrastructure, takes care of updates and scaling, and reduces the operational burden.

- Ideal for organizations focusing on cloud strategies.
- Global availability as data centers are globally distributed.
- Built-in security features

CloudHub 1.0 Block Diagram:

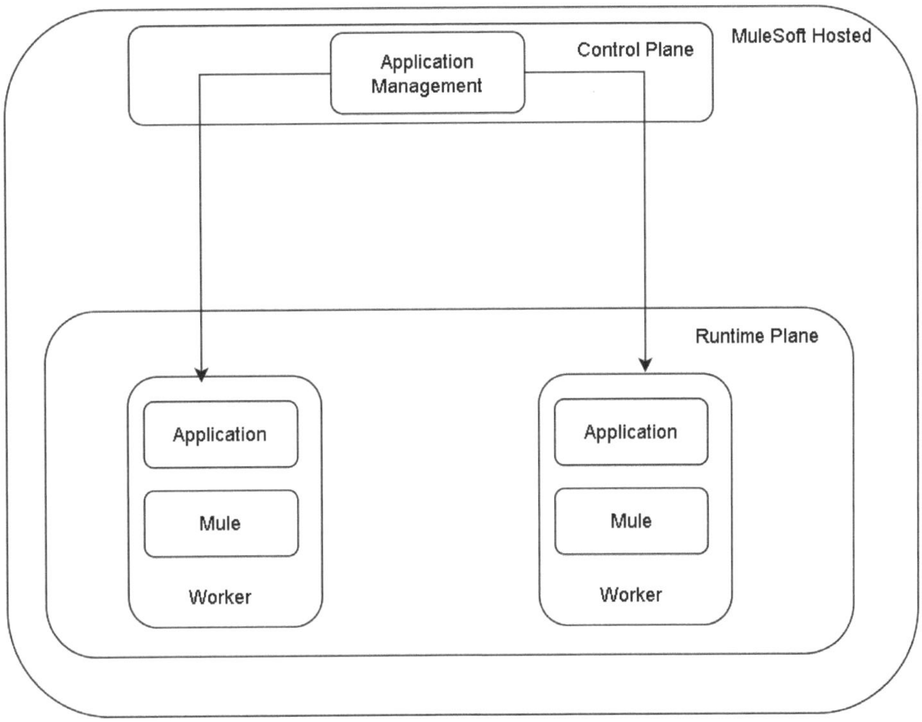

Fig 10.1 CloudHub 1.0 Block Diagram

CloudHub 2.0 Block Diagram:

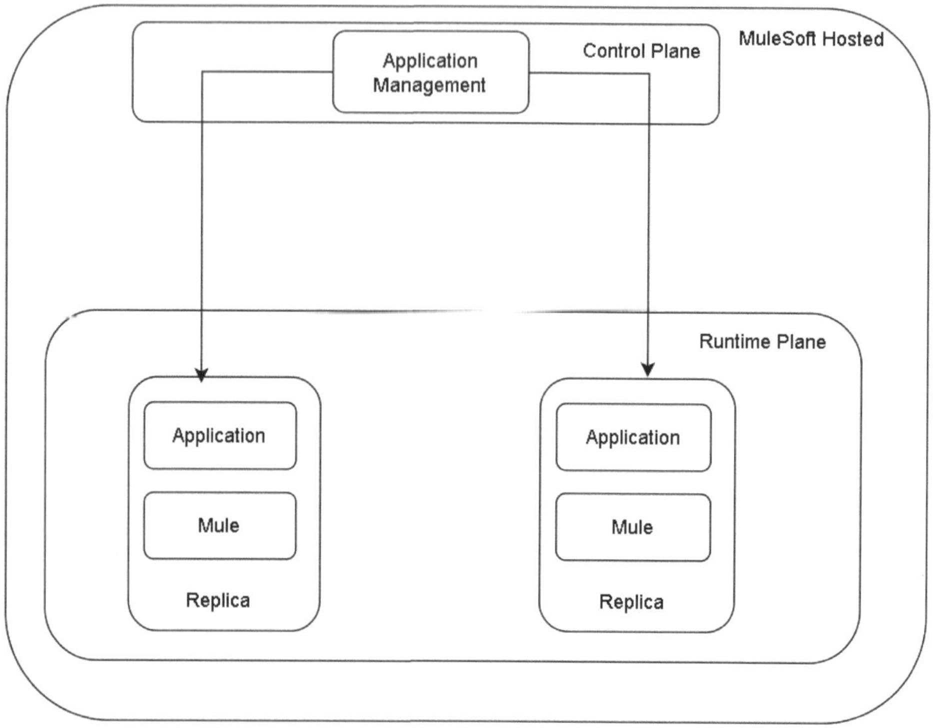

Fig 10.2 CloudHub 2.0 Block Diagram

MuleSoft Runtime Fabric (RTF)

Runtime Fabric is a container-based MuleSoft runtime offering that allows you to deploy Mule applications and API proxies on popular cloud platforms (e.g., AWS, Azure, Google, ROSA, etc.) or on-premises via the Kubernetes Cluster that you can create, configure, and manage.

Benefits:

- The flexibility of deploying a private cloud, public cloud, and on-premises.
- Follows container-based architecture to get built-in support for automatic scaling, failover, and load balancing.
- It works in a hybrid environment where some services run on the cloud, and others run on-premises.
- Complete control over security policies.

RTF Block Diagram:

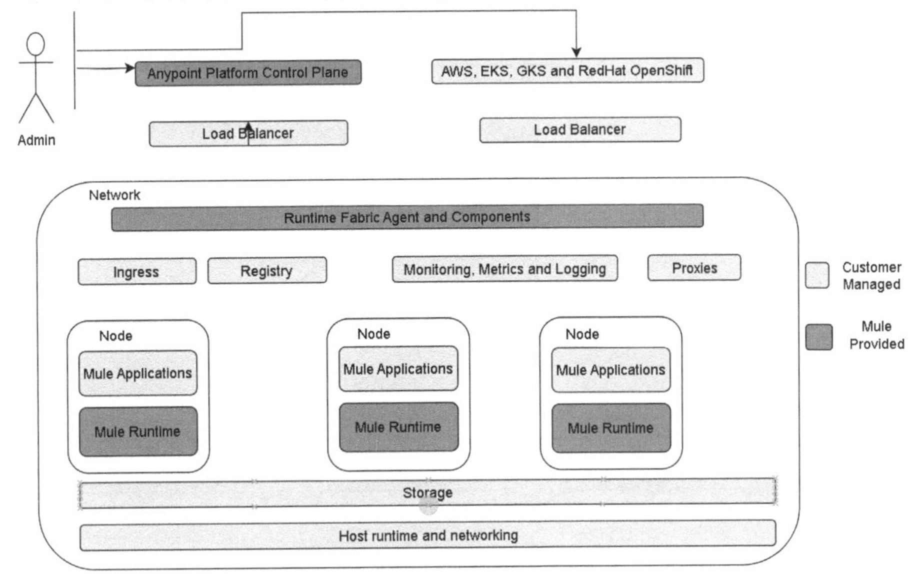

Fig 10.3 RTF Block Diagram

On-Premises

MuleSoft platform can be installed on one's Infrastructure, giving complete control over configurations, resource management, and security. The challenges in this case are high operational overhead due to the requirement of a dedicated DevOps and IT team for maintenance, upgrades, and troubleshooting.

Benefits:

- Complete control over the environment, including security, network connectivity, hardware resource management, etc.
- Scaling is possible, but manual setup and management are required.

In this model, customers have the option to host both the control plane and runtime plane on a customer hosted Infrastructure, as shown below:

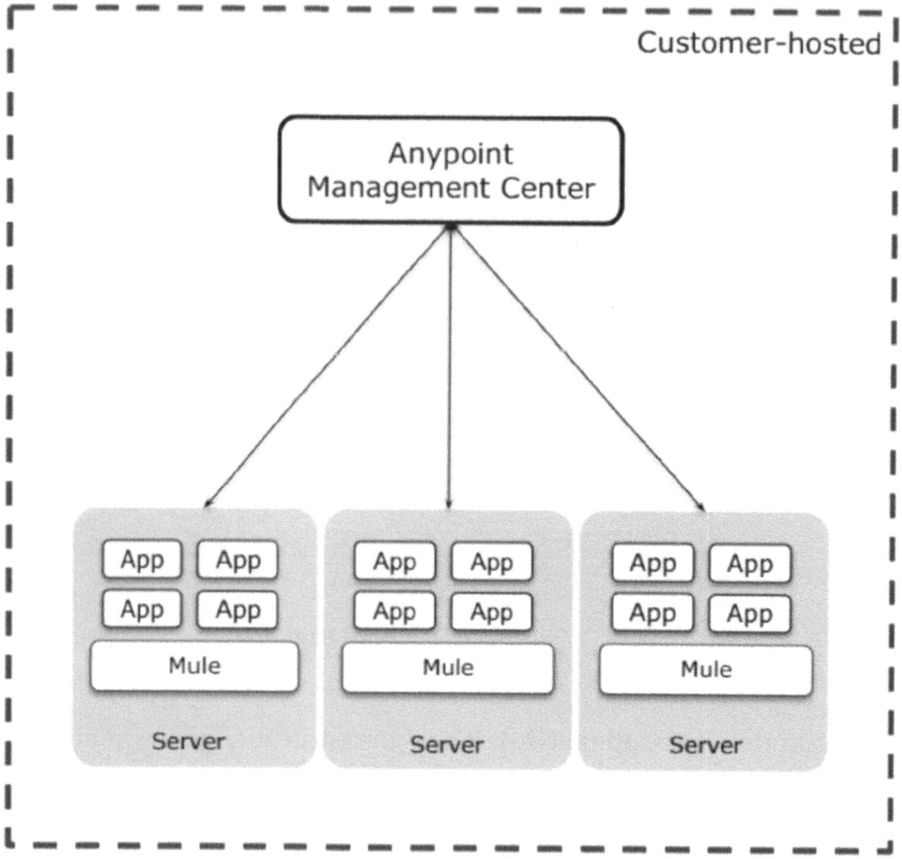

Fig 10.4 Runtime Plane and Control Plane both on Customer Hosted Infrastructure

The other option is to host the control plane on MuleSoft-hosted infrastructure and the runtime plane on Customer-Hosted Infrastructure.

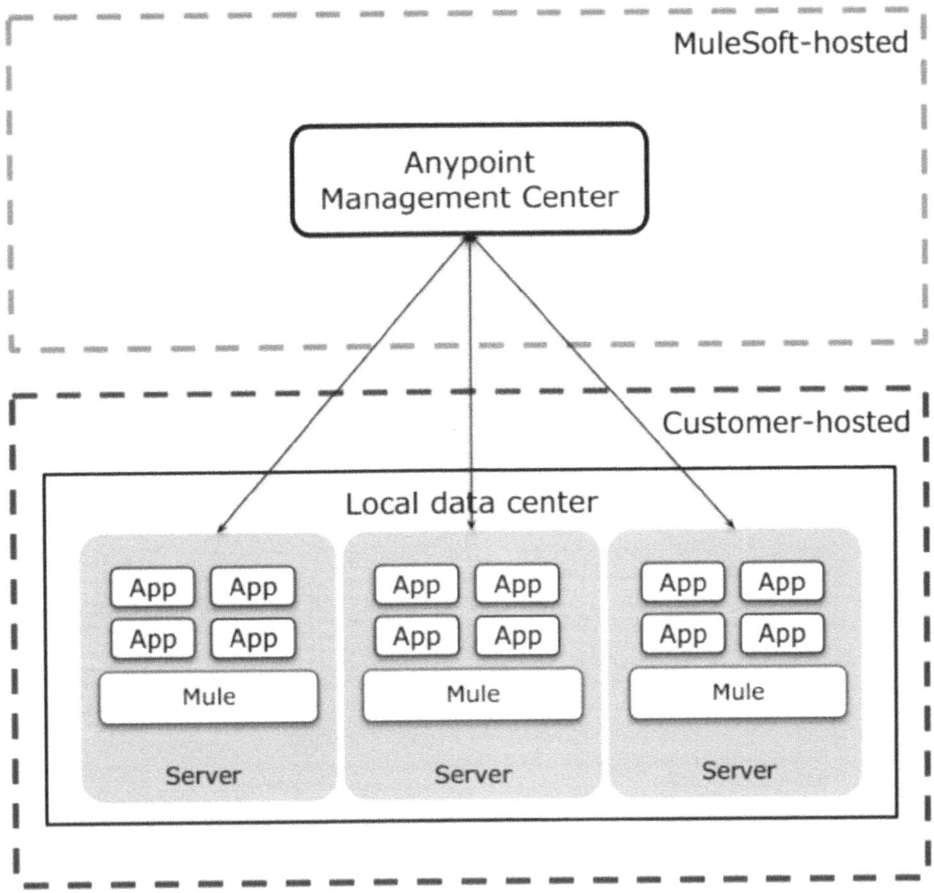

Fig 10.5 Runtime Plane on Customer Hosted Infrastructure and Control Plane on MuleSoft hosted Infrastructure.

The other options are the runtime plane on customer-hosted RTF infrastructure and a control plane on MuleSoft Infrastructure.

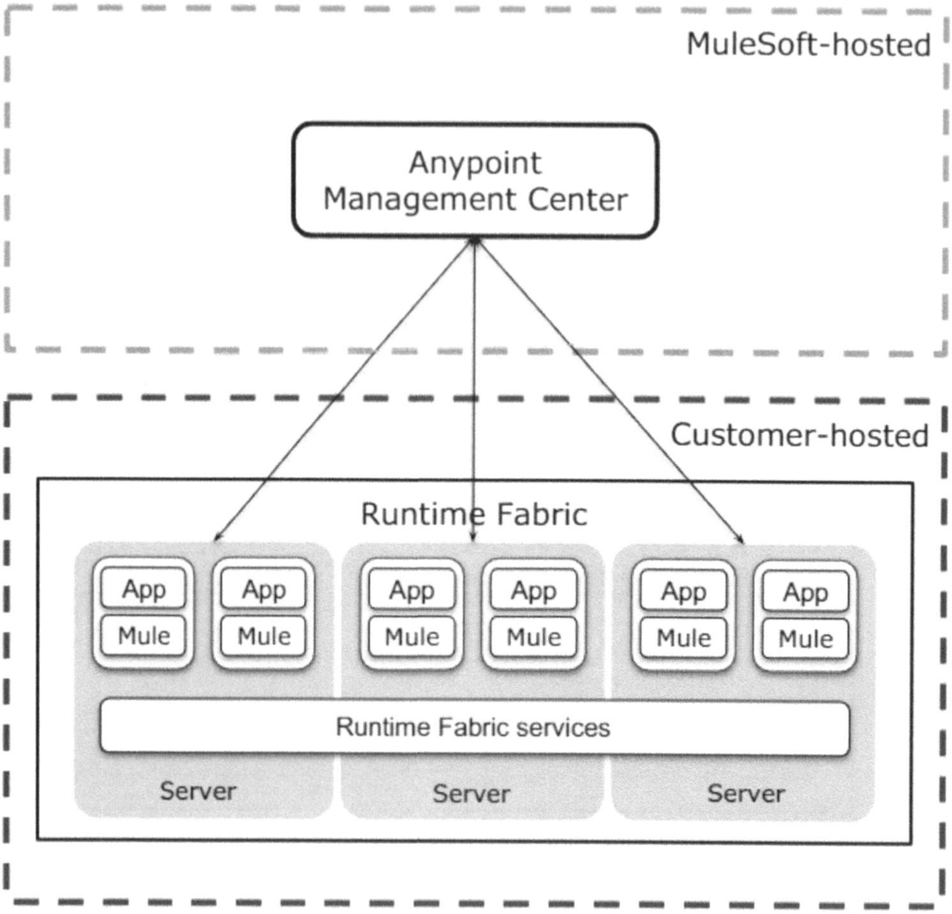

Fig 10.6 Runtime Plane on Runtime Fabric on customer-hosted Infrastructure and Control Plane on MuleSoft hosted Infrastructure.

Sl.No	Features	Hybrid	CloudHub 1.0	CloudHub 2.0	Runtime Fabric (RTF)
1	Architecture & Infrastructure		CloudHub 1.0 is built on top of Virtual Machines (VMs) running on AWS EC2 on various nodes on AWS Cloud Platform. Each application runs	CloudHub 2.0 is built on top of Containers running on Kubernetes on Amazon Elastic Kubernetes Service on various nodes	Provisioning Cloud, setting up Infrastructure, Setting up Networking RTF Installation Hardening Installation

			on a separate worker/VM, a dedicated instance where Mule Runtime is running, and the Mule application gets deployed.	on the AWS Cloud Platform. MuleSoft manages a platform as a service (PaaS) with a multi-tenant architecture where multiple customers share the same Infrastructure, though each customer's applications are isolated.	
2	Application Isolation		AWS EC2 VM running in VPC shared / private	Docker in Pods running on top of EKS shared or private VPC	Docker in Pods running on top of EKS shared or
3	Security	Customer Managed	VPC Level with firewall control for inbound traffic. Outbound traffic not firewalled Static IP for DLB, Static IP for individual VM to be manually provisioned	Private Spaces with firewall control for inbound and outbound traffic Implement tighter security controls, Simplify static IP Management, and customize outbound firewall rules at the private space level.	VPC-level firewall controls inbound and outbound traffic Static IP for Controller Nodes to be manually provisioned
4	Managed By	Customer Managed	Fully Managed by Mulesoft	Fully Managed by Mulesoft	Customer Managed
5	Container	VM or	EC2 VM	Docker	Docker

		Physical server			
6	OS patching	Customer Managed	Fully Managed by Mulesoft	Fully Managed by Mulesoft	Supported (managed nodes)
7	Schedule management	Not supported	Supported	Supported	Not supported
8	Mule patch updates	Requires redeployment	Automated	Automated	Requires redeployment
9	Cluster management	Self-managed	Fully managed	Fully managed (EKS Kubernetes Cluster)	Self-managed
10	Object store		Fully managed (Object Store v2)	Fully managed (Object Store v2)	Supported (Persistent GW)
11	High availability across AZs		Fully managed (with two or more workers)	Fully managed (with two or more replicas)	Supported (with two or more replicas)
12	Secure properties		Supported	Supported	Partially supported
13	Log tailing	Supported outside Anypoint Platform	Fully managed	Fully managed	Supported outside Anypoint Platform
14	Continuous integration deployments	Supported (via API, Maven plugin, Anypoint CLI)	Supported (via API, Maven plugin, Anypoint CLI)	Supported (via API and Maven plugin)	Supported (via API and Maven plugin)
15	Autoscaling				
16	Log forwarding	Manual	Supported	Manual	Manual
17	App monitoring	Fully managed (Anypoint Monitoring)	Fully managed (Anypoint Monitoring)	Fully managed (Anypoint Monitoring)	Fully managed (Anypoint Monitoring)
18	Application isolation	Supported	Supported	Supported	Supported
19	Auto-recovery		Fully managed	Fully managed	Supported
20	Mule		Not supported	Supported	Supported

	clustering				
21	VM manageme nt	Custome r Managed	MuleSoft	MuleSoft	Infrastructure provider/ public cloud
22	Load balancing	Self-managed	MuleSoft	MuleSoft	Self-managed
23	Backup and restore	Self-managed	Fully managed	Fully managed	Self-managed
24	Smallest CPU / Vcore		0.1 VCore	0.1 VCPU = 0.1 Vcore	0.02 VCPU
25	JVM Properties	Supporte d	Supported partially	Overwriting JVM parameters is not supported Overriding default JVM trust stores with custom trust stores not supported	Supported partially
26	Custom Log4j Log forwarding Enable / Disable	Enabled	Enable by Request	Enabled by default for streaming logs to external log collectors	
27	App to App comunicati on		Requires a DLB	Using ports 80 and 443, applications inside a private space can communicate using an internal load balancer via the private endpoint. Note that this depends on the application protocol.	K8 Feature

Summary

- Cloud Hub deployment is suitable for organizations that want a fully managed infrastructure and only want to focus on developing applications. It is also suitable for organizations looking to reduce operational costs and quickly deploy integrations.

- RTF is suitable for an organization that wants to work on hybrid model deployment and integrate with cloud and on-premises services.

- On-premises is suitable for organizations that are strict on regulatory requirements and security.

Ways to Deploy Mule Applications

From Anypoint Studio: Mule applications can be deployed directly in Cloud Hub from Anypoint Studio. Follow the below steps.

- Right-click on the Mule project from Anypoint Studio.

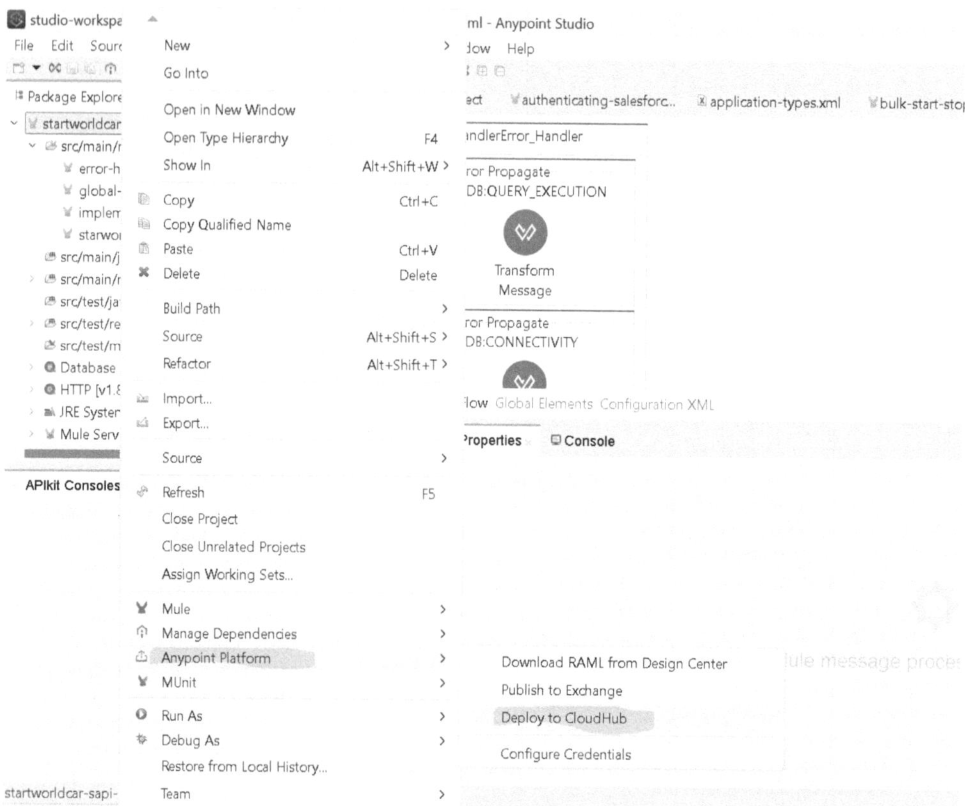

Fig 10.7 Deploying from Anypoint Studio

- If Anypoint Platform credentials are configured already, you will get a screen to select the environment; otherwise, you will get the Platform login screen. Once you log in, you can choose the environment to deploy

- Choose the environment where you want to deploy. It will redirect you to the deployment screen, where you can choose the option Cloud Hub 1.0 or Cloud Hub 2.0 from the drop-down menu. You can also choose the business groups from the drop-down menu. The application name is populated automatically from the Studio.

Fig 10.8 Selecting the Deployment Target

- You can switch the environment as well by clicking on the environment.

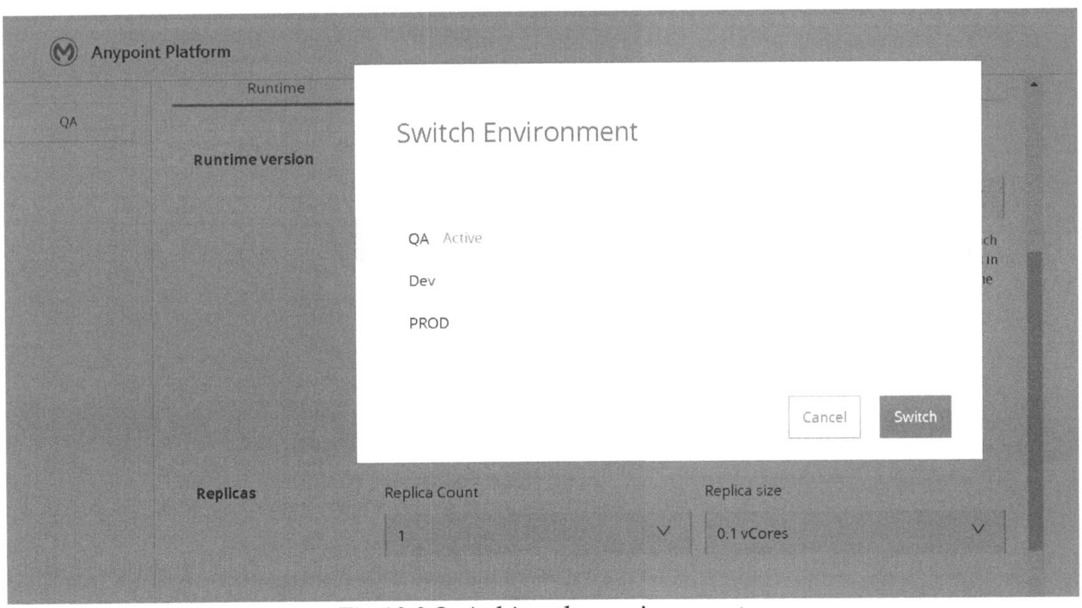

Fig 10.9 Switching the environment.

- Once we select the Cloud Hub, we can choose the number of workers, worker size, and

Java version required for this application. By default, the latest Mule Runtime version is selected. We can change the Runtime version while deploying the application.

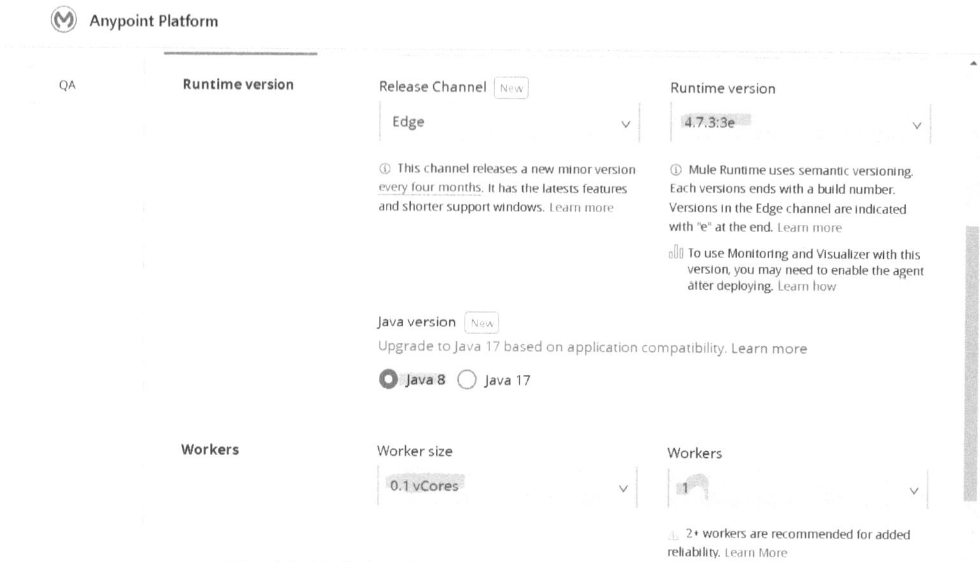

Fig 10.10 Selecting Runtime Configurations

- Select the required Runtime options available.

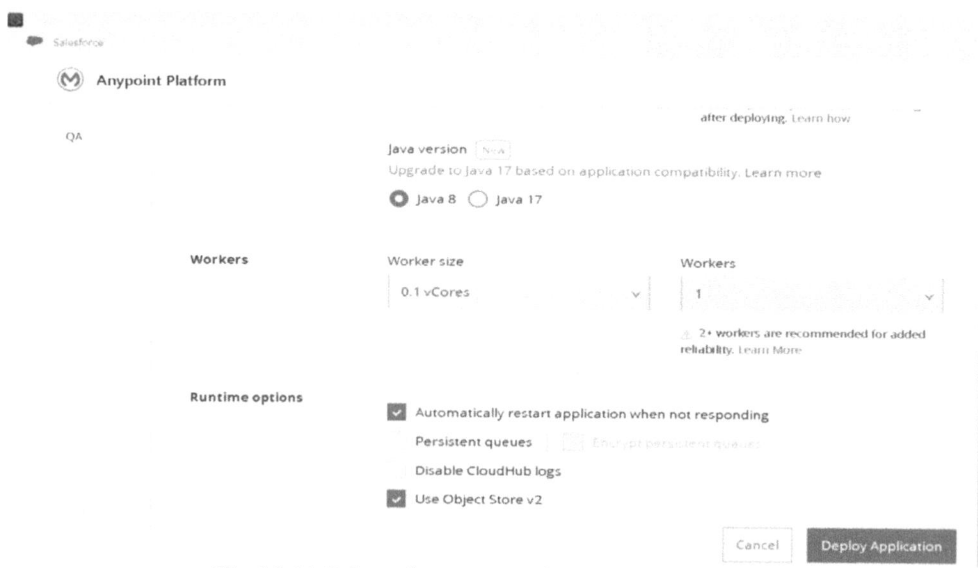

Fig 10.11 Select the required Runtime Options.

- Similarly, you can add the required Runtime Properties, Logging configurations, Insights, and Static IPs. Under Properties, we can pass any runtime configurations, such as the secret key we use to secure the properties.

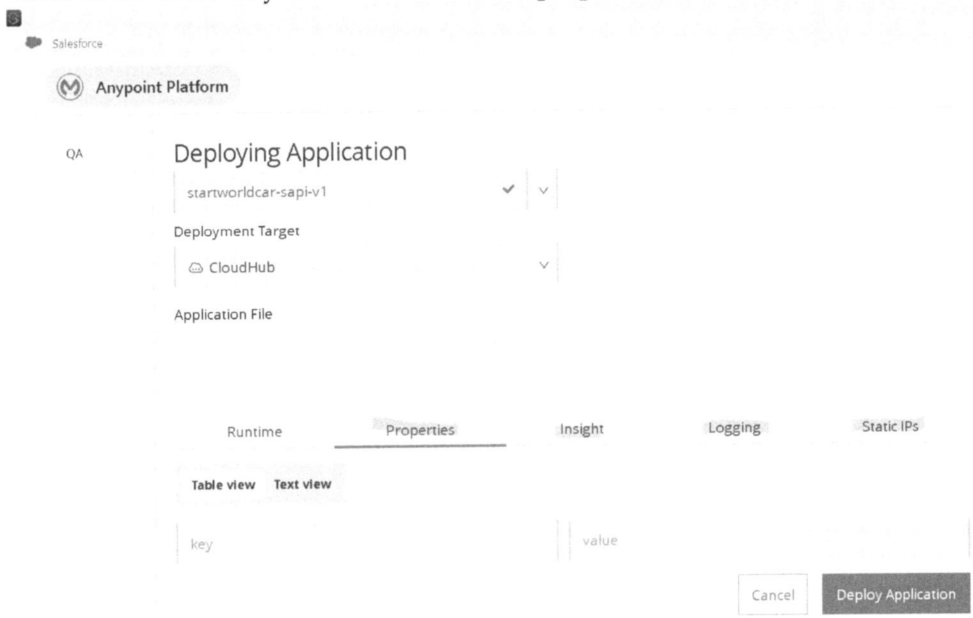

Fig 10.12 Deployment Configurations

- Under Logging, we can choose the log levels for the respective package of the Mule application.

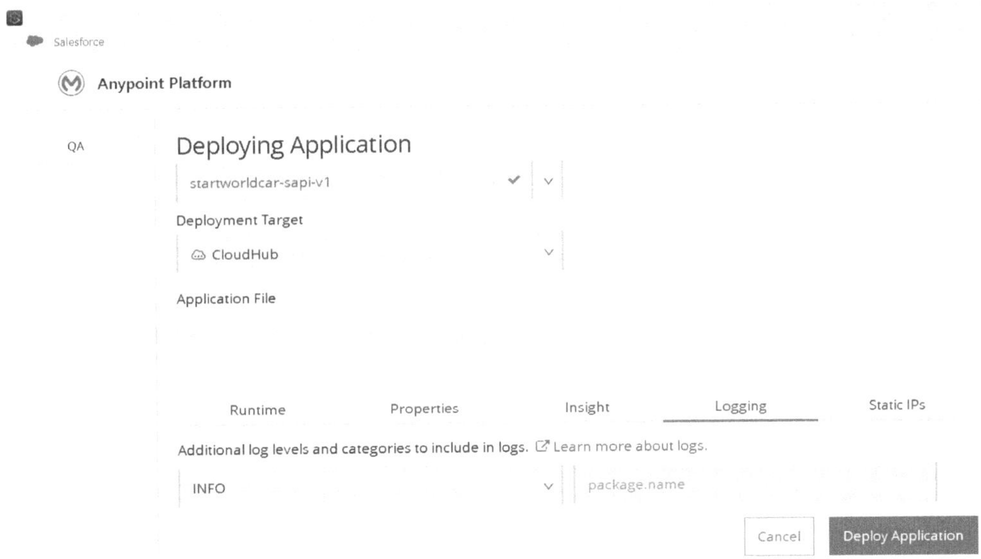

Fig 10.13 Logging Configurations

- Insight configurations allow you to store metadata for Mule transactions. This helps monitor the behavior of the Mule applications and troubleshoot and replay the transactions. By default, this option is disabled. The metadata option allows metadata such as headers, payloads, and context of every transaction to be stored. The Metadata and Replay option allows you to store metadata and replay transactions using the stored metadata. This helps you troubleshoot issues by rerunning them. It is not suggested to select the Metada, Metadata, and Replay options for the long run. Selecting these options impacts data processing and memory consumption.While selecting these options, Anypoint Platform also provides the impact details, which serve as a warning message. Once confirmed, only changes will be applied.

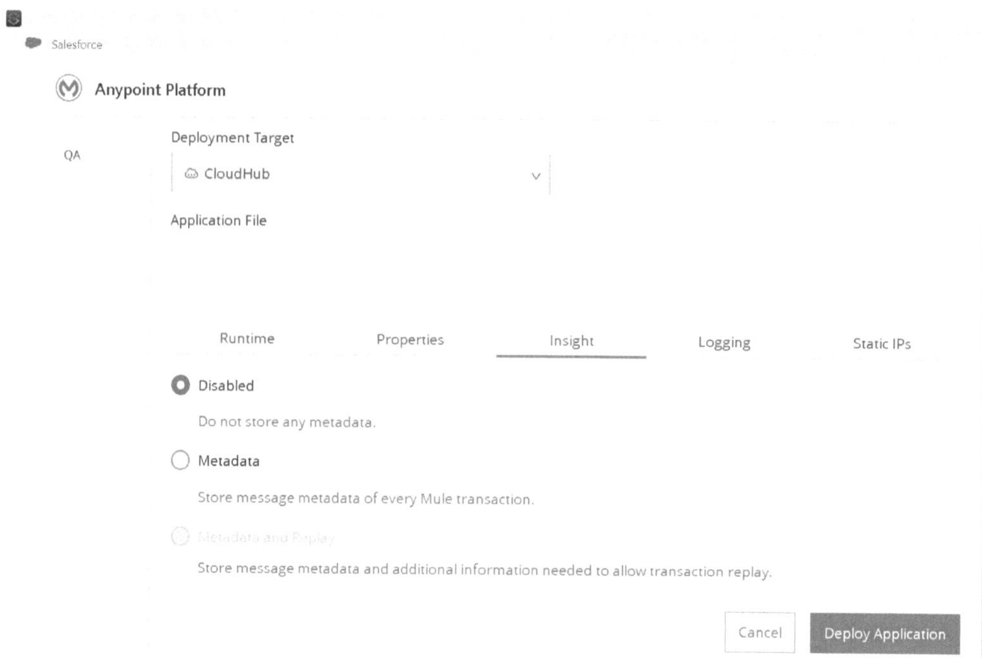

Fig 10.14 Insight Configurations

- Static IPs are required when the Mule application access is required by an external system that requires a fixed IP. This is also required when we apply security policies like whitelisting the IP address. Normally, CloudHub allows the IP address to be configured dynamically for Mule applications, which can be changed for every deployment or during restart. By configuring a Static IP, the IP address will not change during restart or redeployment.

Fig 10.15 Static IPs Configuration

- Once all configurations are selected, click on Deploy Application to deploy the application in Runtime Manager. If we choose Cloud Hub 2.0, the options will be slightly different. Instead of vCore size and workers, we can see the replica count and replica size. The Deployment Model contains two options: Rolling update, which incrementally updates the replicas, and Recreate, which terminates the replicas before redeployment. However, the deployment is faster if you choose the Recreate option.

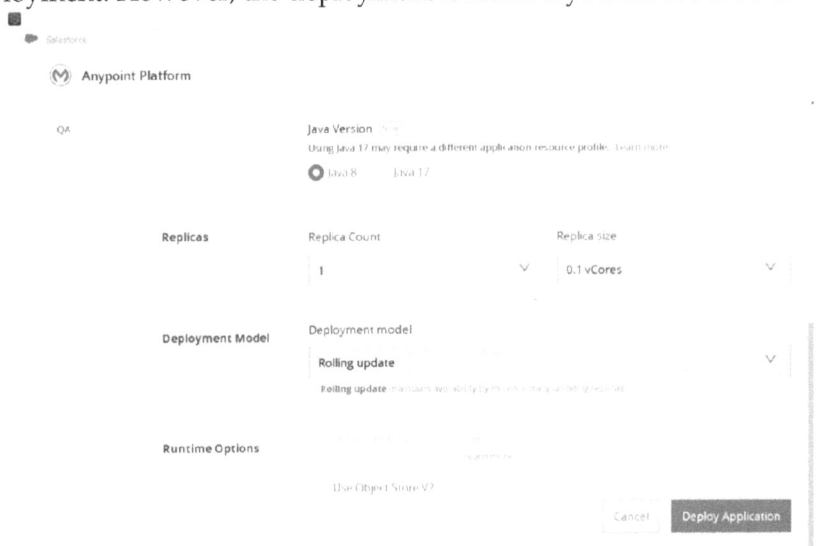

Fig 10.16 CloudHub 2.0 Configurations

- The Properties and Logging configurations are like CloudHub 1.0 for CloudHub 2.0.

Here, there are no Static IPs or Insight configurations available. Ingress is the tab where we can configure how external clients can access the Mule application. It is a load balancer to route the requests.

By default, in Cloud Hub 2.0, the applications are deployed in Shared Space. However, some of the configurations are specific to Private Space.
If the application is being deployed in Private Space, we can add additional public endpoints for the Mule application by clicking on the Add Endpoint button. However, this is not allowed in public spaces. The Path Rewrite options allow rewriting the base path of incoming requests per the application's expected format. The forward SSL Session option forwards the SSL information, like client certificates, to the Mule application.

The option Last Mile Security provides extra security between the ingress and Mule application. It ensures that the connection between the ingress and the Mule application is encrypted.

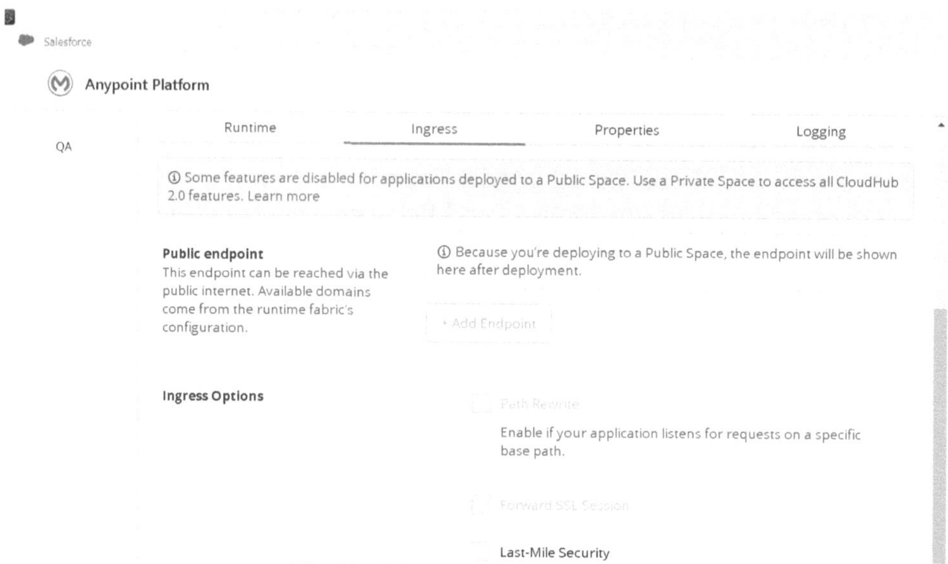

Fig 10.17 Ingress Configurations

Configuring these deployment options allows applications to be deployed to CloudHub from Anypoint Studio.

From Anypoint Platform:
The application can be deployed through Anypoint Platform by uploading the jar file through Runtime Manager

- Export the Mule application as a jar from Studio. Click the project and use the export option. After selecting the export option, a dialog window opens. Select Mule and select the Deployable Archive, as shown in the image.

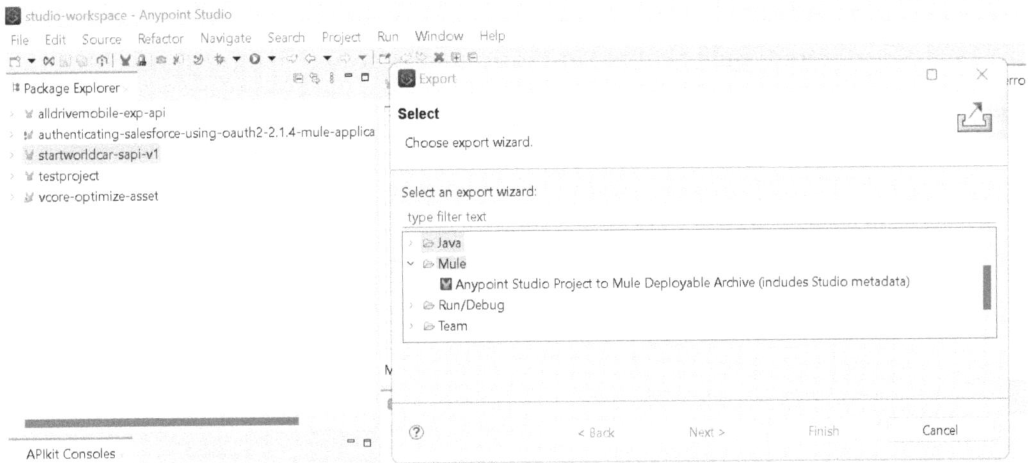

Fig 10.18 Exporting Mule application

- Click on the Next button. Another window will open, where you can browse the location to store the jar file. Select all the default options, such as including the dependencies and all the resources. The jar file will be created in the specified location.
- Login to your Anypoint Platform account
- Go to Runtime Manager
- Select the environment
- Click on Deploy application

Fig 10.19 Deployment Configurations

- Provide the application name and choose the file. The Choose File drop-down menu gives two options: upload the file or import it from the exchange.

- Select the jar file, configure all the required properties and logging levels, and click the Deploy Application button to deploy the application.

In the case of On-Premises RTF deployment, under the Deployment Target drop-down, you can see the configured Mule runtime instances to choose and deploy the applications.

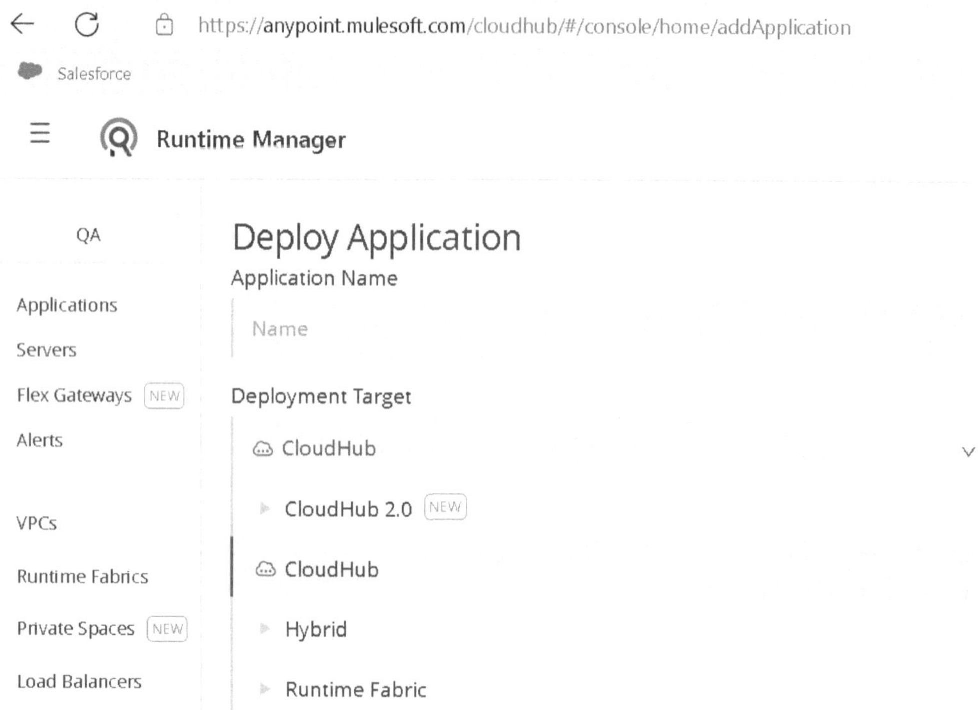

Fig 10.20 Deployment Targets

From CI/CD Pipelines:

MuleSoft applications are Maven-based applications. Based on the deployment model, a Maven plugin configuration must be added in pom.xml. If Mule applications are deployed on MuleSoft CloudHub below, the Mule Maven Plugin must be added to the pom.xml. The plugin automates the application packaging for deployment in CloudHub.

```
<build>
 <plugins>
  <plugin>
   <groupId>org.mule.tools.maven</groupId>
   <artifactId>mule-maven-plugin</artifactId>
   <version>3.5.0</version>
   <extensions>true</extensions>
   <configuration>
    <deploy>
```

```
        <username>${anypoint.username}</username>
        <password>${anypoint.password}</password>
        <environment>${anypoint.env}</environment>
        <target>${anypoint.target}</target>
      </deploy>
    </configuration>
  </plugin>
 </plugins>
</build>
```

If the Mule application needs to be deployed on-premises below, the Mule Maven Plugin needs to be added in the pom.xml

```
<build>
 <plugins>
  <plugin>
   <groupId>org.mule.tools.maven</groupId>
   <artifactId>mule-maven-plugin</artifactId>
   <version>3.5.0</version>
   <extensions>true</extensions>
   <configuration>
    <deployment>
     <target>standalone</target>
     <muleHome/opt/mule/dev</muleHome>
     <host>your.server.com</host> <!-- On-prem Mule server hostname or IP -->
     <port>22</port>
     <user>ssh-username</user>
     <password>your-password</password> ->
    </deployment>
   </configuration>
  </plugin>
 </plugins>
</build>
```

If the Mule application needs to be deployed in RTF below, the Mule Maven Plugin must be added to the pom.xml file.

```
<build>
 <plugins>
  <plugin>
   <groupId>org.mule.tools.maven</groupId>
   <artifactId>mule-maven-plugin</artifactId>
   <version>3.5.0</version>
   <extensions>true</extensions>
   <configuration>
    <cloudHubDeployment>false</cloudHubDeployment> <!-- Disable CloudHub deployment -->
    <anypoint>
     <username>${anypoint.username}</username> <!-- Anypoint Platform username -->
     <password>${anypoint.password}</password> <!-- Anypoint Platform password or token -->
     <organization>${anypoint.organization}</organization> <!-- Anypoint organization ID -->
     <environment>${anypoint.environment}</environment> <!-- Anypoint environment name (e.g.,
dev, prod) -->
    </anypoint>
    <target>RTF</target> <!-- Set target to Runtime Fabric -->
    <targetName>${anypoint.targetName}</targetName> <!-- Name of the Runtime Fabric target -->
    <workers>
     <amount>1</amount> <!-- Number of workers -->
     <type>${anypoint.workerSize}</type> <!-- Worker size (e.g., vCores, memory) -->
    </workers>
    <replicas>2</replicas> <!-- Number of replicas to deploy -->
    <properties>
     <property>
      <key>anypoint.env</key>
      <value>${env.property}</value>
     </property>
    </properties>
   </configuration>
  </plugin>
 </plugins>
</build>
<properties>
 <anypoint.username>your-username</anypoint.username>
 <anypoint.password>your-password</anypoint.password>
 <anypoint.organization>your-organization-id</anypoint.organization>
 <anypoint.environment>dev</anypoint.environment>
 <anypoint.targetName>your-rtf-target</anypoint.targetName>
 <anypoint.workerSize>0.2 vCores</anypoint.workerSize>
</properties>
```

Note: These values can be changed based on the environment setup and settings.
Below is the pictorial representation of the CI/CD process.

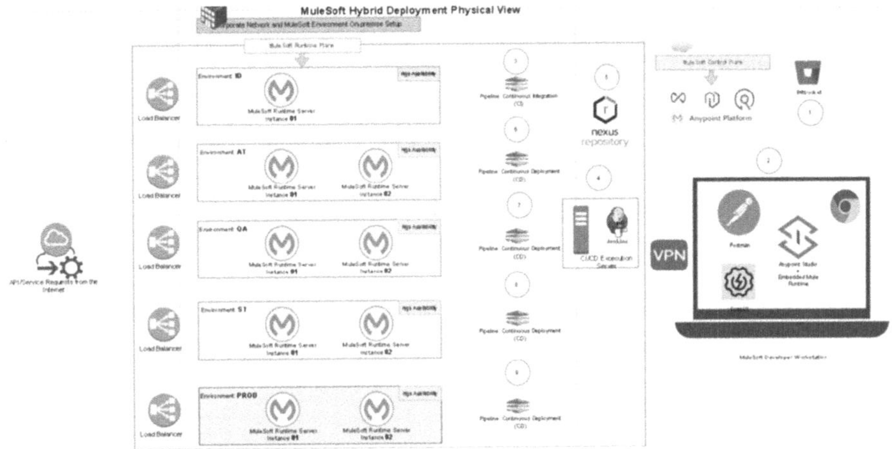

Fig 10.21 DevOps Process

The CI/CD (Continuous Integration/Continuous Deployment) process involves several steps to automate software application build, testing, and deployment. Here is an elaboration on the CI/CD process:

- **Source Code Management (SCM):** Developers commit code changes to a version control system like Git. This is the starting point of the CI/CD process.
- **Continuous Integration (CI)**
  - Step 1 (Trigger): Whenever code changes are pushed to the SCM (e.g., GitHub, GitLab), a webhook triggers the CI pipeline.
  - Step 2 (Build): The CI server (e.g., Jenkins, GitLab CI/CD) pulls the latest code and builds the application. This includes compiling code, resolving dependencies, and creating artifacts (e.g., binaries, Docker images).
  - Step 3 (Automated Tests): Automated tests (unit, integration, and sometimes end-to-end tests) are executed against the built artifacts to ensure code quality and functionality.
  - Step 4 (Static Code Analysis): Tools like SonarQube or ESLint analyze code for bugs, vulnerabilities, and code smells.
  - Step 5 (Artifact Management): The artifacts are stored in a repository (e.g., Nexus, JFrog Artifactory) for future deployment.
- **Continuous Deployment (CD)**
  - Step 6 (Deployment Pipeline): Upon successful build and tests, the CD pipeline automates deployment to various environments (e.g., dev, staging, production).
  - Step 7 (Configuration Management): Configuration files (e.g., environment variables, database connections) are managed and applied based on the deployment environment.

  - Step 8 (Manual Approvals): In some cases, manual approvals are required before promoting changes to production.
  - Step 9 (Monitoring and Logging): Integrated monitoring (e.g., Prometheus, Grafana) and logging (e.g., ELK stack) ensure deployed applications are performing as expected.
- **Continuous Delivery (Optional):** If not deploying directly to production, the CD pipeline ensures the application is always in a deployable state and ready for manual deployment.
- **Feedback Loop:** Throughout the process, feedback is collected on build status, test results, and deployment success/failure to continuously improve development practices.

Each step in the CI/CD process aims to automate and streamline the software delivery lifecycle, ensuring faster release cycles, improved code quality, and better collaboration among development, testing, and operations teams. Let me know if you have any specific questions, or if there is more detail you would like to explore!

Troubleshooting the deployments

We can verify any Mule application deployment-related errors and functionality errors from the logs to troubleshoot them. The table below describes the log's location for various deployments.

Deployment Method	CloudHub	On-premises	RTF
Mule Runtime logs	Runtime Manager logs tab	<MULE_HOME>/logs/ e.g., C:/Mule/logs (in Windows) e.g.,/opt/mule/logs (in Linux)	kubectl logs <pod-name>
Mule Application logs	Runtime Manager logs tab	<MULE_HOME>/apps/<application_name>/logs/	kubectl logs <pod-name>

Based on customer requirements, the logs can be redirected to external tools like Splunk, Datadog, etc. In CloudHub, the log retention period is only 30 days. In this book, we will discuss some of the cases where deployment can fail, how to troubleshoot by reviewing the logs, and how to fix them. Here, we are considering all the examples using CloudHub deployment.

Below is the log for a successful deployment of an application.

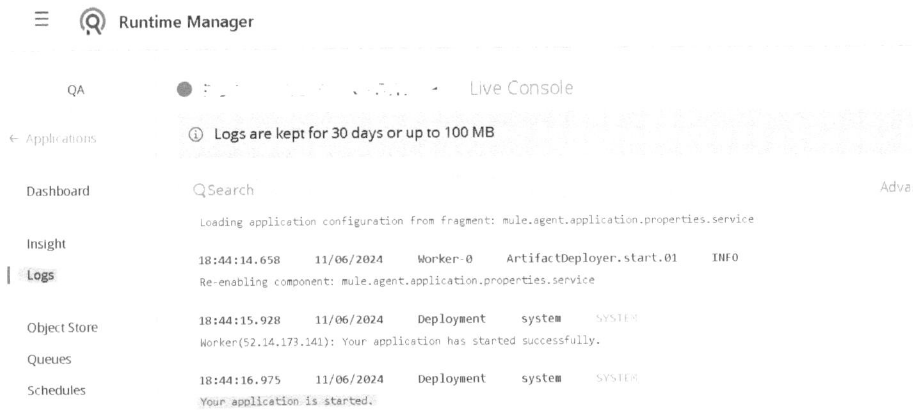

Fig 10.22 Successful Application Deployment

Common mistakes during the deployments

Missing Property: If the property is not defined in the properties file and used in the implementation, the deployment fails. The error in the logs can be seen as below:

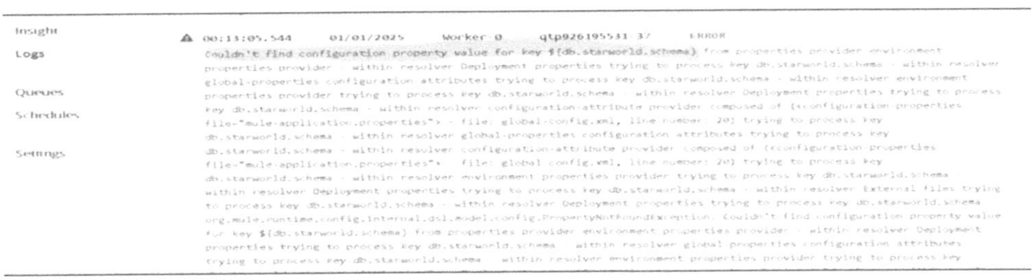

Fig 10.23 PropertyNotFoundException

To resolve this issue, add the property to the mule-application.properties file and try to deploy the application. The application deploys successfully.

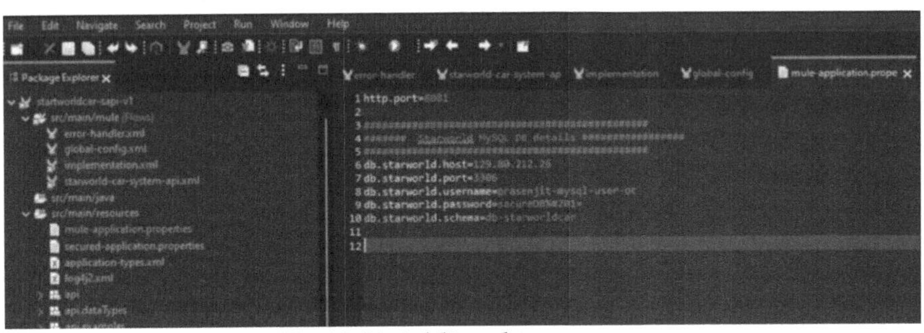

Fig 10.24 Adding the property.

Establishing Communication Link: The application can not be deployed in case of any connection failures to the systems used in the Mule application. This applies to DB, SFTP, FTP, etc. The reason might be that either the system is down or it is not accepting requests from other systems. We see the error below in the logs if the connection is not established to the system during the deployment.

```
2024-12-31 19:11:49.091 ERROR   org.mule.db.commons.shaded.internal.domain.connection.JdbcConnectionFactory [[MuleRuntime].uber.03: [starworldcar-sapi-
v2].uber@org.mule.runtime.core.internal.connection.DefaultConnectivityTesterFactory$1.testConnectivity:81 @3f9e4a1d]: Error while creating connection:
 Message: 'Cannot get connection for URL jdbc:mysql://129.80.212.26:3306/db-starworldcar?logger=org.mule.extension.db.api.logger.MuleMySqlLogger
$$EnhancerByCGLIB$$42140f7b : Communications link failure

The last packet sent successfully to the server was 0 milliseconds ago. The driver has not received any packets from the server.',
 SQLState: '08S01';
 ErrorCode: '0';

java.sql.SQLException: Cannot get connection for URL jdbc:mysql://129.80.212.26:3306/db-starworldcar?logger=org.mule.extension.db.api.logger.MuleMySqlLogger
$$EnhancerByCGLIB$$42140f7b : Communications link failure

The last packet sent successfully to the server was 0 milliseconds ago. The driver has not received any packets from the server.
```

Fig 10.25 Communication Link Error

To fix the issue, the system should allow traffic from the Mule application. This can be achieved by adding some rules to the Firewall or adding the IP of the Mule server by performing IP whitelisting in the system. Also, try to log in to the systems with the same credentials used in the Mule application.

Parsing error from DataWeave script: The deployment can fail if the DataWeave script has a compilation error. Below is one example.

```
2024-12-31 19:54:08.776 ERROR   org.mule.runtime.core.internal.processor.strategy.StreamEmitterProcessingStrategyFactory$StreamEmitterProcessingStrategy
[ArtifactDeployer.start.01]: Exception reached PS subscriber for flow 'get:\cars:starworld-car-system-api-config'
org.mule.runtime.api.exception.MuleRuntimeException: org.mule.runtime.api.exception.DefaultMuleException: Error while parsing script: %dw 2.0
output application/java
---
//if (attributes.queryParams.status != null) ("Select * from `db-starworldcar`.inventory where status = :status") else "Select * from `db-
starworldcar`.inventory"
        at org.mule.runtime.config.internal.factories.FlowRefFactoryBean$StaticFlowRefMessageProcessor.lambda$new$0(FlowRefFactoryBean.java:299)
        at org.mule.runtime.api.util.LazyValue.get(LazyValue.java:75)
        at org.mule.runtime.config.internal.factories.FlowRefFactoryBean$StaticFlowRefMessageProcessor.apply(FlowRefFactoryBean.java:317)
```

Fig 10.26 DataWeave Parsing Error

The application can be deployed after fixing the script errors.

Conclusion

In this chapter, we learned the various deployment options available from MuleSoft and understood the use cases when and how these options can be used. We also learned the various ways to deploy Mule applications and the different configurations that can be used during the deployment of the applications. We also learned how to troubleshoot the logs during the deployment failure. In the next chapter, we will learn how to monitor the deployed Mule applications, the importance of monitoring, and the different options available.

Exercise: Test Your Understanding

Answer the following questions and test your understanding of learning from **Chapter 10**:

Q. 1. What are the different Deployment Options available in MuleSoft?

Q. 2. In CloudHub 1.0, how can we create an isolated network to deploy Mule applications?

Q. 3. What is multi-tenancy?

Q. 4. What are the different ways to deploy Mule applications?

Q. 5. What is the use of Ingress configurations in CloudHub 2.0?

11

Anypoint Code Builder

In this chapter, we will go through the basics of Anypoint Code Builder and its features, as this feature is still evolving. In the future, there is a chance that Anypoint Code Builder will replace Anypoint Studio. Anypoint Code Builder is MuleSoft's newly launched product. It is an Integrated Development Environment (IDE) that enables developers to design, develop, and deploy Mule applications from a single environment. Anypoint Code Builder is available in two flavors. It can be accessed directly from the Anypoint Platform or downloaded as a desktop application. It works using Microsoft Studio Visual Code on the desktop. Both IDEs provide the same capabilities. You can share project snapshots between IDEs by importing and exporting them or using source control systems.

This IDE supports the API development lifecycle in the following ways:

1) Create RAML or OAS specification.
2) Mocking of the service
3) Publish the specification in Anypoint Exchange.
4) Implement the API by importing RAML or OAS specifications, generating the flows, and handling the error.
5) Connect the systems, transform the data into various formats, apply business logic, and manage the events through the Mule application.

In this chapter, we will cover:

- What is Anypoint Code Builder, and how do you get access
- Designing an API specification using Anypoint Code Builder
- Publishing an API specification using Anypoint Code Builder
- Implementing an API using Anypoint Code Builder

Getting Started with Anypoint Code Builder

Anypoint Code Builder can be accessed from the Anypoint Platform as a Cloud IDE and is also available as a desktop IDE. For desktop and cloud IDE, an Anypoint Platform account is required. However, the Anypoint Platform admin should provide the access and necessary permissions to access the Anypoint Code Builder. These permissions can be given by the Admin from Access Management. Under Access Management, we can see Teams and the members assigned to the teams. Select the member and add the permissions as shown below.

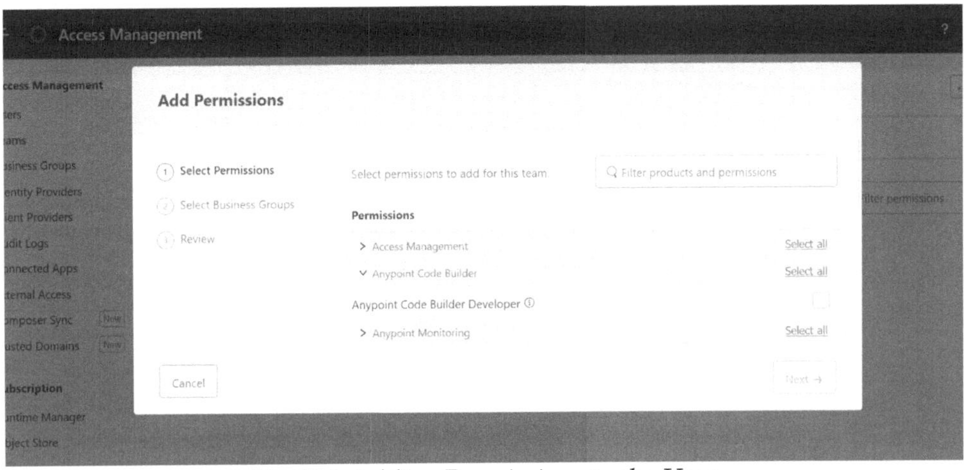

Fig 11.1 Adding Permissions to the User

After assigning the permission, click the "Next" button and select the Business Groups and Environments. After selecting, click on the "Next" button, which will give you a summary of the permissions given. Make sure the Anypoint Code Builder permission is selected, and click on the "Add Permissions" button.

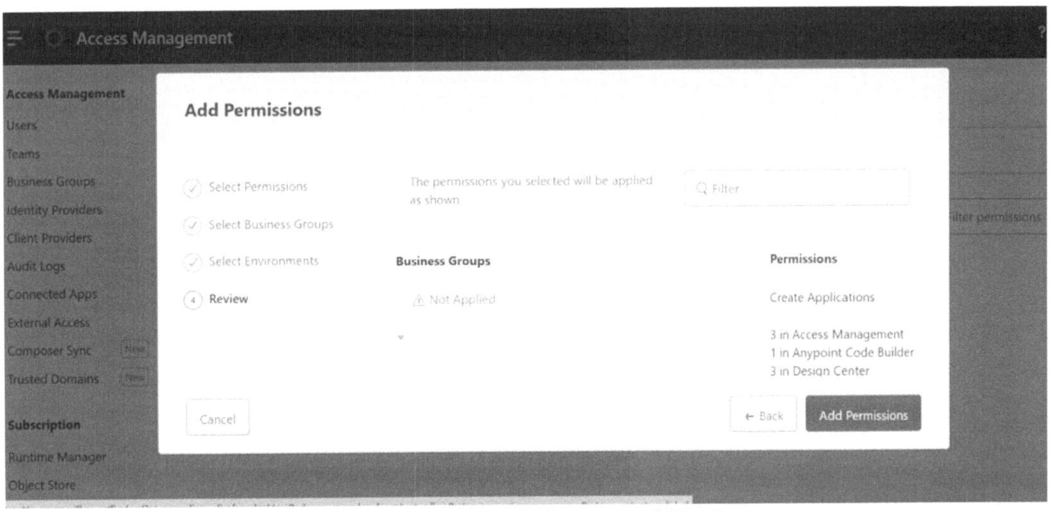

Fig 11.2 Adding Business Group and Environment

Once you have the access, Log in to Anypoint Platform and click on Anypoint Code Builder from the menu. There are two ways to work with Anypoint Code Builder.

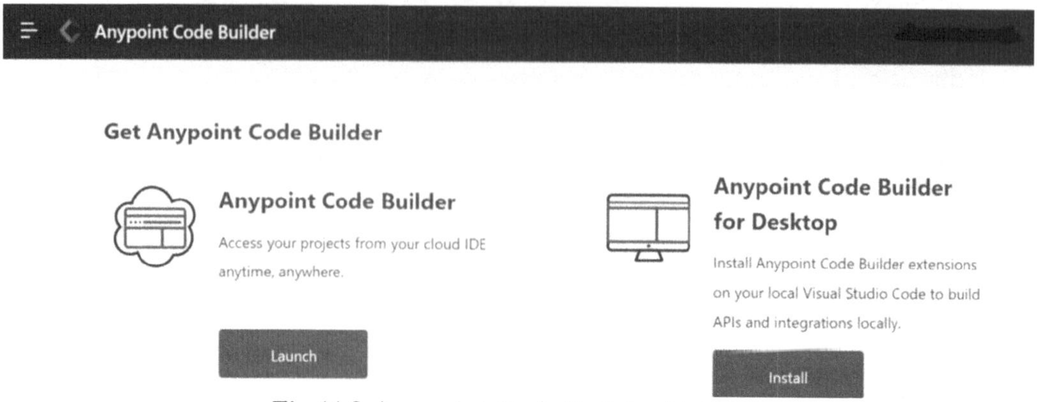

Fig 11.3 Anypoint Code Builder Options

Anypoint Code Builder as Cloud IDE

In this section, we will cover how Anypoint Code Builder is used as an IDE to develop RAML API specifications and implementations. It can also be used to develop Mule APIs the way we develop them in Anypoint Studio.

1) To work on the cloud IDE, click on the launch button. If you want to install the code builder locally, click on the install button.
2) Once you click on the Launch button, your workspace starts getting created in the cloud and opens in a new tab of the browser, as shown below:

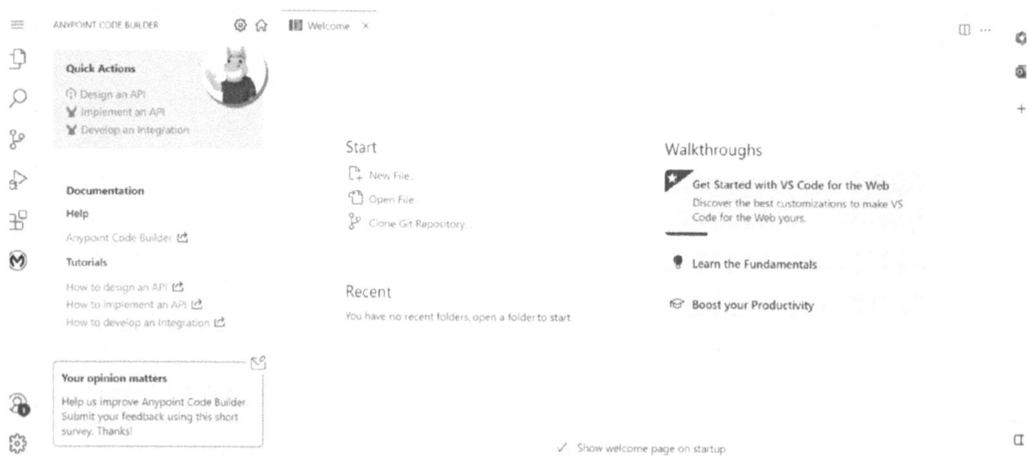

Fig 11.4 Anypoint Code Builder Cloud Workspace

Design an API

To Design an API specification, we will follow these steps:

- We can start designing an API. When you click Design an API, it may prompt you to log in to your Anypoint Platform Account. Once it verifies the credentials, it will open a popup to enter the API Specification and API Fragment details to create.

Select the API specification language according to your choice. You can select a Business Group for which you have the permissions of Anypoint Code Builder. The Project Location is the workspace location. It should not be the root location, which generally doesn't have permission. Select the location for which you have permission. If we select the wrong business group, we will receive a forbidden error, which means that we don't have permission to create the project using the selected business group.

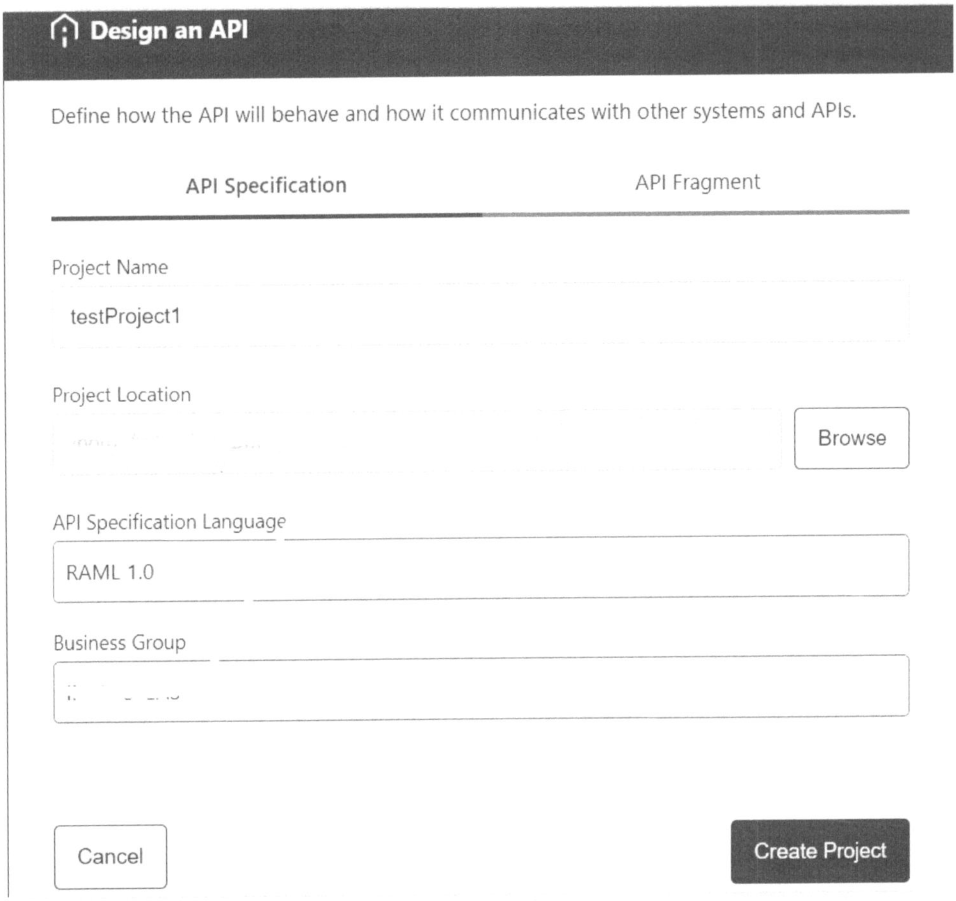

Fig 11.5 Design the API Specification

- To create the API Fragment, go to the API Fragment tab and create the required fragments by providing the business group, location, and language similar to the API specification.

Fig 11.6 API Fragment

- Once the API specification and API fragment are created, the project structure can be seen in Explore,r.

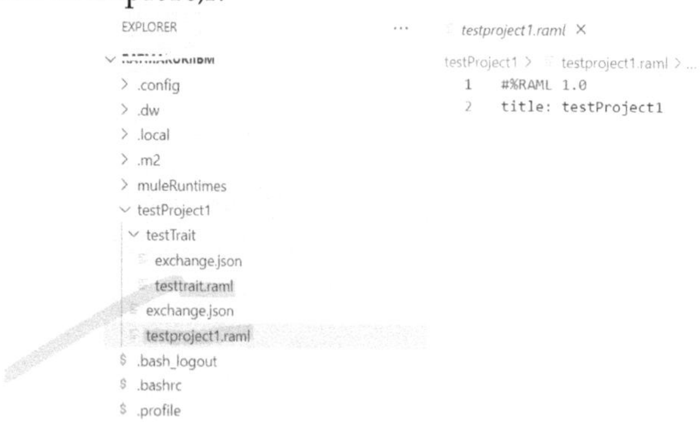

Fig 11.7 Explorer with the Structure

- If there are any errors during project creation, logs can be seen as shown below. The folder is created on the date the project is created. Under the folder, you can see host-related folders and then the corresponding logs.

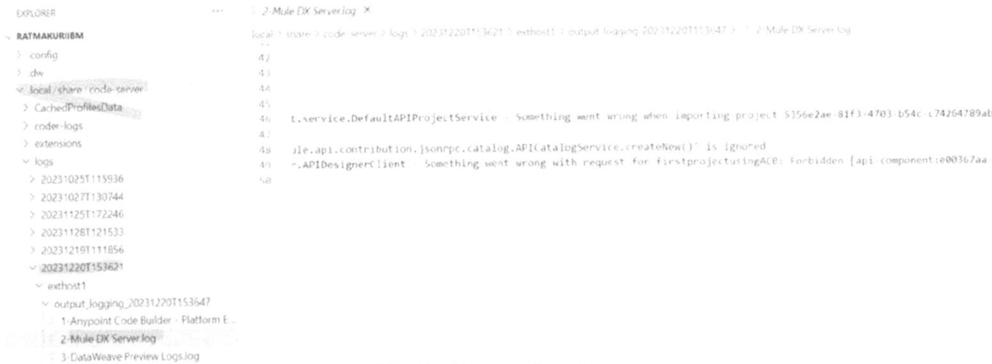

Fig 11.8 Logs location

- Once the API specification is created, we can publish it on Anypoint Exchange. This can be done on the Command Palette by clicking Ctrl+Shift+p in Windows and Cmd+Shift+p in Mac for Cloud IDE. Once the Command Palette is open, search for publish, and you can see the option to publish the specification on Anypoint Exchange, as shown below:

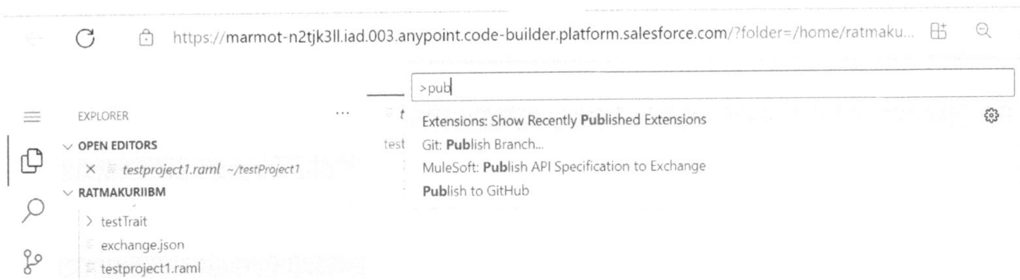

Fig 11.9 Publish API Specification on Anypoint Exchange

We can create folders and files inside the project using the '+' buttons available from the Explorer. Select the folder under which you want to add the folder or file and click the '+' button to create it. By right-clicking, we can permanently delete the folder or file.

Implement an API

We use Anypoint Designer to design the API Specification and fragments. After publishing them on Anypoint Exchange, we use Anypoint Studio to develop the implementation of the API. Using Anypoint Code Builder, we can implement the API directly after publishing the API specification.

- Select the Implement an API link from the Quick Access links. It will open a popup window, as shown in the screen below.

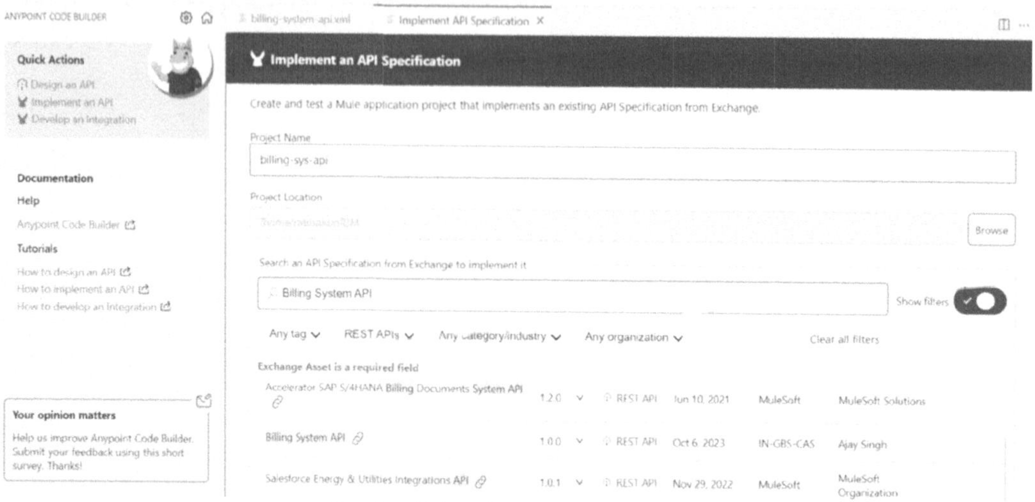

Fig 11.10 Implementing an API

- Enter the project name.
- Browse the project location.
- Select the API specification for which you want to implement the API. To do this, enable the show filters option.
- All the options will be shown. Select the option that meets your requirements. In this case, REST APIs are selected. Once selected, it will show all the API specifications published on the exchange.
- Choose the API specification and click on the Create Project button.
- It will start creating the flows by adding the HTTP listener, APIKit Router, etc., as shown below:

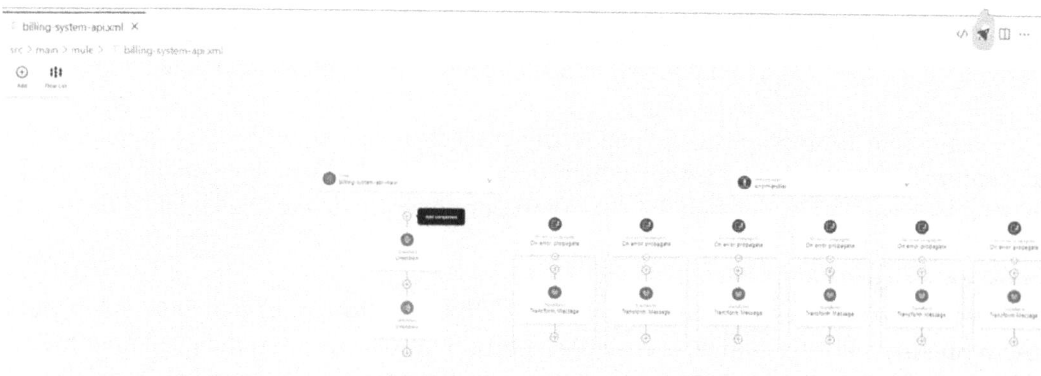

Fig 11.11 Flow and its components

- We can develop further implementation and deploy the API directly on Cloud Hub by clicking the highlighted button at the top right.

- To check all the flows in this implementation, click on the Flow list button at the top left of the canvas, as shown below. It will display all the flows in this implementation. You can select the flow you want to work on, and it will open.

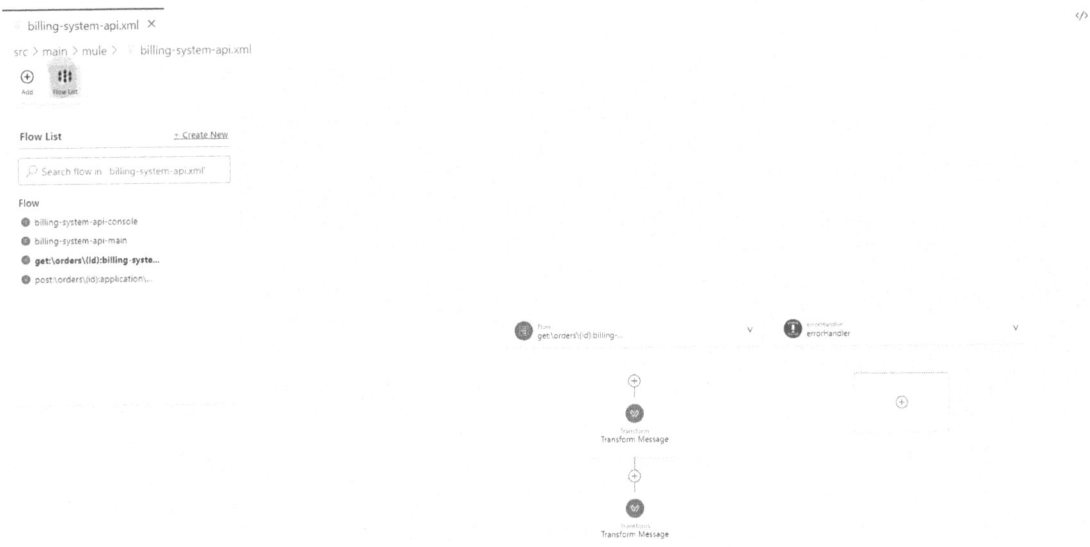

Fig 11.12 List of flows in the API

- We can add new flows by clicking the Add button at the top left, as shown below. This will give you the options on the right side, as shown below:

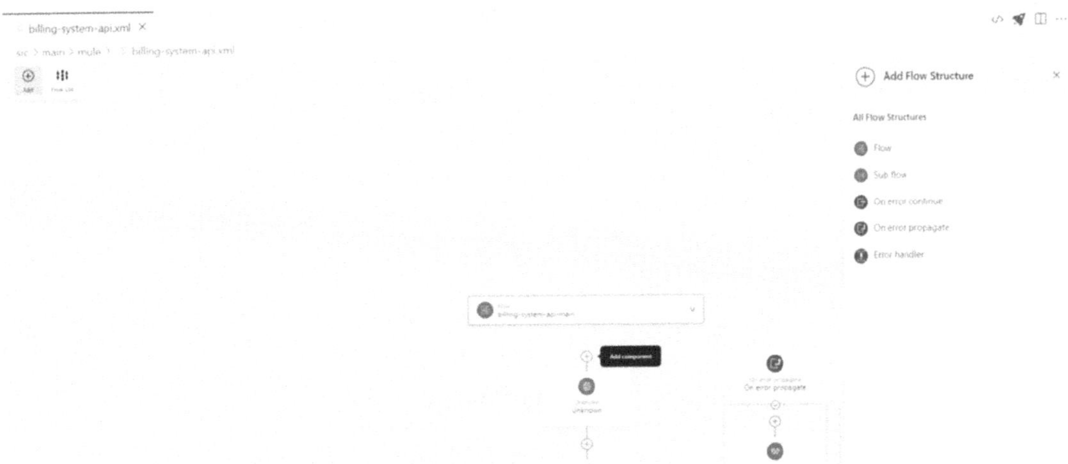

Fig 11.13 Adding new flows

- We can add components, connectors, and snippets by clicking on the '+' in the flow.

This will open the Palette to choose the components, connectors, and snippets, as shown in the screen below:

Fig 11.14 Adding components to the flows

- In the below example, we tried to add the built-in snippet Database Insert, as shown below. We can also download the snippets from Anypoint Exchange by clicking the exchange button next to the search box. When we add them, the dependencies will be added automatically.

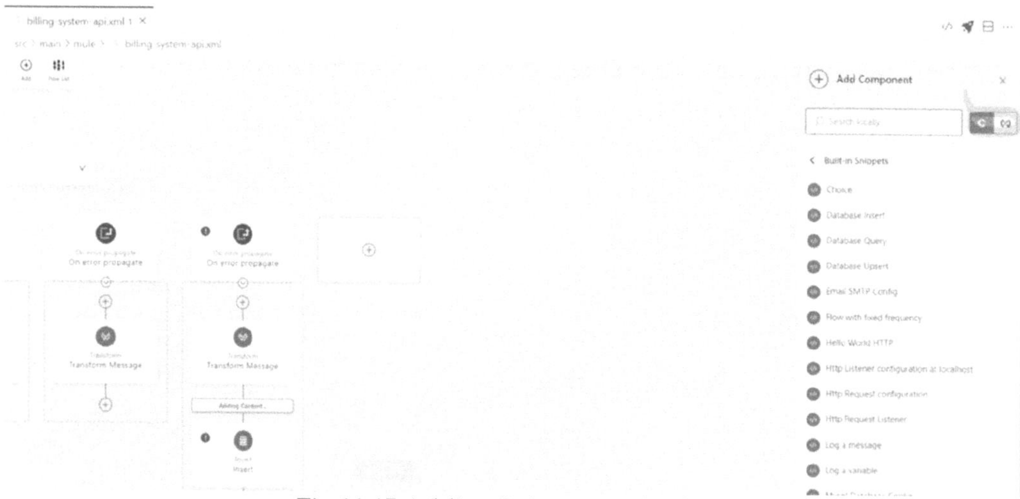

Fig 11.15 Adding Snippets to the flow

- API Implementation can be opened as XML by clicking the "Open in text editor" button at the top right.

Fig 11.16 XML code of the API Implementation

- Clicking the toggle panel at the top right allows us to see the problem, debugging, and console editors.

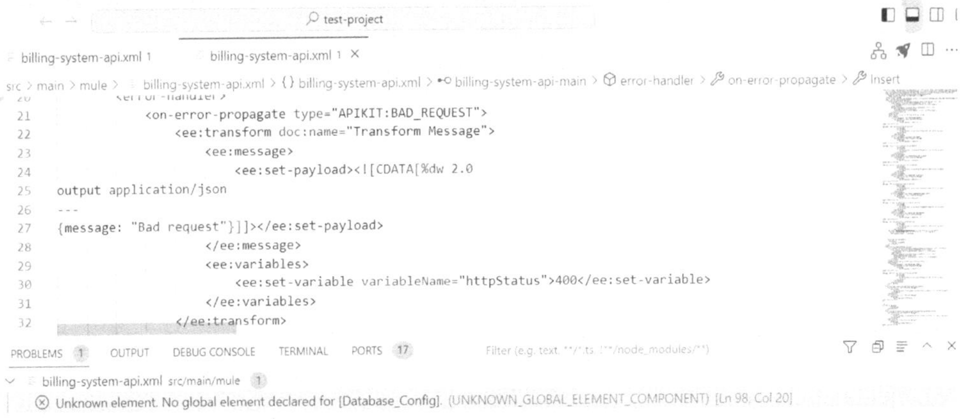

Fig 11.17 Various Editors

Anypoint Code Builder as Desktop IDE

To work on the Desktop version of the Anypoint Code Builder, click on the **Install** button from Fig 11.18 Anypoint Code Builder Options. It will allow you to install Visual Studio and Anypoint Extensions.

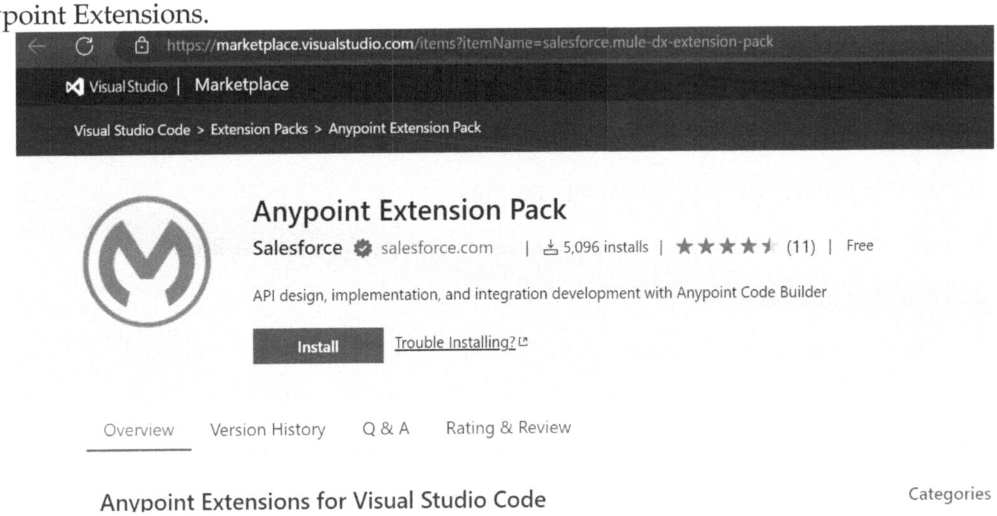

Fig 11.18 Anypoint Extension Pack for Visual Studio

We can also perform all the functionalities on the desktop version, which we discussed in Cloud IDE. To open the Command Palette in the desktop IDE, go to View and select the Command Palette. Ctrl+Shift+p also works.

Anypoint Code Builder Features

Anypoint Code Builder helps developers develop Mule APIs intelligently using AI capabilities. Anypoint Code Builder improves the developer's productivity by providing the features below:

1) A browser-based IDE so that one can work from anywhere.
2) Graphical interface to create integration flows.
3) Snippets are used to speed up development and follow best practices.
4) Interactive Debugger
5) Validation support
6) Visual Studio Extensions

Conclusion

Anypoint Code Builder is the next-generation IDE provided by MuleSoft to design, build, and deploy Mule APIs intelligently using the power of AI. These APIs can be developed using either cloud IDE or desktop IDE. The IDE has an easy interface, debugging tools, syntax highlighting, and the capability to connect version control systems. It has the Command Palette to access the commonly used commands quickly—code snippets to follow the best practices and fasten the development. In the next chapter, we will learn about the importance of using Integration design patterns and their advantages. We will also discuss how some of the design patterns are incorporated in our use case.

Exercise: Test Your Understanding

Answer the following questions and test your understanding of learning from `Chapter 11`:

`Q. 1.` What is the use of Anypoint Code Builder?

`Q. 2.` How many types of flavors are available in Anypoint Code Builder?

`Q. 3.` How do I get access to Anypoint Code Builder?

`Q. 4.` What are the features of Anypoint Code Builder?

`Q. 5.` What must be installed to work with Anypoint Code Builder as a Desktop IDE?

12

Integration Patterns – MuleSoft Connectors

Integration patterns are standardized solutions, practices for the problems which we face in our integration between various systems, applications, and services. Integration patterns provide structured approach to connect different systems by making complex integrations manageable and reliable. These patterns help in building robust, scalable and maintainable integration solutions while processing data exchange, communication between systems and process automation across various diversative platforms.

Integration Patterns: Below are some of the major integration patterns which we need to consider in the integrated solutions.

1) Messaging Patterns - Messaging patterns enable asynchronous communication between systems, ensuring flexibility and decoupling.
   a) Routing the messages to different system based on specific criteria.
      - **Connectors**: Scatter Gather (parallel broadcasting of the same message), Choice Router (routing messages based on specific criteria).

Mule 4 Sample code:

```
<flow name="routingFlow">
    <http:listener config-ref="HTTP_Listener_Config" path="/route" />
    <choice>
        <when expression="#[payload.type == 'order']">
            <set-payload value="Routing to order service" />
        </when>
        <otherwise>
            <set-payload value="Routing to default service" />
        </otherwise>
    </choice>
</flow>
```

   b) Message Transformation: Converts data formats (e.g., XML to JSON).
      - **Connectors:** XML-to-JSON Transformer (simple, direct XML–JSON conversion), DataWeave (flexible or more complex transformations)

Mule 4 Sample Code

```
<flow name="transformFlow">
    <http:listener config-ref="HTTP_Listener_Config" path="/transform" />
    <xml-to-json-transformer />
</flow>
```

c) Filtering the messages based on some criteria - Removes irrelevant messages based on conditions..
   - **Connectors:** Choice Router, (Route messages that meet the criteria to the main path, and drop or log the rest) Validation Module (Perform validations, and if they fail, trigger an error path that effectively filters out invalid messages).

Mule 4 Sample Code

```
<flow name="filterFlow">
    <http:listener config-ref="HTTP_Listener_Config" path="/filter" />
    <choice>
        <when expression="#[payload.priority == 'high']">
            <set-payload value="High priority message" />
        </when>
        <otherwise>
            <logger message="Message ignored" />
        </otherwise>
    </choice>
</flow>
```

2) Batch Integration Patterns - Used for processing large volumes of data in a controlled manner.
   a) Batch Processing: Processing of large volumes of data in chunks.
      - **Connectors:** Database (Ideal for batch jobs that read from or write to relational tables), File (Ideal for batch jobs that handle large file-based inputs/outputs e.g., CSV, XML).

Mule 4 Sample Code

```
<batch:job name="batchJob">
    <batch:input>
        <db:select config-ref="Database_Config" doc:name="Retrieve Records"
            SELECT * FROM orders WHERE status = 'pending';
        </db:select>
    </batch:input>
    <batch:process-records>
        <logger level="INFO" message="Processing record #[payload]" />
    </batch:process-records>
    <batch:on-complete>
        <logger message="Batch job completed!" />
    </batch:on-complete>
</batch:job>
```

3) Enterprise Integration Patterns

a) Publish-Subscribe: Publishers sends message to a topic and subscribers consumes the message.

- **Connectors:** VM Connector (limited scope, but still capable of pub-sub **within** the same Mule application or cluster), JMS (uses topics for pub-sub if you already have JMS connector), Anypoint MQ (cloud-based pub-sub solution via **exchanges** and bound queues).

Mule 4 Sample Code

```
<flow name="publishFlow">
    <http:listener config-ref="HTTP_Listener_Config" path="/publish" />
    <vm:publish queueName="notifications" />
</flow>

<flow name="subscribeFlow">
    <vm:listener queueName="notifications" />
    <logger message="Subscriber received: #[payload]" />
</flow>
```

b) Event-Driven: Actions are triggered by events which allows real time processing and responsiveness.

- **Connectors:** Webhooks (let external systems push event notifications to Mule in real time), HTTP Listener (Mule entry point for receiving those event notifications (or any other real-time calls)

Mule 4 Sample Code

```
<flow name="eventFlow">
    <http:listener config-ref="HTTP_Listener_Config" path="/event" />
    <logger message="Event received: #[payload]" />
</flow>
```

c) Request-Reply: Requester sends a request to an application and waits for the response back from the application.

Key Use Cases:

- Requesting a service response, such as fetching order status.
- Sending a query and expecting immediate results.

- **Connectors:** HTTP Request (Synchronous calls to external services via REST/SOAP), JMS (Typically asynchronous, but can be adapted to request-reply using **temporary reply queues** and **correlation IDs**), Database (Naturally synchronous queries/updates, returning results immediately)

Mule 4 Sample Code

```
<flow name="requestReplyFlow">
    <http:listener config-ref="HTTP_Listener_Config" path="/request" />
    <http:request config-ref="TargetService" path="/getDetails" method="POST">
        <set-payload value="#[payload]" />
    </http:request>
    <logger message="Response: #[payload]" level="INFO" />
</flow>
```

d) Guaranteed Delivery: Ensure that the message delivery happens at least once without any fail.

Key Use Cases:

- Financial transactions.
- Inventory updates in distributed systems.

- **Connectors:** JMS (with **persistent** messages and **transactional** flows ensures reliability within on-prem or self-managed brokers), Anypoint MQ (**fully managed**, **cloud-based** messaging service with built-in **durability** and **retries** to prevent message loss)

Mule 4 Sample Code

```
<flow name="guaranteedDeliveryFlow">
    <http:listener config-ref="HTTP_Listener_Config" path="/send" />
    <jms:publish config-ref="ActiveMQ_Config" queueName="criticalQueue" />
    <logger message="Message successfully queued." level="INFO" />
</flow>

<flow name="deliveryHandlerFlow">
    <jms:listener config-ref="ActiveMQ_Config" queueName="criticalQueue" />
    <logger message="Processing message: #[payload]" level="INFO" />
</flow>
```

e) Transactional Operations: Maintain the consistency across the systems by ensuring all the operations are either by making successful or fail.

Key Use Cases:

- Processing payments where debits and credits must match.
- Multi-step workflows like order creation and inventory updates.
    - **Connectors:** JMS (**Supports local or XA transactions** in Mule)

Mule 4 Sample Code

```
<flow name="transactionFlow">
    <http:listener config-ref="HTTP_Listener_Config" path="/processTransaction"
    <transaction>
        <db:update config-ref="Database_Config">
            UPDATE accounts SET balance = balance - 100 WHERE id = '123';
        </db:update>
        <db:update config-ref="Database_Config">
            UPDATE accounts SET balance = balance + 100 WHERE id = '456';
```

4) Data Integration Patterns: These patterns can be implemented to

a) Multiple applications access the same database.
b) Synchronizing the data in multiple databases.
c) Aggregating the data from multiple datasets to a single dataset.

Key Use Cases:

- Generating a consolidated customer report.
    - **Connectors:** Database, HTTP Request - these connectors can work together to:
        - **Read/Write** from multiple DBs.
        - **Call external services** or APIs for additional data.
        - **Combine** all sources in Mule (using DataWeave) for **consolidated outputs**.

Mule 4 Sample Code

```
<flow name="aggregationFlow">
    <http:listener config-ref="HTTP_Listener_Config" path="/aggregate" />
    <scatter-gather>
        <http:request config-ref="ServiceA" path="/dataA" />
        <http:request config-ref="ServiceB" path="/dataB" />
    </scatter-gather>
    <logger message="Aggregated response: #[payload]" />
</flow>
```

d) Replicating the data from one database to another database.

Key Use Cases:

- Synchronizing data from a central ERP to regional systems

Connectors: Database (Direct approach—query from source, insert into target), File (Batch or staged approach—export data to files, then load into the target system.)

Mule 4 Sample Code

```
<flow name="replicationFlow">
    <http:listener config-ref="HTTP_Listener_Config" path="/replicate" />
    <db:select config-ref="Source_DB" doc:name="Fetch Data">
        SELECT * FROM orders WHERE status = 'pending';
    </db:select>
    <foreach>
        <db:insert config-ref="Target_DB" />
    </foreach>
</flow>
```

5) Service Integration Patterns: These patterns can be implemented to

a) Orchestrating multiple services to complete one business process.

b) Creating a service broker to route requests to appropriate services.

Key Use Cases:

- Load balancing across multiple services
- Connectors: HTTP Request (to invoke external APIs/services), Choice Router (to conditionally route or load balance)

Mule 4 Sample Code

```
<flow name="serviceBrokerFlow">
    <http:listener config-ref="HTTP_Listener_Config" path="/broker" />
    <choice>
        <when expression="#[payload.service == 'ServiceA']">
            <http:request config-ref="ServiceA_Config" />
        </when>
        <otherwise>
            <http:request config-ref="ServiceB_Config" />
        </otherwise>
    </choice>
</flow>
```

c) Circuit Breaker prevents to execute the requests which is supposed to fail due to the system non-availability and gives the time to the system to recover.

Key Use Cases:

- Preventing system-wide downtime due to a single point of failure
- Connectors: HTTP Listener (as the entry point for incoming requests), Error Handling Module (to track failures, open/close the circuit, and decide whether to call the downstream service or return a fallback)

Mule 4 Sample Code

```
<flow name="circuitBreakerFlow">
    <http:listener config-ref="HTTP_Listener_Config" path="/service" />
    <try>
        <http:request config-ref="Unstable_Service" path="/data" />
    </try>
    <catch-exception-strategy>
        <logger message="Service unavailable. Returning fallback response."
        <set-payload value="Fallback response" />
    </catch-exception-strategy>
</flow>
```

d) Applying reconnection or retry mechanism for failed operations to couple of times.

6) Application Integration Patterns

a) Invoking a remote procedure on a remote application.

b) Implementing common business logic so that multiple application shares this logic.

- Connectors: HTTP Request Connector(flexible option to invoke remote REST endpoints) Web Service Consumer (SOAP) Connector(Mule's built-in SOAP connector that consumes WSDL-based services)

7) File Transfer Patterns

a) Batch data transfer: Data files transferred from one system to another at scheduled intervals. These are asynchronous integrations.

Key Use Cases:

- Nightly transfer of sales data to a data warehouse
    - **Connectors:** File (for local or network-based file operations), SFTP (or secure remote file transfers)

Mule 4 Sample Code

```
<flow name="batchFileTransfer">
    <scheduler frequency="24h" />
    <file:read path="/data/input" />
    <ftp:write config-ref="FTP_Config" path="/data/output" />
</flow>
```

b) Real Time data transfer: Data is transferred as soon as it is available in the source system. This enables real time data transfer.

Key Use Cases:

- Streaming sensor data to a monitoring system
- Connectors: File (Ideal when the source system writes files locally or to a shared drive), SFTP (Ideal when files are placed on a remote server and need secure transfer)

Mule 4 Sample Code

```
<flow name="realTimeFileTransfer">
    <file:listener path="/data/incoming" />
    <ftp:write config-ref="FTP_Config" path="/data/output" />
</flow>
```

Pattern	Connectors
Routing Messages	HTTP Listener, Choice Router
Message Transformation	DataWeave, XML-to-JSON Transformer
Publish-Subscribe	VM, JMS, Anypoint MQ
Batch Processing	File, Database
Request-Reply	HTTP Request, JMS, Database
Guaranteed Delivery	JMS, Anypoint MQ
Transactional Operations	Database, JMS, Transactions Module

Data Aggregation	Scatter-Gather, HTTP Request
File Transfer	File, FTP
Service Broker	HTTP Listener, Choice Router
Circuit Breaker	HTTP Listener, Error Handling

Best Practices and Anti-Patterns

Best Practices

- Decouple using asynchronous messaging where possible
- Use canonical data models for reusability
- Adopt a layered approach (API-led or microservices)

Common Pitfalls

- Over-reliance on synchronous calls leading to bottlenecks
- Not planning for failure or not having a rollback strategy
- Lack of proper monitoring and logging

Security Considerations

Authentication and Authorization

- OAuth 2.0, JWT, API Keys
- Zero Trust principles

Encryption and Secure Communication

- TLS/SSL, data-at-rest encryption
- Message-level encryption in integration flows

Compliance and Audit

- Managing data privacy (GDPR, HIPAA)
- Tracking changes and ensuring data lineage

Conclusion

In this chapter, we understand that the different integration patterns and the advantages of the integration patterns. Best Practices needs to be followed while implementing the integration patterns.

Exercise: Test Your Understanding

Answer the following questions and test your understanding of learning from `Chapter 12`:

`Q. 1.` Design a solution using the **Publish-Subscribe pattern** to send sales updates from a retail POS system to a CRM, an analytics tool, and an inventory management system. Implement the solution using Mule 4?

`Q. 2.` Your guaranteed delivery system is currently experiencing a backlog of undelivered messages in the queue. Act by outlining the steps required to debug the issue and enhance the system's reliability.

`Q. 3.` Consider two use cases where transactional operations are essential and describe how you would implement them using MuleSoft.

`Q. 4.` Imagine integrating a payroll system with a bank for salary disbursements; which integration patterns would you use? Please provide a detailed explanation of your choice.

`Q. 5.` Enhance the Routing Messages pattern by introducing a fallback service that processes orders when the primary services are unavailable.

Appendix-A

Answers - Test your understanding

CHAPTER 1

Answers to test your understanding, **Chapter 1**

Ans.1. Enterprise Integration is the process of connecting various business units, systems, and applications within the organization and sometimes outside the organization.

Ans.2. There are various benefits of integration. To name a few

- Reduces the dependency of IT departments.
- Data migration from one system to another.
- Simply the process of connecting other systems and applications

Ans.3. Reusability is the process of identifying the common assets which can be used in multiple applications at enterprise level to maintain consistency and modularity.

Ans.4. Migration pattern refers to migrating of the data from one system to another using various types of integrations like ETL, Batch integrations, Event based integration patterns.

Ans.5. Some of the best practices of Enterprise Integration are:

- Make sure there is no data loss between the systems.
- Use of Connectors provided by the framework.
- Creating microservices instead of Monolithic applications

CHAPTER 2

Answers to test your understanding, **Chapter 2**

Ans.1. The Restful API Modeling Language (RAML) defines the API specification. RAML has various advantages. We can create various reusable assets and use them in multiple API specifications.

Ans.2. Anypoint Designer.

Ans.3. Fragments are reusable assets that can be developed using Anypoint Designer and published on Anypoint Exchange. They can also be reused in multiple API specifications.

Ans.4. Datatypes, Security Schemes, Resource Types.

Ans.5. Data Types define the request and response of payloads. They are also helpful for validating the data or requesting a payload when the consumer calls the API.

CHAPTER 3

Answers to test your understanding, **Chapter 3**

Ans.1. POST, GET, DELETE, PATCH, PUT, OPTIONS

Ans.2. SOAP

Ans.3. This option creates the APIKit router and the flows for the defined resource methods in the RAML specification.

Ans.4. WSDL

Ans.5. The following are the different ways of creating a Mule project:

- Importing the RAML from the Design Center
- Importing the RAML from local
- Importing the published API from Exchange

Ans.6. APIKit Router, the resource flows, and the supported methods are created automatically.

CHAPTER 4

Answers to test your understanding, **Chapter 4**

Ans.1. Center for Enablement(C4E) team by adding employees from different Line of Business (LOB) teams.

Ans.2. Define the best practices for the API development, Identify the reusable assets, Identify the Key Performance Indicators, etc.

Ans.3. Managing and setting various configuration values for Mule applications.

Ans.4. C

Ans.5. **{method}-yyyy**. The method is the **HTTP** method for which the flow is created, and it is the name of the flow, e.g., get-order-details

CHAPTER 5

Answers to test your understanding, **Chapter 5**

Ans.1. To protect sensitive data.

Ans.2. Ways of securing properties:

a) Using Secure Properties Generator Online Tool

b) By downloading the security tools jar

c) Using Secure Configuration Property Extension

d) Using Anypoint Enterprise Security Module

Ans.3. secure::

Ans.4. Runtime configuration

Ans.5. Global Configuration (**global.xml**)

CHAPTER 6

Answers to test your understanding, **Chapter 6**

Ans.1. Dataweave code divided into:

- **Header**: Defines metadata, such as namespaces, input types, and functions.
- **Payload** Section: The core transformation logic.
- **Output** Section: Specifies the format of the output data

Ans.2. DataWeave expressions allow you to extract, filter, map, and transform data from one format to another.

Ans.3. Different Editors to write DataWeave:

- Using Anypoint Studio
- Using DataWeave Playground

Ans.4. **Update** operator updates values in objects, arrays, or specified data structure fields with new values.

Ans.5. **Range** operator is used to generate a sequence of numbers

CHAPTER 7

Answers to test your understanding, **Chapter 7**

Ans.1. Using the preview button of DatwWeave

Ans.2. It is a reusable library which can be used in any Mule Project.

Ans.3. **mapObject** returns the output payload as object whereas **pluck** returns as array

Ans.4. **map** function is used to iterate an **array** and the output returns is also an array

Ans.5. It can be applied over arrays, and as the name says, it reduces the lambda expression and replaces the accumulator with the new result.

CHAPTER 8

Answers to test your understanding, **Chapter 8**

Ans.1. The Global Error Handler can handle multiple Error Errors as per the requirement. This can be referenced inside the flow inside their Error Error handling section to handle multiple errors.

Ans.2. When you want to catch an error, perform custom logic (like logging or compensatory actions) and allow the flow to continue executing.

Ans.3. **Try** scope is used to catch the errors inside the processor level.

Ans.4. Raise Error is used to generate custom error during the processing.

Ans.5. **causedBy** can be used in DataWeave code to propagate the Error.

CHAPTER 9

Answers to test your understanding, **Chapter 9**

Ans.1. Horizontal scaling can achieve by increasing the workers.

Ans.2. Vertical scaling can be achieved by increasing the size of the workers.

Ans.3. **Client ID Enforcement** and **Basic Authentication.**

Ans.4. Rate limiting is restricting the API requests for a specific time. E.g 100 request per second. Rate limiting with SLA is restricting API requests with service level agreements with respect to a specific client. For example, Client A can make 100 requests per second, and Client B can make 1000 requests per second.

Ans.5. API Autodiscovery is a feature in MuleSoft that allows a deployed Mule application to connect with Anypoint Platform Api Manager to manage the API.

CHAPTER 10

Answers to test your understanding, **Chapter 10**

Ans.1. CloudHub with 1.0 and 2.0, RTF, On-premises.

Ans.2. By creating a Virtual Private Cloud.

Ans.3. Sharing the resources between the applications.

Ans.4. Using Anypoint Studio, Upload the jar file from Anypoint Platform Using the pipelines.

Ans.5. We can configure how external clients can access the Mule application.

CHAPTER 11

Answers to test your understanding, `Chapter 11`

`Ans.1.` Anypoint Code Builder is used to design, develop, and deploy MuleSoft applications and APIs. It provides a modern IDE experience with features like flow design, code editing, debugging, and deployment capabilities within the Anypoint Platform.

`Ans.2.` Anypoint Code Builder is available in two flavors:

- **Web IDE**: Runs directly in your browser within Anypoint Platform.
- **Desktop IDE**: An extension available for Visual Studio Code to work locally.

`Ans.3.` You can access Anypoint Code Builder:

- For Web IDE: Log in to Anypoint Platform and navigate to Design Center to launch it.
- For Desktop IDE: Install the Anypoint Code Builder extension from the Visual Studio Code marketplace and authenticate with your Anypoint Platform account.

`Ans.4.` Key features include:

- Visual flow design with drag-and-drop components
- Full code editing with syntax highlighting and IntelliSense
- Debugging and testing tools
- API design and development integration
- Deployment to CloudHub or Runtime Fabric
- Git integration for version control.

`Ans.5.` To use Anypoint Code Builder as a Desktop IDE, you must install:

- Visual Studio Code (VS Code) on your local machine.

Anypoint Code Builder extension from the VS Code Marketplace.

CHAPTER 12

Answers to test your understanding, `Chapter 12`

`Ans.1.` In this scenario, the **Publish-Subscribe pattern** can be used to broadcast sales updates to multiple subscribers (CRM, analytics tool, and inventory system). Below is the Mule 4 configuration:

```
<flow name="publishSalesUpdatesFlow">
    <http:listener config-ref="HTTP_Listener_Config" path="/sales-update" />
    <vm:publish queueName="salesUpdates" />
</flow>

<flow name="crmSubscriberFlow">
    <vm:listener queueName="salesUpdates" />
    <http:request config-ref="CRM_Service" path="/update-sales" method="POST">
        <set-payload value="#[payload]" />
    </http:request>
</flow>

<flow name="analyticsSubscriberFlow">
    <vm:listener queueName="salesUpdates" />
    <http:request config-ref="Analytics_Service" path="/analytics" method="POST">
        <set-payload value="#[payload]" />
    </http:request>
</flow>

<flow name="inventorySubscriberFlow">
    <vm:listener queueName="salesUpdates" />
    <http:request config-ref="Inventory_Service" path="/inventory-update" method="
        <set-payload value="#[payload]" />
    </http:request>
</flow>
```

Explanation:

- **Publish Flow:** Receives sales updates from the POS system and publishes them to a queue (salesUpdates).
- **Subscriber Flows:** Three separate flows listen to the queue and forward updates to CRM, analytics, and inventory systems.

`Ans.2.` Steps to Debug and Resolve:

- **Check Message Broker Status:**
    - Ensure the JMS or Anypoint MQ broker is running.
    - Look for errors in the broker logs.
- **Verify Queue Configuration:**
    - Check if the queue (criticalQueue) is correctly configured (e.g., persistent storage is enabled).
- **Monitor Consumers:**
    - Ensure that all subscriber flows are active and listening to the queue.
    - Verify the connectors are properly authenticated (e.g., JMS credentials).
- **Analyze Dead Letter Queue (DLQ):**

- Check if messages are moved to a DLQ due to repeated failures.
    - Resolve the root cause (e.g., failed processing logic).
- **Test Connectivity**:
    - Use test tools (e.g., curl or Postman) to verify connectivity between the Mule app and the message broker.
- **Implement Backoff and Retry Logic**:
    - Add retries with exponential backoff to handle transient failures in consumers.

Ans.3. The following are the two apps in consideration:

- **Bank Transfer Between Accounts:**
    - When transferring money, the debit and credit operations must occur as a single transaction.
    - **Implementation**: Use Mule's **Transaction Scope** to ensure both dB: update queries (debit and credit) are executed atomically.

Mule 4 Implementation

```
<flow name="bankTransferFlow">
    <http:listener config-ref="HTTP_Listener_Config" path="/transfer" />
    <transaction>
        <db:update config-ref="Database_Config">
            UPDATE accounts SET balance = balance - #[vars.amount] WHERE id = #[vai
        </db:update>
        <db:update config-ref="Database_Config">
            UPDATE accounts SET balance = balance + #[vars.amount] WHERE id = #[vai
        </db:update>
    </transaction>
    <logger message="Transfer completed successfully!" level="INFO" />
</flow>
```

- **Order Creation and Inventory Update**
    - When creating an order, reduce inventory stock and create an order record. Both operations must succeed together.
    - **Implementation**: Use a transaction scope to ensure both db:insert (order creation) and db:update (inventory update) succeed or fail as a unit.

Mule 4 Implementation

```
<flow name="createOrderFlow">
    <http:listener config-ref="HTTP_Listener_Config" path="/create-order" />
    <transaction>
        <db:insert config-ref="Database_Config">
            INSERT INTO orders (order_id, customer_id, product_id, quantity) VALUES
                #[vars.orderId], #[vars.customerId], #[vars.productId], #[vars.quar
        </db:insert>
        <db:update config-ref="Database_Config">
            UPDATE inventory SET stock = stock - #[vars.quantity] WHERE product_id
        </db:update>
    </transaction>
    <logger message="Order created successfully!" level="INFO" />
</flow>
```

Ans.4. Explanation:

- Guaranteed Delivery: To ensure salary messages are not lost during transfer.
- Transactional Operations: To ensure all salary disbursements are committed or rolled back if one operation fails.
- Batch Processing: To process salaries for large employee datasets efficiently.

Example Implementation:

```
<flow name="salaryDisbursementFlow">
    <http:listener config-ref="HTTP_Listener_Config" path="/pay-salaries" />
    <batch:job>
        <batch:input>
            <db:select config-ref="Database_Config">
                SELECT * FROM salaries WHERE status = 'pending';
            </db:select>
        </batch:input>
        <batch:process-records>
            <transaction>
                <http:request config-ref="Bank_API" method="POST" path="/disburse-s
                    <set-payload value="#[payload]" />
                </http:request>
                <db:update config-ref="Database_Config">
                    UPDATE salaries SET status = 'processed' WHERE id = #[payload.s
                </db:update>
            </transaction>
        </batch:process-records>
        <batch:on-complete>
            <logger message="All salaries processed successfully!" />
        </batch:on-complete>
    </batch:job>
</flow>
```

Ans.5. Enhance the routing flow with a fallback mechanism that redirects unprocessed orders to a backup service.

Mule 4 Implementation

```
<flow name="routingFlowWithFallback">
    <http:listener config-ref="HTTP_Listener_Config" path="/process-order" />
    <choice>
        <when expression="#[payload.region == 'US']">
            <http:request config-ref="US_OrderService" path="/process" />
        </when>
        <when expression="#[payload.region == 'EU']">
            <http:request config-ref="EU_OrderService" path="/process" />
        </when>
        <otherwise>
            <http:request config-ref="Fallback_OrderService" path="/process-fallba
        </otherwise>
    </choice>
</flow>
```

Explanation: If no specific service matches the region, the Fallback_OrderService ensures the order is still processed.